IGWEBUIKE PHILOSOPHY AND COMPLEMENTARY RELATIONS

Ikechukwu Anthony KANU

authorHOUSE®

AuthorHouse™ UK
1663 Liberty Drive
Bloomington, IN 47403 USA
www.authorhouse.co.uk
Phone: UK TFN: 0800 0148641 (Toll Free inside the UK)
        UK Local: (02) 0369 56322 (+44 20 3695 6322 from outside the UK)

Published by AuthorHouse 06/20/2022

ISBN: 978-1-6655-9970-2 (sc)
ISBN: 978-1-6655-9971-9 (e)

In Memory
of
Sir Emmanuel Nwafor Kanu, KSJI
An Igwebuike Philosopher

CONTENTS

INTRODUCTION

In this work, *Igwebuike* is employed as a unifying concept of African thought, especially, that aspect concerning the human person's conception of the spiritual and material universe in which he or she lives. It is an explanatory theory or principle that interprets the puzzle of our complex relationship with the non-corporal world and human social life, that is, major social institutions that ensure social continuity and group identity, and further, underpins the epistemological manifestations of the human person's universe.

Different thinkers from different backgrounds in this book have brought different tastes of *Igwebuike* perspective on the table of discourse on *Igwebuike* philosophy. A co-relation between *Igwebuike* and the African worldview was made, followed by a study of the relevance of *Igwebuike* philosophy within the context of insecurity. The Igbo kola nut, being a very important symbol in Igbo ontology is studied in relation to *Igwebuike* philosophy. There is also the study of the relevance of *Igwebuike* philosophy and the management of corona virus pandemic (Covid-19); it also studies *Igwebuike* as the basis for science and technology in Africa and the key to understanding African traditional religion.

Recently, the struggle towards the liberation of African women has taken a centre stage in efforts towards liberation. *Igwebuike* principle is also employed in this regard showing how it stands for respect for alterity, equality and equity. There is also an evaluation of the relationship between *Igwebuike* and belongingness, and the place of consciousness in the understanding of *Igwebuike* philosophy. This was concluded with a chapter on the relationship between *Igwebuike* philosophy and human resource management.

This piece remains a major contribution to the corpus of literature on *Igwebuike* philosophy. I, therefore, introduce this piece to all lovers of African philosophy, religion and culture.

'IGWEBUIKE' AS A CONCEPTUALIZATION OF IGBO-AFRICAN WORLDVIEW

Ikechukwu Anthony KANU
Department of Philosophy and Religious Studies
Tansian University Umunya, Anambra State
ikee_mario@yahoo.com

EXECUTIVE SUMMARY

The relationships in the African universe point to the fact of the dynamics of a personal and universal world, and the reality that the human person is a composition of lived embodiment with the world while at the same time experiencing his/her own body. This interaction between the personal world of the human person and the universal world is possible because, just as the heart of the human person is in the body, so is the body of the human person in the world. As a being in the world, the human person nourishes the world through creativity, while the world nourishes and sustains the human person. This interaction between the personal and universal worlds is a very important element in the understanding of the dynamics in the African worldview. It is in this regard that the African worldview can be described as an inter-subjective and complementary universe. It is a universe that remains in being by maintaining a balance in the relationships between complementary realities. This complementary and relational nature of the universe affects the way the African understands and interprets reality around him/her. This notwithstanding, with the recent studies in the area of Igwebuike philosophy and theology, the present researcher makes a co-relation between Igwebuike and the African worldview. This work discovered that Igwebuike is a conceptualization of the African worldview. It, therefore, understands Igwebuike as the African worldview, and the African worldview as Igwebuike. For the purpose of this research, the Igwebuike complementary approach would be employed.

Keywords: *Igwebuike*, Complementarity, Inter-subjectivity, Worldview, Universe, African

INTRODUCTION

The concept, 'worldview' (*Weltanschauung*), was popularized by German philosophers. Heidegger considers worldview within the context of distinguishing *Weltanschauung* from philosophy, to be a fixed interpretation of the universe of beings, as opposed to philosophy

1

as the study of being. He further suggests that fundamental ontology could demonstrate the condition of possibility for something like worldview (Heidegger, 1975). In this sense, he distinguishes philosophy from worldview, while making it clear that philosophy as wisdom of the world and life is a provider of worldview. In this, he was quite unlike Hegel, Dilthey, Nietzsche, and Jaspers, who more or less equated philosophy with worldview.

The concept, worldview, had a very specific meaning for Freud. He defines it as "an intellectual construction which solves all the problems of our existence uniformly on the basis of one overriding hypothesis, which, accordingly, leaves no question unanswered and in which everything that interests us finds its fixed place" (1933, p. 158). This definition was to aid his distinction between rational or scientific worldview from religious or philosophical worldview. He argues that the age of modernity marks the emergence of the rational or scientific worldview and the bowing out of religious or philosophical worldview. While the religious and philosophical worldviews place realities beyond the reach of human understanding, the rational or scientific worldview sees reality as ultimately transparent to the power of human cognition.

Dilthey analyses worldview within the context of hermeneutics. Dilthey (1954) understands worldview as hermeneutical constructs, conveying the meaning of the world, thus, the interpretation of worldviews helps us to get at the meaning of reality, just as the interpretation of language helps to understand a text. According to Rickman (1988), Dilthey presents worldviews as:

> A special case of methodological *Verstehen* (interpretative examination of phenomena) in the human sciences, involving description, abstraction, analysis, typification, comparison, and generalization. It [a worldview] attempts to reproduce or re-evoke at the conceptual level the original content of what is "there for us" in lived experience (p. 327).

Schleiermacher understands worldview as an element that makes our knowledge of God complete. For Emmanuel Kant, worldview is a world-intuition 'mundus sensibilis', which determines contemplation, apprehension and interpretation of being in the world of man. In the contention of Schelling, worldview is the summation-scheme for the understanding of the real world (Okonkwo, 2002a&b).

While these perspectives of worldview from German philosophers introduce us to the discourse on worldview, this paper focuses on the African worldview, that is, how the African interprets the universe around him and how he relates the individual elements of his world to each other. With the recent studies in the area of *Igwebuike* philosophy and theology, the present researcher makes a co-relation between *Igwebuike* and the African worldview. As a result of the content of *Igwebuike* and the place it occupies in African ontology in relation to the concept of African worldview, it would be argued in this piece that *Igwebuike* is a conceptualization of the African worldview. *Igwebuike* is, therefore, understood as the African worldview, and the African worldview as *Igwebuike*.

WHAT IS AFRICAN WORLDVIEW?

African worldview refers to the African theory of the universe, which includes the manner of conceiving the world and the place of humanity in this world in relation to other realities. The African worldview forms a 'life system' that the African holds on to consciously or unconsciously which serves as an interpretative framework for the interpretation and conception of reality. Writing on the philosophy of the Igbo-speaking people, Nwala (1985) defines worldview as:

> The complex of beliefs, habits, laws, customs and traditions of a people. It includes the overall picture they have about reality, the universe, life and existence; their attitude to life and things in general; what they do and think of; what life is; what things are worth striving to attain; what man's place is in the scheme of things; whether or not man has an immortal soul; whether or not life has a meaning and purpose, etc… worldview is enmeshed in the practical life of the people; in particular in the economic, political, social, artistic and religious life (p. 26).

Worldview is, therefore, at the centre of our thoughts and expressions through actions and the institutions of society, like education, politics, fender, sense of family, religion, arts, social interactions, health care, etc.

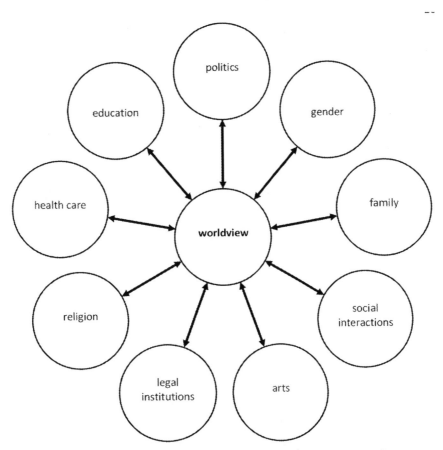

Figure 1: Walsh and Middleton (cited in Kara 2011)

Just like any other worldview, the African worldview has the following characteristics: It is mutually exclusive, which also gives it its unique identity; it is assumption-based; it has a strong sense of assurance and provides Africans with techniques to manipulate their world.

It is like the lens (glasses, sunglasses) through which the African looks at the world around him. In this sense, the African worldview colours everything that the African sees. Although we have one universe, one world, one existence, but how the African understands it, interacts with it, and lives it depends on his lens, that is, his worldview. The African worldview, therefore, affects everything the African sees, notices, etc., and, therefore, affects the way he/she relates to it. It is the worldview that guides, directs, orients the African; it takes him to where he is, where he is going to and shapes how he intends to get there. It is the same worldview that shapes the African personality and culture and serves as a filter and framework. It sifts and sorts, accepts and rejects, and gives context to the life of the African; it interprets, explains and imparts meaning to realities, such as God, universe, the self, etc.

The African worldview gives answers to the following questions: What is the origin of the universe? What is the ultimate and prime reality? What sustains the universe? What is the basic nature of the environmental universe? What is the place of the human person in the world? What is death and what happens after death? Is there any need for morality? Etc. The answers it gives to these questions shapes the life of the African. In providing answers to these questions, the African worldview provides an intellectual construct that provides unified solutions or answers to these fundamental questions in a way that blends the multiplicity of beings, values and duties. This intellectual construct may be expressed in African mythical narratives, songs, proverbs, parables, drama, prayers, etc. It is essentially the underlying thought link that holds together the African value system, philosophy of life, social conduct, morality, folklores, myths, rites, rituals, norms, rules, ideas, cognitive mappings and theologies.

THE RELIGIOUS AND RELATIONAL CHARACTER OF AFRICAN WORLDVIEW

There are different types of worldviews: there is the religious worldview that is based on the belief in a universal spirit: God, deity or divine entity. This divine entity has established a moral order which is known to human beings, and human beings have a moral duty to obey it as it has future consequences in relation to life after death. The religious worldview has a comprehensive perception of the world, putting into consideration the seen and unseen realities. Contrary to the religious worldview, there are non-religious worldviews. These include the mythological worldview, especially when it uses myths, folklore or legends believed to be supernatural and true for the interpretation of nature, universe, events and humanity. The distinction between religious and mythological worldviews, not withstanding, a mythological worldview can also be a religious worldview. Non-religious worldviews also include the philosophical worldview, which uses logical reasoning, mathematics and speculation to interpret and provide answers to fundamental questions about reality. The third is the scientific worldview, which uses the premises and findings of science in explaining the meaning of life, morality, creation, etc. Although it is more exact and authentic, it does not provide meaning to existence as it is limited to the material realm.

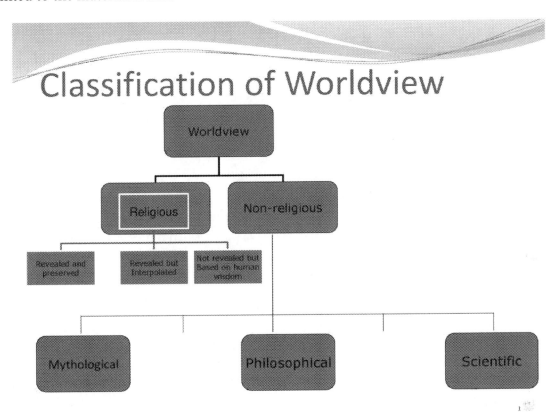

Figure 2: Carmel M. (https://slideplayer.com/user/15613762)

These classifications notwithstanding, the basic question looming at the horizon is: what is the nature of the African worldview? There is copious font of literature available on the African worldview. One needs to glance at the works of eminent scholars like Wambutda (1986), Ejizu (1986), Achebe (1958), Onuoha (1987), Metuh (1987), Quarcoopome (1987), Arinze (1970), Madu (2004) and Kanu (2012). Very significant to their analysis is an underlying principle that speaks of the African worldview as basically religious, which gives a sense of purpose and direction to the lives of people and enables them to act purposefully and exercise a measure of control over their environment. Thus, Okonkwo (2002b) argues that it is difficult, if not impossible, to separate the African person as 'homo religiosus' from his 'mundus sensibilis'.

One cannot talk about the African worldview without making reference to the place of the God, deities, ancestors, etc., in it, and the place of the human person in relation to the other elements of the African universe. The presence of and relationship between the human person and God, the deities, the ancestors, etc., and the strong influence that these divinities have in the day-to-day life experience of the African introduce a wide sense of the sacred and mystery in the African universe. It is such that it is difficult to separate other dimensions of the life of the African from his personal inclinations to the divine. Mbiti (1970) puts this succinctly:

> Wherever the African is, there is his religion. He carries it to the fields where he is sowing seeds or harvesting new crop, he takes it with him to a beer parlour or to attend a funeral ceremony; and if he is educated, he takes religion with him to the examination room at school or in the university; if he is a politician, he takes it to the house of parliament. (p. 2).

In the contention of Njoku (2004), this is such that:

> The African man had many taboos to observe, and many daily rituals to perform, either to appease the community or the divinities. If he was not an indirect or unconscious slave of the dominant conscious, he held perpetual allegiance to one divinity or another. If he was 'free' with men, he was not free with nature or his environment. Suppose community and environment allow him to live his life with fewer burdens, he would still have to pay the debts owed by his past ancestors. (p. 57).

What makes the African worldview religious is not just because of the presence of God, the deities and ancestors, etc., but the relationship that is operative between the human person and these divine realities. More so, this religious dimension has great influence on the African worldview, as it shapes the worldview of individual persons or people. This perspective has great implications for the Latin origin of religion as *religare,* which means 'to bind together'. It is around this process and degree of binding or relationship between the African and the divine elements of his universe that religion takes its place. In this relation within the context of the religious universe, the *Igwebuike* character of the African universe begins to emerge. Through this relationship, the divine does for man what he cannot do for himself and man does for the divine what they cannot do for themselves. It is a relationship of not only of survival but a display of the beauty of being with the other. It is this ideology of being in relation to the other that *Igwebuike* captures.

IGWEBUIKE CHARACTER OF THE AFRICAN WORLDVIEW

Igwe bu ike is an Igbo proverb and also a typical Igbo name. Igbo proverbs and names are among the major traditional vessels in which African philosophy, religion and culture have continued to be preserved. Mbiti (1970) writes that: "It is in proverbs that we find the remains of the oldest forms of African religious and philosophical wisdom" (p.89). They contain the wisdom and experience of the African people, usually of several ages gathered and summed up in one expression. Proverbs spring from the people and represent the voice of the people and express the interpretation of their beliefs, principles of life and conduct. It expresses the moral attitudes of a given culture, and reflects the hopes, achievements and failings of a people (Kanu, 2018). This is to say that beyond the linguistic expression lies a deeper meaning, that is, the spirit of the letter. Beyond the literal sense, *Igwebuike* is understood as providing an ontological horizon that presents being as that which possesses a relational character of mutual relations (Kanu, 2016c).

Igwebuike is a combination of three Igbo words. It can be understood as a word or a sentence: as a word, it is written as *Igwebuike*, and as a sentence, it is written as, *Igwe bu ike,* with the component words enjoying some independence in terms of space. Literally, *Igwe* is a noun which means 'number' or 'multitude,' usually a large number or population. The number or population in perspective are entities with ontological identities and significances, which are, however, part of an existential order in which every entity is in relation to the other. *Bu* is a verb, which means *is*. *Ike* is a noun, which means *strength* or *power* (Kanu, 2016a&b). *Igwe, bu* and *Ike* put together, means 'number is strength' or 'number is power' (Kanu, 2017f). However, beyond the literal sense of *Igwebuike,* it means *otu obi* (one heart and one soul) – *cor unum et anima una.*

The need for *otu obi* or solidarity in the African universe is anchored on the fact that the universe in which the African lives is a world of probabilities. An Igbo proverb says: "If a thing remains one, then nothing remains". This is because the power or strength generated by a person is not strong enough to withstand the existential gamble of life, as the chances of being overcome are on the high side, thus the need for an existential backing. There is also an African proverb that says: "while going to the toilet in the morning ensure that you carry two sticks". The sticks were used for cleaning oneself after using the convenience. But because there is always the high probability of the stick falling into the pit, it is always advisable to take a second stick, just in case. With two sticks one has a greater assurance of cleaning oneself up after using the toilet; the higher the number, the greater the preparedness towards minimizing the casualty of life. The second stick is also necessary in case of a second coming or remainder of the output. In a metaphoric sense, it is used within the Igbo linguistic setting to refer to relational engagement in the world, accomplished in solidarity and complementarity, and the powerful and insurmountable force therein (Kanu, 2017g). The closest words to it in English are complementarity, solidarity and harmony.

The main principles of the African worldview that makes it *Igwebuike* and *Igwebuike* the African worldview include: the interconnectedness of reality; the spiritual nature of the human person that creates a basis for connection to other spiritual beings in the African universe; the collective or inclusive nature of the family structure; the ones of mind, body and spirit; and the value of interpersonal relations.

THE STRUCTURE OF THE AFRICAN UNIVERSE

The African universe has physical and spiritual dimensions (Unah, 2009). At the spirit realm, God is the Chief Being, and sits at the apex of power. In the physical world, human beings dominate, occupying the central position (Onunwa, 1994). The human beings form a "microcosm" on which converge the innumerable forces and influences from the beings that inhabit the other arms of the universe.

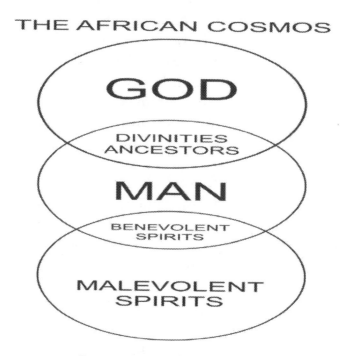

Figure 1: Kanu (2013 & 2015)

The diagram above, with three circles, represents the spiritual worlds of God (*Chukwu*) and the spirits and the physical world of human beings that overlap and, thus, interact. Thus, Ekwealor (1990) stresses that "It is important to note that although the Igbo universe is divided into these three broad structures, there is the possibility of certain elements to move from one structure to another to commune with other elements" (p. 30). In the African universe, there is really no distinction between the physical and spiritual worlds, between the visible and invisible, the sacred and profane. There is a corporate existence of reality in the African universe and this corporate existence is not brought to an end by the death of the human person but extends into the hereafter. It is in this regard that the African speaks of his death as a return to the world of the ancestors. In this interaction, human beings commune with God, the angels, the ancestors, and vice versa. The African world is, therefore, an interactive universe.

Taking the foregoing into consideration, it can be concluded that the African universe has basic characteristic features which include: unified view of reality: the profane and the sacred cannot be separated, as they interact through divination, sacrifices, libations, etc; and a strong sense of community: there is an intricate web of relationship between the living, the dead and the yet to be born.

THE HUMAN PERSON IN THE AFRICAN INTERACTIVE UNIVERSE

African religion and thought is anthropocentric. Man is at the centre of the universe. Mbiti (1970), therefore, asserts that "Man is at the very centre of existence and African people see everything else in its relation to this central position of man… it is as if God exists for the sake of man" (p. 92). Corroborating Mbiti's position, Metuh (1991), avers that "Everything else in African worldview seems to get its bearing and significance from the position, meaning and end of man" (p. 109). The idea of God, divinities, ancestors, rituals, sacrifices etc., are only useful to the extent that they serve the needs of the human person. However, the human person is a being that has its origin and finality in the Supreme Being. This implies that the human person in the African universe is best understood in his relationship with God his creator, with whom, from the Igbo perspective, he is ontologically linked through his *chi*, the spark or emanation of God in each person. He comes into the world as a force amidst forces and interacting with forces. Good status, good health and prosperity are signs of the well-being of a person's life-force, and man struggles to preserve it through an appropriate relationship with the spiritual forces around him.

This relationship is maintained through a community of channels:

a. Libation

Libation is prayer usually said in the morning time. However, libation can also be offered during ceremonies, meetings and gatherings using *oji* (kola nut) and *mmanya-oku* (hot drink), the food and drink of the gods. It is through libation that the African tries to normalize or balance the relationship between the three worlds. This libation is made to God through the agency of the ancestors and other deities. The Igbo believe that it is through gifts that they can gain God's favour. There is an aphorism that says, *enyepu dibia ego, obuo mkpologwu n'ajo-ofia* (when a medicine man is well paid, he seeks the vital roots even in the evil forest).

b. Divination

Divination involves a process of inquiry. People who wish to know why certain things happen, how to solve certain problems, and so on, go to diviners. This is usually done through the agency of a particular deity. The Igbo would say *Onye amaghi ebe mmiri bidoro maba ya, anaghi ama ebe okwusiri* (He who does not know where rain started beating him cannot know where it stopped).

9

c. Religious Festivals, Rituals and Ceremonies

Religious festivals and rituals such as New Yam festivals, harvest seasons, hunting seasons and planting season festivals are activities that demonstrate and express belief and faith in God and the spirit world. During these ceremonies, what God or the spirits have done for human beings are commemorated; rituals are done and powers obtained from the spirit world. Describing the function of rituals, Steyne (1992) writes that "Rituals sustain and generate the myth underlying the belief system, while it also binds people together socially" (p. 95). For instance, the Igbo's celebration of the New Yam festival is connected to the month of *Ahiajioku*. It is a time when they give thanks to *Chukwu* and his deans and the ancestors for granting them a bountiful harvest for the year. Igbo traditional marriage ceremonies also provide an opportunity for communion with the ancestors, as the Igbo invoke their blessings upon the newly married couples.

d. Professional communicators with the spirit world

In the African world, as Egbeke (2001) observes, when the African speaks of an accident or the unexpected event, he does not speak in terms of chance, but in terms of an event whose cause is not yet known. Because of the need to trace the causes of these events and conditions, counteract them and appease or punish those behind them, the African employs the help of sacred specialists like the priests, rain makers, medicine men, etc., as professional communicators with the spirit world to go into the spirit world and find out what is wrong.

These four channels are not the only channels through which the human person relates with the other elements in his universe; we can also speak of dreams, visions, etc.

CONCLUSION

The relationships in the African universe point to the fact of the dynamics of a personal and universal world, and the reality that the human person is a composition of lived embodiment with the world, while at the same time experiencing his/her own body. This interaction between the personal world of the human person and the universal world is possible because, just as the heart of the human person is in the body, so is the body of the human person in the world. Being in the world, the human person nourishes the world through creativity, while the world nourishes and sustains his being in diverse ways.

Every interaction between the human person and the world begins from the personal trading scheme of 'my world,' which creates consciousness and understanding of both the personal and universal worlds. It also triggers the consciousness of abstraction that affects a relational understanding of consciousness and a universal world - 'our world'. The concept of 'my world' which leads to 'our world' through sense abstraction expresses what Okonkwo (2020) calls the "personal and objective living communicative fieldwork of a world" (p. 71) that is made present to 'me' and to 'us' and also the familiar place of life experiment. At the level of logic, it seems more appropriate to speak of the discovery of 'my world' before the discovery of 'our world'. But in reality, once you are conscious of 'my world,' it implies that you are already in 'our world,' as you can only discover 'your world' in relation to 'our world'.

This relationship made possible as a result of the presence of both personal and universal worlds within the African context is conceptualized by *Igwebuike*. It captures the inter-subjectivity of the African universe in terms of complementarity. Thus, *Igwebuike* becomes like a 'control box' that determines thinking, action or doing and values. It exerts a strong influence in shaping the life of individuals and the community as a whole, thereby, unifying the African thought and life. It is within this context that *Igwebuike* is understood as the African worldview, and the African worldview as *Igwebuike*.

REFERENCES

Achebe, C. (1958). *The things fall apart*. England: Heinemann.

Arinze, F. (1970). *Sacrifice in Igbo religion* Ibadan: Ibadan University Press.

Dilthey, Wilhelm. *The Essence of Philosophy*. Trans. Stephen A. Emery and William T. Emery. Chapel Hill: The University of North Carolina Press, 1954.

Egbeke, A. (2001). *Metaphysics: An introduction*. Enugu: Donze.

Ejizu, C. I. O. (1986). *Igbo ritual symbols*. Enugu: Fourth Dimension.

Ekwealor, C. C. (1990). The Igbo world-view: A general survey. E. Oguegbu (Ed.). *The humanities and all of us* (pp.29-33). Onisha: Watehword.

Freud, Sigmund (1933). New introductory lectures on psycho-analysis. *SE*, 22: 1-182.

Heidegger, M. (1975). *The basic problems of phenomenology*. Indiana

Ijiomah, C. (2005). African philosophy's contribution to the dialogue on reality issues. *Sankofa: Journal of the Humanities. 3. 1.* 81 – 90.

Kanu, I. A. (2012 a). The secularity of sacredness of the priestly office in African traditional societies. *Journal of Integrative Humanism. 2. 1.* 219-225.

Kanu, I. A. (2012 b). A metaphysical epistemological study of African Medical practitioners. In O. E. Ezenweke and I. A. Kanu (2012). *Issues in African traditional religion and philosophy (227-240).* Jos: Fab Anieh.

Kanu, I. A. (2013). The Dimensions of African Cosmology. *Filosofia Theoretica: Journal of African Philosophy, Culture and Religion, Vol. 2. No. 2.* pp. 533-555.

Kanu, I. A. (2015a). *African philosophy: An ontologico-existential hermeneutic approach to classical and contemporary issues.* Nigeria: Augustinian Publications.

Kanu, I. A. (2016a). Igwebuike as an Igbo-African Hermeneutics of Globalisation. *IGWEBUIKE: An African Journal of Arts and Humanities,* Vol. 2 No.1. pp. 61-66.

Kanu, I. A. (2016a). Igwebuike as the consummate foundation of African Bioethical principles. *An African journal of Arts and Humanities* Vol. 2. No.1 June, pp.23-40.

Kanu, I. A. (2016b) Igwebuike as an Expressive Modality of Being in African ontology. *Journal of Environmental and Construction Management. 6. 3.* pp.12-21.

Kanu, I. A. (2017e). Igwebuike as an Igbo-African modality of peace and conflict resolution. *Journal of African Traditional Religion and Philosophy Scholars. Vol. 1. No. 1. pp. 31-40.*

Kanu, I. A. (2017g). Igwebuike and the logic (Nka) of African philosophy. *Igwebuike: An African Journal of Arts and Humanities. 3. 1.* pp. 1-13.

Kanu, I. A. (2018). *Igwe Bu Ike* as an Igbo-African Hermeneutics of National Development. *Igbo Studies Review. No. 6.* pp. 59-83.

Kanu, I. A. (2014). Being and the categories of being in Igbo philosophy. *African Journal of Humanities. Volume 1. Issue 1.* pp. 144-159.

Kanu, I. A. (2014a). Igbo proverbs as *depositum* of Igbo-African philosophy. *International Journal of Humanities and Social Sciences. Vol. 4. No. 1.* pp. 164-168.

Kanu, I. A. (2014a). Suicide in Igbo-African ontology. *Developing Countries Studies. Vol. 4. No. 5.* USA. pp. 27-38.

Kanu, I. A. (2014b). Suffering in Igbo-African Ontology. *Research on Humanities and Social Sciences. Vol. 4. No. 5.* pp. 8-13.

Kanu, I. A. (2014b). The place of Igbo myths in Igbo-African philosophy. *American Journal of Contemporary Research. Vol. 4. No. 2.* pp. 98-102.

Kanu, I. A. (2015). African traditional democracy with particular reference to the Yoruba and Igbo political systems. *International Journal of Philosophy and Public Affairs.* Vol. 2. No. 3. pp. 147-160.

Kanu, I. A. (2015). *Personal identity and punishment in John Locke* (A Dissertation for the Award of Master of Arts Degree in Philosophy- Metaphysics), University of Nigeria, Nsukka, Enugu State.

Kanu, I. A. (2015a). *African philosophy: An ontologico-existential hermeneutic approach to classical and contemporary issues.* Nigeria: Augustinian Publications.

Kanu, I. A. (Ed.) (2016a). *Complementary ontology: Provocative essays on Innocent Asouzu's African philosophy of integration for progressive transformation.* Germany: Lambert Academic Publishing.

Kanu, I. A. (Ed.) (2016b). *Ibuanyidanda: A complementary systematic inquiry. Reflections on Innocent Asouzu's African philosophy.* Germany: Lambert Academic Publishing.

Kanu, I. A. (2016). *Igbo-African Christology: A cultural Christological construct in Post-Missionary Africa.* Germany: Lambert Publications.

Kanu, I. A. (2016a). African traditional folk songs as dialogue between education and entertainment. *Cambridge International Journal of Contemporary Education Research.* 6. 6. pp. 53-64.

Kara M. K. (2011). An Exploration of Worldview and Conceptions of Nature of Science among Science Teachers at a Private Christian High School. https://www.semanticscholar.org/paper/An-Exploration-of-Worldview-and-Conceptions-of-of-a-Kits/7a839bed677eaa2f282bf8dca6feb2afba18f0e0.

Madu, J. E. (1997). *Fundamentals of religious studies.* Calabar: Franecloh.

Madu, J. E. (2004). *Symbolism in African cosmology: The Igbo perspective.* Nnamdi Azikiwe University, Awka, Anambra State. Lecture Note.

Mbiti, J. S. (1970). *African religions and philosophy.* Nairobi: East African Educational Publishers.

Metuh, E. I. (1987). *Comparative studies of African Traditional Religion.* Onitsha: Imico.

Metuh, I. E. (1991). *African religions in western conceptual schemes.* Jos: Imico

Njoku, F.O.C. (2004). *Development and African philosophy: A theoretical reconstruction of African socio-political economy.* New England: Universe.

Nwala, T. U. (1985). *Igbo philosophy: The philosophy of the Igbo speaking peoples of Nigeria.* Ikeja-Lags: Lantern Books.

Okonkwo J. I. (2020). *Uwa m:* The Igbo phenomenology of existential perception. *Okpulo Journal of Arts and Cultural Heritage.* Vol. 2. No. 3. 71-82.

Okonkwo, I. J. (2002a). World-view and life-forms crisis of a Nigerian philosophy of culture. An appraisal. *Journal of Nigerian Languages and Culture.* Vol. 4. 171-182.

Okonkwo, I. J. (2002b). Religious language and Igbo-folks media: The crisis situation of modern trends of evangelization. In Okonkwo, I. J. Et al (Eds.). *Elements of Igbo Traditional Religious Practice* (pp. 8-27). Imo: Ministry of Information and Culture.

Onunwa, U. (1994). The individual and community in African Traditional Religion and society. *The Mankind Quarterly. 34. 3.* 249 – 260.

Onuoha, E. (1987). *Four contrasting world-views.* Enugu: Express.

Parinder, G. D. (1961). *West African religion.* London: Epworth.

Quarcoopome, T. N. (1987). West African traditional religion. Ibadan: African Universities Press.

Rickman, H. P. (1988). *Dilthey Today: A Critical Appraisal of the Contemporary Relevance of His Work.* New York: Greenwood Press.

Steyne, D. M. (1992). *In step with the god of the nations: A biblical theology of missions.* Houston: Touch.

Unah, J. (2009). Ontologico – epistemological background to authentic African socio-economic and political institutions. A F. Uduigwomen (Ed.). *From footmarks to landmarks on African philosophy* (264 – 278). Lagos: O. O. P.

Wambutda, D. N. (1986). The interplay between cosmology and theology: A. matrix for African theologizing. In A. Oduyoye (Ed.). *The state of Christian theology in Nigeria, 1980-81,* (38-49). Ibadan: Day Star.

IGWEBUIKE ATTRIBUTES IN THE MEDIEVAL FRENCH SYSTEM: A REVIEW OF CHARLEMAGNE'S LEADERSHIP IN "LA CHANSON DE ROLAND"

Jude I. Onebunne, PhD
Department of Philosophy
Nnamdi Azikiwe University, Awka
juno.anyi@gmail.com
&

Sylvia Chinazom Ezeaka
Department of Modern European Languages
Nnamdi Azikiwe University, Awka
cs.ezeaka@unizik.edu.ng

EXECUTIVE SUMMARY

The fact that the society is filled with human beings, and not only a single being, justifies the Supreme Being's intentions for all beings to relate with each other and work together to achieve a common goal. As such, the logical understanding of the Igbo adage "A nyukoo amiri onu, o gbaa ufufu" simply depicts the Igwebuike philosophy which propagates the limited nature of the individual person and uplifts the unity of the collective human person in achieving far greater positive results. As early as the middle ages, France has recorded a great success in unity, and regretted every form of betrayal and division; hence, the title "La Belle France " was not a misconception of aesthetics and glamour, rather, the beauty in unity, togetherness and solidarity. La chanson de Roland clearly conveys Charlemagne's victorious achievements in the medieval period, which was not by mere fortress, rather by unity and solidarity. Unfortunately, the regrettable destruction that befell his reign was as a result of disunity in the form of betrayal, treachery and division. This paper will significantly unveil the importance of solidarity, the need to be unified as a nation to fight insecurity and maintain national peace. Political analysis of the role of unity in Charlemagne's ruling class and solidarity skills utilized to overcome problems will be deployed, while the integration of the principles of Igwebuike philosophy for national security and peace are strongly recommended.

Keywords: Igwebuike, Kanu Ikechukwu Anthony, National unity, Igbo-African, Peace, Solidarity, Charlemagne

INTRODUCTION

A quick glance at the history of the attainment of freedom and independence of many African countries reveals a couple of outstanding leaders, freedom fighters, true heroes of their time, and patriots who once championed solidarity movements and conquered as well as set the moral and political tones for their societies. Such leaders as Julius Nyerere of Tanzania, Nnamdi Azikiwe of Nigeria, Kwame Nkrumah of Ghana, Nelson Mandela of South Africa, etc., have proved that unity and solidarity is a working strategy for Africa. History reminds us that the success of any organization - religious or secular, state or nation - is highly dependent on the quality of its leadership. Leadership, void of dictatorship and one which upholds unity, complementarity, friendship and solidarity, records substantial success and progress. In this regard and in the spirit of integration and togetherness, *Igwebuike* philosophy propagates principles of good leadership.

Igwebuike philosophy developed over time by Professor Kanu Ikechukwu Anthony is one that is described with an Igbo word, but with a universal relevance and appeal. Nonetheless, it is not limited to the Igbo or African society, rather a universal ideology that believes in the incarnation and confirmation of the universal relevance of its principles. *Igwebuike*, which literally translates to unity is strength, reflects in different Igbo proverbial representations to support its ideology; this philosophy can be well addressed with some collection of Igbo proverbs (Kanu, 2014). These proverbs are not mere collections of words; rather, they are words of communal wisdom that speaks the echoes of ancestral truth which society should do well to hearken to. "*A nyukoo amiri onu, o gbaa ufufu*" defines the power of unity and working together in peace and harmony to achieve common positive results. In this regard, the society is made to understand that working as a group in harmony is far better than individual actions. Solidarity in the face of conflict is an insurmountable force which is most likely to conquer. The Igbo tradition in its totality has always upheld solidarity because of the great success it has known so far in cultural wars and inter-boundary conflicts, hence the agreement of the adage "*Gidi gidi bu ugwu eze*" (Kanu, 2015a&b). Humans are often taught to develop the spirit of oneness, or group solidarity and brotherhood. Igbo culture cannot define complementarily without tracing it to the adage: "*Egbe beru Ugo beru,*" and this is a principle on which the *Igwebuike* philosophy is rooted. This Igbo adage (whose cultural emblem is the eagle and the hawk perching on the same tree branch) is the Igbo version of the concept of Ubuntu, which is common among many other African groups (Kanu, 2016a&b). This concept implies that there is room enough for all. Your existence and well-being does not threaten the Igbo existence and its well-being because the Igbo tradition believes that there is room for all. The Igbo world and religious views demand that the stranger and alien be treated with utmost care, respect and courtesy. In this spirit of oneness, the structure and idea of this proverb has been altered, thereby replacing the wordings to reflect love and concern for others. This renders it *thus: "let the kite perch, let the eagle perch as well, anyone that does not want the other to perch, let its wing not be broken; rather, it should show its mate where to perch"* (Kanu, 2017a&b). All should try to live in peace. Those who do not want peace with others, or insist on causing disharmony have only themselves to be blamed; thus, peaceful coexistence is encouraged and taught. *Igwebuike* also depicts the extension of hand of brotherhood and friendship as a principle of unity which promotes love amongst neighbours, hence the understanding that no man is an island and no man can exist alone because the African tradition does not overlook human intervention. *"Okwa Mmadu k'eji aka,"* therefore, establishes a very strong link between *Igwebuike* philosophy and the structure of the African universe.

> It is a universe of particularities that, however, exist in a thermodynamic system- where every creature as an independent but interacting entity, negotiates another's existential highway for mutual survival (Kanu, 2019).

A closer look at the literal meaning of *Igwebuike* as *strength/power in numbers,* Kanu insists that it rests on the philosophy of solidarity and complementarity; thus, to live outside the parameters of these principles is simply to suffer alienation. *Igwebuike* understands every individual reality as part and completion of the whole, and presents being as that which possesses a relational character of mutual relations (Kanu, 2019 & 2018). Mbiti classically proverbializes this relationship between beings thus: *"I am because we are and since we are, therefore I am"* (Mbiti, 1970). The Igbo cosmology, on its part, having long accepted the potency of unity in resolving issues mutually, depicts its puissance in the proverbs *"Otu osisi anaghi emebe ohia,"* which literally means: A tree does not make a forest. This portrays the importance of numbers; the existence of many trees to create a forest. Asouzu airs his views on the importance of many to successfully achieve a common positive and efficient goal:

> It is also a view that maintains that by the coming together of the individual or parts, a viable and sustainable whole will emerge, and by this, the parts will get to the brim purpose of their existence (Asouzu, 2004).

Prior to this, no particular tree is more important than the other in this concept. No matter how small, tiny or less leaves a particular tree bears, its role in the creation of a forest cannot be overlooked; its existence in the circle is very important. In the human existence, the tree depicts human beings, and none can exist alone; we all need each other to survive. In one way or the other, everything man does needs one form of human interaction or intervention. The earlier proverb entails a relative adage: *"otu aziza anaghi aza ezi,"* which entails that a stick of broom cannot sweep; therefore, sticks of broom put together make up a lever for sweeping. Man cannot ignore the existence and importance of another because forces properly together constitute a power to be reckoned with. Looking at the second adage in its totality solves a bigger problem when applied in unity. Sweeping a small square space with a single stick of broom will take ages and still not achieve a good result, whereas using many sticks of broom jointly tied together does not just make the work a lot easier; it will save time and make the environment very clean. The rich entrepreneurs in the society today did not become rich because they wanted to, nor do the poor make a choice of poverty over riches. Alas, the wealthy didn't even achieve the status quo on their own accord, hence the importance of the existence of the poor masses in the society today. This supports Kanu's presentation of *Igwebuike* thus:

> It is a fact of life that no human person can claim to know everything; and so the need of the other to complement one's knowledge. (Kanu, 2016)

A man with an idea only visualizes how to materialize his ideas using the tools produced and manufactured by other humans and expose them for consumption in the market occupied by other humans, rich or poor. Both depend on the materialized idea of other humans and in turn make him wealthy - everything runs concurrently. Should an intelligent man exist alone in the society, the scene is completely static because he degenerates with his useless ideas in his head. An idea or dream belongs to one man who adopts the tools produced by another to visualize his own ideas, and he finally solicits for other humans to consume his items to help him complete his dream. A human existing alone cannot assume the responsibilities of other humans to affect his success or survival; all humans have their specific role in the lives and success of other humans, consciously or unconsciously. This sense of unity, friendship, complementarity and solidarity among the community is evident in the philosophy of Tempels: *'Beings forces' of the universe are not a multiple of independent forces placed in juxtaposition from being to being* (Tempels, 1959). Therefore, humans are dependent on others for existence. Mbiti also airs his view on the coexistence of humans thus:

> The world of forces is held like a spider's web of which no single thread can be caused to vibrate without shaking the whole network. (Mbiti, 1970)

No man is an island and his existence can never circle around him alone. Even if an idea comes from one man, he needs other forms of human intervention to actualize that idea and bring it into form. The effect of one relatively manifests in other beings because of coexistence and unavoidable connection between one and other, hence the saying *"Otu aka ruta mmanu, ozuo ora."* This adage summons us to look out for one other to ensure nothing goes wrong at one end; whatever goes wrong affects those at the other end. A company owned by an entrepreneur needs the hard work of many to grow, because the survival of many depends on the company's progress. Should by disorderliness, carefree attitude and selfishness the company suffers liquidity, although owned by an individual, it will automatically force many into the labour market. Therefore, unity should be a perennial goal because it is an important value for any society, and for the entire global community. In order for this to become a reality, it is necessary to establish a consensus about fundamental values, and work to extend the principles of peace, equity and well-being, to establish a basic principle of mutual recognition and reciprocity.

UNITY AND DIVISION IN THE MIDDLE AGES FRENCH SOCIETY

A quick run through the political history of France during the middle ages shows clearly the positive impact of unity, and negative default of division and disunity in the leadership and national security of the French society. During the later years of Charlemagne's rule, the Vikings made advances along the northern and western perimeters of his kingdom, but they lost severally because Charlemagne had always based his leadership on solidarity and complementarity. The French text titled *La chanson de Roland* depicts Charlemagne's leadership era, and one could see different levels of success it attained in unity and solidarity, and the destruction meted out to a divided sect, evidently visualizing the *Igwebuike* principle of solidarity *"gidi gidi bu ugwu eze."* Charlemagne was well-known all over France for his might and immeasurable power in the battlefield, and cities and countries were terrified at the mention of his name and at war because he had a great army that fought in unity and looked out for one another. They fought with love for their troop and with immense enthusiasm for the glory of their country. Charlemagne had already conquered all the cities around, except Saragosse which was ruled by Marsille, and it was clear that the city was Charlemagne's next land to conquer. The opponents, already terrified of Charlemagne's might, honourably sought for reconciliation and surrendered under Emperor Charlemagne's rule, rather than facing scandalous death and momentary slavery as they were no measure to the his power. The emperor had always had a strategy of protecting his warriors by means of ambush, whereby they stampeded at different points and ambushed the enemy in case they tried to overpower the armies in the battle field. This complementary approach gained him huge success in the battle field, upholding France as the most powerful country in the entire region.

Charlemagne already tired of fighting, and overwhelmed by the huge success he had attained as the emperor, accepted Marsille's peace offer and sent a messenger, Ganelon, who happened to be Roland's Stepfather, to seal the treaty between the two cities. Ganelon, who was already enraged with jealousy for Roland the chief guard, saw him as enemy and planned revenge by exposing their secret of success to the <u>Saracens</u>. He alienated with the Saracens and formed a new form of friendship with them, thereby informing them of how they could ambush the rear guard of Charlemagne's army, which would surely be led by Roland as the Franks picked their way back to Spain through the mountain valleys. He helped the Saracens plan this evil attack just to eliminate Roland, thereby exposing his country to harm and danger. Ganelon, in this regard, possesses an object of division in an existing unified circled by exposing a guarded secret that has helped them achieve success, not minding the fact that the same single act might unleash terror and disaster upon the entire country. He only aimed at achieving his selfish goals of killing a singular being that his existence was entangled to his own and that of his country. This form of alienation has helped the Saracen attain a pact to their long-awaited confusion as to the reason for Charlemagne's great success. Although the friendship was to a disadvantage to the Frankish army, it would lead to their success, portraying the importance of friendship and hospitality to strangers. Ganelon helped the Saracens achieve the *Igwebuike* principle of *"mmadu k'eji aka"* to plan their movement against the Franks.

Exactly as the traitor Ganelon predicted, Roland gallantly volunteered as usual to lead the rear guard with the clear intention of standing guard to protect his people against sudden ambush, while Olivier and Turpin, his friends and most trusted ally in the army, accompanied him in the rear. Unfortunately, according to plan, and well-prepared in great numbers, the warriors of Saragosse ambushed them at Ronceavaux; Roland and his men were overwhelmed by their sheer number. In unity, they still fought, not knowing that their solidarity circle had been tampered with by an insider, alas, the enemy had taken advantage of the power in number tactics they had always been deployed against them, and fought back gainfully. Hence, unity cannot be defined without solidarity, because the existence of a ravager in the circle sabotages all efforts to succeed, thereby annihilating the unity and peace amongst them. At this point, the unity of Roland's army has been sabotaged because they were unprepared and scattered on their way back home. They never expected a huge fight from the same country that had already paid allegiance and tendered loyalty to the emperor's leadership. Ironically, the opponents deployed the *Igwebuike* principle of *"a nyukoo amiri onu, o gbaa ufufu"* to encircle them and confuse them before they could make a decision to restore their sanity.

Oliver and Turpin, having seen how badly outnumbered they were, asked Roland to blow on his Oliphant (trumpet) made out of an elephant tusk, and seek help from the emperor. This had always been their alibi in time of uncertainty and unexpected confrontation. Unfortunately, Roland proudly declined to the suggestion, believing that they needed no help and could fight any number the Saraceneans came up with. Although they fought magnificently, and with great enthusiasm and spirit of patriotism to protect their great country "la belle France", there was no way they could have held off the great number of the Saracenean army, and the battle began to turn clearly against them. It then dawned on Roland that it was now too late to ask for help from Charlemagne. He blew his Oliphant anyway, so that at least, the emperor should become aware of evil that had befallen his great warriors and seek to avenge them. Roland blew so hard that his temples burst and afterwards he died a glorious martyr's death for his beautiful country; his friends also died in the battle field. Unity and solidarity had always been the key to success for Charlemagne's army. Roland's pride cost his life and that of his dear friends. It was clear that the Frankish army was always victorious by virtue of solidarity. Roland was unaware that the Saracenean army had gained knowledge of their secret and applied the idea of fighting in numbers, instead of sending few to the death field and saving some for a later challenge. Roland always trusted their might and the efficient unity that existed among them, unaware that the circle had already leaked and endangered their lives. Ganelon, on the other part, exposed the entire country to great danger, just to achieve his selfish aim, thereby wasting the blood of the innocent, hence, the Igwebuike proverbial warning against disunity *"otu aka ruta mmanu, o zuo ora"*. Charlemagne and his army angrily fought back the Saracens, killed them in numbers, took over their properties and chased them into the river Ebro where they all drowned. This literary work of the French middle ages was not fictional; rather, it brought to light the importance of unity and its reckoned success as well as described the challenges and disadvantages of disunity to national progress. The real France society after Charlemagne's reign continued to experience change in the system across decades, pending the unified relationship integrated in the existing leadership during each period.

After Charlemagne's death in 814, unfortunately, his successor Charles le Bald was incapable of maintaining political unity as his predecessor, and the empire began to crumble under his reign. The Vikings, who had earlier made advances along the northern and western perimeters of the kingdom under Charlemagne's reign but lost severally, escalated their advances, this time their dreaded longboats sailed up the River Loire, Seine and other inland waterways. They took advantage of the disunity in France during Charles reign and achieved great success. They wreaked havoc and spread terror, murdering people and burning down churches; eventually, they sacked Paris. The history of medieval France transcended into a new era with the election of Hugh Capet (940–996), but his political unimportance weighed against the powerful barons who elected him. Hugh lost the Spanish principalities again due to his inability to give in to solidarity and complementarity, thereby restricting his greatest achievement to just being a ruling king. In order to secure his succession, seeing the extent of failure his leadership suffered, Hugh allowed his son, Robert the Pious, to be crowned king before his demise. Robert II, as King, sought solace in unity and met Holy Roman Emperor Henry II in 1023 on the borderline. They agreed to end all claims over each other's realm, setting a new stage of Capetian and Ottonian relationships. Although a king weak in power, Robert II's efforts were considerable, and that was as a result of mutual understanding and having faith in brotherhood and unity. Unity gave his era an advantage over the leadership of his predecessors. He construed with the fact that he was weak and cannot prosper on his own and sought solace in his ruling quarters and achieved success, even greater than the mighty kings he succeeded. The reign of Robert II was quite important because it involved the Peace and Truce of God. His surviving charters implied that he relied heavily on the Church to rule France. Robert II crowned his son, Hugh Magnus, as king of the Franks at age 10 to secure the succession, but Hugh Magnus rebelled against his father and died fighting him in 1025. His second son, Henry I, was crowned as co-ruler with his father (1027 – 1060), and reigned after his father's death in 1031, but was one of the weakest kings of Franks because he trusted himself alone and never believed in human intervention. He handed over to King Philip I who reigned from 1060 to 1108 and handed the mantle down to Louis VI.

It was from Louis VI onward that royal authority became more accepted. The king, who was more a soldier and warrior than a scholar, launched regular attacks on his vassals due to his greedy and ambitious nature. Hhe raised so much fortune from his vassals, and his bad nature made fun of the royal image and earned him an unpopular king. From 1127, having recorded fame without honour and respect, he sorted the advice of a skilled religious statesman, Abbot Suger, whose political advice was extremely valuable. Louis VI successfully defeated both militarily and politically, but his insatiable greedy nature never eluded his person, and he went against his statesman advice and had landed possessions confiscated and military campaigns mounted against those questioning his leadership. Autocracy and dictatorship was mounted on the people and this drastic policy clearly imposed some royal authority on Paris and its surrounding areas. When Louis VI died in 1137, much progress had been forcefully and illegally achieved towards strengthening Capetian authority, but King Louis VII, upon his succession as king after Louis VI, heeded religiously to Abbot Suger's advice and enjoyed greater moral authority over France than his predecessors. Powerful vassals willingly paid homage to the French king, unlike his predecessor, who forcefully took over the vassals and imposed heavy rules on the people. The succession of kingship in the medieval France has evidently shown the extent of success which true leadership by virtue of unity, complementarity, brotherhood, love for others, solidarity and oneness has achieved in the course of time. Apparently, situation worsens at a point where selfishness and self-centeredness, lack of trust and disunity became the order of the day. Unity restores sanity, stability, and orderliness in a country, and these virtues promisingly help the nation achieve economic, political, social and financial greatness.

IGWEBUIKE AS A RESPONSE TO NATIONAL INSTABILITY

Life rests on the mutual need for human beings to come together and form a community of similitude; *Igwebuike* works best when we respect one another's needs and life circumstances, as respect for one's needs breeds love and reduces the tendency of injustice and wickedness in the society. *Igwebuike*, in the spirit of unity, does not work when we attempt to coerce shame or inflict guilt upon one another, no matter how subtle. No doubt, human relation is a difficult task because we are all different people from very different spheres of life. Nonetheless, we are not necessarily immediate allies, nor are we one another's greatest enemy, therefore, the similarity amongst us should prevail to ascertain attainment of unity amongst all. We believe we have different ideologies and values, but we still share important norms, especially the common belief in basic human rights and the need to live communally in respect and dignity. We believe we must protect this planet, our air, water, earth and food, or we will all die; therefore, unity must be prioritized to achieve these goals. The current situation of the existing COVID-19 pandemic has exposed the fact that affluence is not a guarantee to good life. The rich have always believed they are independent and untouchable in the society because they have attained a prominent financial status which is capable of shielding them from imminent danger. Currently, the entire world is on Corona virus rampage, and in some countries like Nigeria, it seems the rich are the most affected and the wealth acquired through dehumanization and poor leadership has been unable to protect them from the dangers of the disease. All along, had the leadership of the country in the spirit of Igwebuike principle of love, oneness and friendship considered the good health of its citizens and the poor masses, it would have provided the country with befitting hospitals and good health care centers; rather, they depended confidently on their financial ability to sustain the health of their family members by moving to countries with efficient health system while neglecting the citizens. Today, their financial status can neither help the rich nor the poor, everybody is paying the price of greed and disunity existing in the country; health security has failed completely in the system.

The purpose of solidarity is to build our movement, and to embody our mutual care and concern for justice. Chandran defines solidarity thus:

> Solidarity can be simply a way of lifestyle, to support one or more and stick by him in good and bad, as well as his success and failures. (Chadran, 2014)

The definition above could mean a lot more than just its literal sense, because people are necessarily dependent on each other in different ways. When solidarity requires one to follow a group's social and moral rules, they usually have non-instrumental reasons to obey these rules as ways of standing in solidarity and unity with others. Solidarity often grounds reasons to follow somewhat defective rules, and improve their social moral rules in order to pull them in line with the group's ideals, which in turn has lots of limitations to refine oneself and grow.

Solidarity can be referred to as a value *par excellence,* being characterized by mutual collaboration between individuals which makes it possible to overcome the most terrible disasters, such as wars, plagues, bad leadership, destructive trend, etc. This applies as well to helping relatives, friends and acquaintances who find themselves in difficult situations, so that they can overcome obstacles and move forward. The belief that the leadership of the country is engrossed in corruption is a common understanding, including the belief that the global corporate and political institutions are serving only the interests of the rich and continue endlessly to sap the poor of their scourging sweat and effort. But at a point, one wants to break out and achieve success. The oppressed are tired of been abused, voices wish to be heard. There is a mutual agreement that it's time for a fundamental and radical change. There is only one way to speak out; it is for voices to come together and echo in a thunderous manner that will disrupt the serenity of the entire land. The only way voices can be heard loud and clear is through solidarity. Solidarity is the voice of oneness, togetherness and the only way diversity becomes strength of the weak. We build movements and protect one another's lives and rights, the interest being mutual and equal - existence of mutual love, human and group interest at heart, and integrity to strongly hold on to one another to avoid the outbreak of sabotage. In essence, unadulterated solidarity implies great success, critically applying the form of social behavior for the purpose of creating cohesion and social ties that unite the members of a partnership with each other.

There is need for the integration of human relation in performance and practices that are complementary to each other. However, the concept of complementarity suffers from a lack of operational clarity and has been essentially approached from a statistical standpoint that has limited the understanding of the overall system. Complementarity posits that human social coordination is the product of structured psychological inclination linked to corresponding cultural paradigms. A hungry person needs more than bread to survive, because today's bread might not be his problems. He might have the day's bread but is bothered about his hopeless tomorrow; he needs inner peace, and this is the only remedy to his psychological derangement. The rich are not free of this trauma of lack of financial abundance, implying peace; whereas, undue acquisition of so much fund, management and spending are bigger problems on their own. Peace remains the answer to existing problems in the society, and this can be achieved through oneness, complementarity with oneself and other humans. Every human has the innate and congenital need to experience peace and an environment that is void of conflicts. Trees and animals need no peace because nature has blessed them with a peaceful existence. It is unnecessary to hold animal pets in higher regard than fellow humans, because they only agree and respect man's wishes in an animalistic manner which their nature has subjected to. They are created as animals and tend to behave as such, but humans possess understanding and individual differences; therefore, tolerance in adversity is a virtue to be emulated and deployed in general relation with fellow humans to achieve peace of mind. Humans need peace for an enduring co-existence.

The peace that extends to other humans emanates naturally from one's self and inner satisfaction; man can only remain at peace with other men when he has achieved inner peace with himself. Ralph Waldo Emerson once said: *The reason why the world lacks unity, and lies broken and in heaps, is because man is in disunity with himself"*. He clearly establishes the need for individual restoration of inner peace to be able to relate properly with other humans in unity and brotherhood. As difficult as humility and tolerance towards diverse human negative attitude are, peace of mind accelerates discipline and grants a better chance of understanding, and ensures logical approach to human behaviour and individual differences. Unfortunately, the society today bedrocks on other people's faults, and carelessly analyzes these faults to exhibit their intolerance. Humans neglect their own weaknesses, and look at other people's weaknesses. Resolving conflicts, as the principle of the *Igwebuike* philosophy does, is not limited to the Igbo-African culture, and ensuring peace is a world phenomenon that is peculiar to all humans all over the world. Conflict resolution and world peace, as we all know is very important in our lives and is essential to our overall well-being. However, it has regrettably eluded us over the years, not just emphasizing on a particular nation but the entire globe. It has been hindered by different disastrous factors like war, conflicts, diseases, and disagreements throughout human epoch, which have left our entire world and humans in a dilapidating and deplorable state, be it in their emotional, psychological, physical and financial strata.

This research has studied the reality of disunity which characterizes being, the positive dynamics the society could benefit in appreciation of *Igwebuike* as an option for social relationship and leadership goals. Within this context, it looks into the echoes of the medieval French government in the leadership system of France and called for the need for change in Nigerian and generally African political qualities. It describes humans being as beings that should in all aspect deploy other human relations for better survival. It sees the leadership of a nation in the values of the society as a communal responsibility, which everyone is held responsible for its success and failure as well. This work, therefore, suggests as a solution to saving Nigeria from instability (and extends to Africa) from already existing or further emergent political upheaval: there must be a conscious policy of leadership that integrates the local context of the Igbo-African cultural belief of *Igwebuike* principles into its leadership visions. *Igwebuike* potency for achieving national unity should not be overlooked as its principles can help to either prevent or attack problems emanating from bad leadership qualities.

CONCLUSION

Igwebuike philosophy is a true manifestation of the African spirit, *I am because we are* with great emphasis on its translation, *unity is Strength*. An ideology that defines the true essence of human relationship with others, such that mutual relationship, it is a great force which rightly combines and exhibits forces to be reckoned with. Kanu upholds *Igwebuike* as the kind of bond or strength in collaboration and community spirit, and an indication of the necessity of synergy to amplify the value of African communal spirit towards achieving success or anything meaningful in life. The principles of *Igwebuike*, exhibited in this paper as unity, complementarity, friendship and solidarity, are the basis on which this philosophy is well-defined, thus giving them an Igbo-African cultural representation, not limiting the philosophy to the Igbo culture alone, rather giving it cultural amplification and elaboration as preachers of world unity. Elaborating on *Igwebuike* as a philosophy conspicuous in the French society and already perceptible as early as in the middle ages, its success in leadership and other spheres of national progress cannot be overlooked; therefore, it is a commendable approach and serves as a solution to existing problems in our nation today. These principles allow us to overcome the adversities that present themselves throughout life. A person or nation which acts on these principles does not hesitate to collaborate with and support all those who are in disadvantaged situations, in contrast to people who are indifferent to the needs of others and are more self-centered. Therefore, in team spirit, we must encourage an attitude of *Igwebuike* in individuals, since unity can be seen as the basis of many other human values. In a special way, it helps one to develop valuable friendships in family and social settings, and helps nations to attain growth and progress.

REFERENCES

Asouzu, I. I. (2004). *The methods and principles of complementary reflection in and beyond African philosophy*. Calabar: University of Calabar Press.

Barrette, J., Carrière, J. (2003). *Organizational Performance and Complementarity in Human Resources Management Practice*. Journals des Relations Industrielles / Journal of Industrial Relations, Vol. 58, No. 3.

Cadot-Colin, A. (2010, Réécrit) *La Chanson de Roland*. ISBN : 2218944782. Editions Hatier, Paris.

Chandran, R. (2014). Solidarity – The Need for Survival and Existence. *Global Education Magazine*. http://www.globaleducationmagazine.com/solidarity-survival-existence/

Henderson, C. R. (1905). *Social Solidarity in France*. American Journal of Sociology, Vol. 11, No. 2. USA, University of Chicago Press

Kanu, I. A. (2015). *Igwebuike as an Igbo-African Philosophy for National Unity*. A paper presented at the 2015 Faculty of Arts International Conference, Nnamdi Azikiwe University, Awka, Anambra State.

Kanu, I. A. (2016). *Igwebuike as an Igbo-African hermeneutic of globalization*. Igwebuike: An African Journal of Arts and Humanities. Vol. 2, No. 1.

Kanu I. A. (2018). *Sources of Igwebuike Philosophy: Towards A Socio-Cultural Foundation*. International Journal of Religion and Human Relations. Vol. 9, No 1.

Kanu, I.A. (2019). *On the Origin and Principles of Igwebuike Philosophy*. Journal of

Religion and Human Relations. Volume 11, No. 1.

Kanu I. A. (2015b). *A hermeneutic approach to African traditional religion, theology and philosophy*. Nigeria: Augustinian Publications.

Kanu I. A. (2017). *Igwebuikeconomics*: Towards an inclusive economy for economic development. *Igwebuike: An African Journal of Arts and Humanities. Vol. 3. No. 6. 113-140.*

Kanu I. A. (2017). Sources of *Igwebuike* philosophy. *International Journal of Religion and Human Relations. 9. 1. pp. 1-23.*

Kanu, A. I. (2016a). *Igwebuike* as a trend in African philosophy. *IGWEBUIKE: An African Journal of Arts and Humanities. 2. 1. 97-101.*

Kanu, A. I. (2017c). *Igwebuike* as an Igbo-African philosophy of inclusive leadership. *Igwebuike: An African Journal of Arts and Humanities. Vol. 3 No 7. pp. 165-183.*

Kanu, A. I. (2017d). *Igwebuike* philosophy and the issue of national development. *Igwebuike: An African Journal of Arts and Humanities. Vol. 3 No 6. pp. 16-50.*

Kanu, A. I. (2017f). *Igwebuike* as an Igbo-African ethic of reciprocity. *IGWEBUIKE: An African Journal of Arts and Humanities. 3. 2. pp. 153-160.*

Kanu, I. A. (2014). *Igwebuikology* as an Igbo-African philosophy for Catholic-Pentecostal relations. *Jos Studies. 22. pp.87-98.*

Kanu, I. A. (2015a). *African philosophy: An ontologico-existential hermeneutic approach to classical and contemporary issues.* Nigeria: Augustinian Publications.

Kanu, I. A. (2015b). *Igwebuike as an ontological precondition for African ethics.* International Conference of the Society for Research and Academic Excellence. University of Nigeria, Nsukka. 14th -16th September.

Kanu, I. A. (2015c). *Igwebuike as an Igbo-African philosophy of education.* A paper presented at the International Conference on Law, Education and Humanities. 25th -26th November 2015 University of Paris, France.

Kanu, I. A. (Ed.) (2016a). *Complementary ontology: Provocative essays on Innocent Asouzu's African philosophy of integration for progressive transformation.* Germany: Lambert Academic Publishing.

Kanu, I. A. (Ed.) (2016b). *Ibuanyidanda: A complementary systematic inquiry. Reflections on Innocent Asouzu's African philosophy.* Germany: Lambert Academic Publishing.

Kanu, I. A. (2017). *Igwebuike* as an Igbo-African philosophy for Christian-Muslim relations in Northern Nigeria. In Mahmoud Misaeli (Ed.). *Spirituality and Global Ethics* (pp. 300-310). United Kingdom: Cambridge Scholars.

Kanu, I. A. (2017). *Igwebuike* as an Igbo-African philosophy for the protection of the environment. *Nightingale International Journal of Humanities and Social Sciences.* Vol. 3. No. 4. pp. 28-38.

Kanu, I. A. (2017). *Igwebuike* as the hermeneutic of individuality and communality in African ontology. *NAJOP: Nasara Journal of Philosophy.* Vol. 2. No. 1. pp. 162-179.

Kanu, I. A. (2017a). *Igwebuike* and question of superiority in the scientific community of knowledge. *Igwebuike: An African Journal of Arts and Humanities.*Vol.3 No1. pp. 131-138.

Kanu, I. A. (2017a). *Igwebuike as a philosophical attribute of Africa in portraying the image of life.* A paper presented at the 2017 Oracle of Wisdom International Conference by the Department of Philosophy, Tansian University, Umunya, Anambra State, 27-29 April.

Mbiti, J. (1970). *African religions and philosophy.* Nairobi: East African Educational.

Tempels, P. (1959). *Bantu Philosophy.* Paris: Presence Africaine.

THE IGBO-AFRICAN KOLA NUT AS A SYMBOLIC MANIFESTATION OF 'IGWEBUIKE' PHILOSOPHY

Ikechukwu Anthony KANU
Department of Philosophy and Religious Studies
Tansian University Umunya, Anambra State
ikee_mario@yahoo.com

EXECUTIVE SUMMARY

Among the Igbo of eastern Nigeria, symbols are not only important, but have become indispensable in their daily lives. Several symbols used include: Ofo, which is a symbol of authority; Ogu, the symbol of innocence; Ikenga, a symbol of strength, uprightness, success, integrity and ancestry; Mbari, the symbol of culture and aesthetics; Mmanwu, the symbol of the ancestors; Udara, the symbol of fertility, procreation and abundance. All these symbols among the Igbo put together are not as important as the symbolic expressions of the Igbo kola nut (Oji Igbo) 'cola acuminata'. It is among the greatest, if not the greatest symbol among the Igbo, and belongs to the mysteries of Igbo history, culture and tradition. It symbolizes the well-acclaimed Igbo hospitality, and manifests goodwill. It is used to settle disputes and make peace, and serves as a link between human beings and the divine. This work studied the Igbo kola nut in relation to its symbolic expression of Igwebuike philosophy. Igwebuike, at the philosophical level, provides an ontological horizon that presents being as that which possesses a relational character of mutual relations. Taking from the Igwebuike worldview, which places the human person at the centre of the universe, the kola nut was employed to advance the understanding of the human person's relationship with fellow human beings, and the relationship between human beings and the gods, ancestors, etc. This piece discovered that the kola nut expresses Igwebuike philosophy which is the operative condition of the Igbo universe. For the purpose of this study, the Igwebuike holistic and complementary approaches were employed.

Keywords: Oji, Igbo Kola Nut, Africa, *Igwebuike*, Complementarity, symbol, philosophy

INTRODUCTION

The African is a *homo symbolicus*, and one does not need to live long among them to discover that symbols occupy a very significant place in their life. As representational beings, they have a distinctive character of creating and using symbols to communicate evocative messages that represent aspects of their lives or those around them. The African is, therefore, not just a symbol-making being, but a symbolizing being. Farchild (1965) describes a symbol as:

> ...that which stands for something else particularly a relatively concrete explicit representation of a more generalized, diffuse, intangible object or group of objects. A very large part of social processes is caused on by use of symbols such as words, money, certificates and pictures. A true symbol excites reactions similar to, though perhaps not quite as intense as those created by the original object. (p. 314).

It is from the above perspective that Madu (2011) maintains that symbolism implies the practice of using acts, sounds, objects or other means which are not of importance in themselves for directing attention to something that is considered important.

Among the Igbo of eastern Nigeria, several symbols are used to direction attention to significant realities; symbols like the *Ofo,* which symbolizes authority; *Ogu,* the symbol of innocence; *Ikenga*, a symbol of strength, uprightness, success, integrity and ancestory; *Mbari*, the symbol of culture and aesthetics; *Mmanwu*, the symbol of the ancestors; and *Udara*, the symbol of fertility, procreation and abundance. All these symbols among the Igbo put together are not as important as the Igbo kola nut (Oji Igbo) *cola acuminata*. It is among the greatest, if not the greatest symbol among the Igbo. Of the many cultural symbols in Igboland, none has received attention like the kola nut. It is very important and central to the life and ceremonies of the Igbo.

This work studies the Igbo kola nut in relation to its symbolic expression of *Igwebuike* philosophy. *Igwebuike,* at the philosophical level, provides an ontological horizon that presents being as that which possesses a relational character of mutual relations. Taking from the *Igwebuike* worldview, which places the human person at the centre of the universe, the kola nut, as a symbolic expression, will be studied to see to what extent it expresses the understanding of the human person as a being relationship with fellow human beings and the divine: gods, ancestors, etc.

THE IGBO KOLA NUT IN IGBO-AFRICAN RELIGION AND CULTURE

For the Igbo, the kola nut goes beyond the red and yellow seed that you find in trays sold on the streets and in kiosks. It is not just the biannual crop grown and stored in sacks and baskets (Kanu, 2015a). It is a food that must be eaten with relish; it commands adoration and many accolades and must be attended to with deserving feast. It unites the living and the dead, and symbolizes a feast of togetherness, love and trust. The kola nut is a symbol of life *ndu;* this is why the Igbo say: "He that brings kola brings life" (Kanu, 2019).

Uchendu (1965) refers to the kola nut as "the greatest symbol of Igbo hospitality. It always comes first. 'It is the king'"(p. 74). And because of the important place it occupies, presenting it is very ceremonial. The ceremony begins with the presentation of the kola nut to the guests through the next ranking male after which it is returned to the host. It is usually presented alongside with white chalk (*nzu*), alligator pepper, garden egg, bitter kola, groundnut butter (*Okwa ose*) in a wooden dish (*Okwa oji*). Inside the wooden dish is added a knife for the breaking of the kola. Even if the visitor is just a person, more than one kola nut is presented in case the visitor may need to take one back home. Anything less than two must be presented with apologies before any other ritual commences. The presentation is followed by a prayer, said by the host if he is the eldest; if not, the prayer is said by the eldest person present. During the prayer, *Chukwu* is invoked with incantations garnished with proverbs and prayers for life, good health, prosperity, children, peace, justice, etc. After the prayer, the kola nut is broken into its various lobes; this is followed by distribution and chewing. It is expected that everyone present would partake in the kola nut to avoid the euphoria of suspicion.

Figure 1: *The Kola Nut: Culled from www.pinterest.com*

As the heart beat of the Igbo culture and tradition, the Igbo kola nut is used for several purposes, which include:

1. **To welcome a visitor**
   To welcome a visitor with a kola is to receive the visitor into one's life. It is also a sign that you wish the visitor life.

2. **To open a prayer**
   It is used for prayers and sacred communion because of the special place it occupies among the gods.

3. **For rites, rituals and ceremonies**

   It is what the gods, ancestors and men eat together during these ceremonies.

4. **Food and nutrition**

   It is a food that contains caffeine, theobromine, tannins, potassium, magnesium, glycosides, etc.

5. **Commerce**

   It is bought and sold just like any other goods and services.

6. **Cleansing**

   It is used for ritual of cleansing of a person, property or place.

7. **Flavoring**

   It is used for flavoring food, drinks and beverages. In 1886, Pendergrast (2000) observes that it was used to flavor coca cola.

8. **Oath-taking, covenant and settlement of disputes**

   When used during these circumstances, it is employed to call on God to be a witness.

9. **Divination and prophecy**

   Usually it is broken into lobes and cast on the ground, then the diviner makes an interpretation.

10. **Sacrifice and worship**

    This is very important as it is a sacred meal, the meal of the gods.

11. **Receiving a new day**

    It is used in the morning during invocatory poems and prayers.

12. **Medical and mystical uses**

    Because of its nutritive value, it has health consequences. It helps strengthen the tooth enamel surface.

Every kola nut can be broken into lobes, and these lobes signify numbers. And number is very important for the African. Some have one lobe, some two lobes, some three, some four, some five, some six and some seven. One can also find a kola nut with more than seven lobes.

The kKola nut with one lobe is a dumb kola (*Oji Ogbi*). It is also called the kola nut of the spirits (*Oji Mmuo*), round kola nut (*Oji Ifilifi or nkpurukakpu*), kola nut of the mystical circle or zero kola nut(*Oji Akwu na Ogbi or Obi*); it is not eaten by human beings because it belongs to *Chukwu*; *Chukwu* is a spirit (*Chukwu bu mmuo*). A one-lobed kola nut is neither male nor female, since *Chukwu* is one and indivisible in nature.

When it has two lobes, it is called *oji gworo,* symbolizing male and female. It is an elliptical gender shadow of *oji ogbi* and the first child of the one-lobed kola nut. It is the *cola nitida.* Just like the one-lobed kola nut, it belongs to the spirits and is not used for religious and cultural celebrations in Igbo land. However, it can be eaten after some prayers.

Three-lobed kola nut is called *Oji Ikenga (Ike eji aga,* Ikenga is a spirit of power and achievement*)* or *Oji Dike* (the kola nut of the brave or valiant), or *Oji Echichi* (the kola nut of titled people). It is the masculine kola. As a matter of principle, it is eaten only by warriors, brave men, the consecrated or the ordained. It is not eaten by women, except for those who may be seeking for a male child.

The kola with four lobes (*Oji Aka ano*) is the kola of peace (*Oji Udo*) and blessings (*Oji Ngozi*), the kola nut of the four market days (*Oji ahia na ano ubosi na ano: Afor, Nkwor, Eke* and *Orie*). It also symbolizes completeness (*izu zuru oke,* referring to the four market days). It is the kola nut for both male and female genders (*Oji nwoke na nwayi*), and thus considered the most gender-sensitive kola. It is also called the kola nut of the family (*Oji ezinuno*) because it is believed to unite the family.

The kola with five lobes is the kola of procreation (*Oji omumu*), protection, of industry and achievement (*Oji aka na okpa*), of wealth (*Oji una or Oji ubalaka*), progress and good luck (*Oji sirili werere*). Whenever it is broken and shared, it is a sign that things will go well. It came from the four-lobed kola; however, unlike the four-lobed kola with two males and two females, the five-lobed kola comes with three males and two females.

The kola with six lobes is called the kola nut of the ancestors (*Oji ndi chie*), or the kola that doubles the Ikenga kola (*Oji Ikenga abuo*). It is also called the covenant kola nut (*Oji Ogbugbandu*), the kola nut of communion (*Oji Oriko*) or the kola nut of blood and spirit ties (*Oji Umume na Umuite*). It is the kola of blood and spirit, and thus, indicative of communion with the ancestors. No wonder the smallest part of it is not eaten but given to the ancestors. It is used to make peace, covenant ties, taking of oath and punishment of offenders.

The last is the seven-lobed kola, which is known as the kola nut of perfection of man and spirit (*Oji asaa mmadu asaa mmuo*), consummations, fulfillment, and completeness (*Oji kpurugede*), the kola nut of the titled cow killer (*Oji ogbuefi*), the kola nut of Ozo title and prophecy (*Oji ozo na amuma*), the kola nut of celebration and festivities (*Oji emume na mmemme*), the kola nut of law and judgment (*Oji iwu na ikpe*). It is also the kola of endlessness or eternity. Thus, the Igbo would say: *Uwam uwa asaa; asaa ndu na anwuanwu; ikpa naasaa mmiri naasaa* (Kanu, 2015b).

THE KOLA NUT AND THE EXPRESSION OF *IGWEBUIKE* PHILOSOPHY

Igwe bu ike is an Igbo proverb and also a typical Igbo name. Igbo proverbs and names are among the major traditional vessels where African philosophy, religion and culture have continued to be preserved. They contain the wisdom and experience of the African people, usually of several ages gathered and summed up in one expression (Kanu, 2018a). Thus, beyond the linguistic expression lies a deeper meaning. It is at the philosophical level that *Igwebuike* is understood as providing an ontological horizon that presents being as that which possesses a relational character of mutual relations (Kanu, 2016a).

The expression, *Igwebuike*, is a combination of three Igbo words. It can be understood as a word or a sentence: as a word, it is written as *Igwebuike*, and as a sentence, it is written as, *Igwe bu ike*, with the component words enjoying some independence in terms of space. Literally, *Igwe* is a noun which means 'number' or 'multitude,' usually a large number or population. The number or population in perspective are entities with ontological identities and significances; however, they are part of an existential order in which every entity is in relation to the other. *Bu* is a verb, which means *is*. *Ike* is a noun, which means *strength* or *power* (Kanu, 2016b). *Igwe, bu* and *Ike* put together, means 'number is strength' or 'number is power' (Kanu, 2017a). However, beyond the literal sense of *Igwebuike*, it means *otu obi* (one heart and one soul) – *cor unum et anima una*. In a metaphoric sense, it is used within the Igbo linguistic setting to refer to relational engagement in the world, accomplished in solidarity and complementarity, and the powerful and insurmountable force therein (Kanu, 2017b). The closest words to it in English are complementarity, solidarity and harmony.

If *Igwebuike* provides an ontological horizon that presents being as that which possesses a relational character of mutual relations, the major question looming at the horizon is how the kola nut symbolizes this mutual relational character. It is in this regard that kola nut symbols of human/human and human/divine relationships will be studied.

1. The Kola nut Symbol of Divine/Human Relationship

The kola nut is a sacred symbol among the Igbo, and it tells the story of the Igbo religious reality. It is, therefore, not surprising that, in relation to its beginnings, the kola nut is presented in Igbo mythologies as belonging to the plant world of the spirits and has remained associated with the spirit world. Umeogu (2019) gives several mythical stories in this regard; however, the following three are of relevance to this research:

1. The autochthonous origin of the kola nut holds that it was planted by *Chukwu* as the first tree planted on Igbo land. It was planted by *Chukwu* so that the fruits would serve as fruits for both the gods and human beings. It was also planted that it may become the gateway of communion between spirits and human beings.

2. A second myth holds that the gods lived on kola nuts and sacrifices. Usually, when they were offered sacrifices, they consumed the sacrifice with kola nut. Human beings used sacrifices to invoke the presence of the gods so as to attend to human needs or challenges. During one of such invocations and the appearance of the gods in Igbo land, they forgot to return with some of the kola nuts that they had brought to eat their sacrifice with. The kola nut then sprouted and became a cherished tree in Igbo land.

3. A third myth has it that the founding fathers of Igbo land paid a visit to the gods. As part of the welcome ceremony, the gods went to their orchard, plugged a fruit and offered it to the founding fathers of Igbo land. On their return home, these founding fathers returned with the kola nut to Igbo land, planted it and began using it in the world of human beings. Since then, it has been used for welcoming visitors, rituals, ceremonies, etc.

Because of the sacred dimension of the kola nut, it has been regarded as a symbol of sacred communion between human beings and the gods, spirits, ancestors, etc. Thus, during the blessing of the kola nut, Osamugha (2006) observes that the prayer below is said:

God in heaven come and eat kola.
Unfathomable God, come and eat kola.
King who is the final arbiter, come and eat kola
Our ancestors, recent and remote, come and eat kola (p. 10).

From the foregoing, the kola nut has been used by the Igbo in their relationships with the divine. It is at this level that the kola nut is understood as a symbol of divine and human relations. Through the kola nut, human beings do for the divine what they cannot do for themselves, and through it too, they appeal to the gods to do for them (human beings) what they cannot do for themselves. This communion between human beings and the gods is symbolized in and attained through the use of kola nut. There are special events when and where it is used by human beings in their relationship with the divine. These times include:

a. **Prayer**
It is very important in prayer because the kola nut speaks, and also used to communicate between human beings and the gods. It is so important that in every gathering of the Igbo it is employed for the opening prayer. Nzekwu (1966) presents a typical Igbo prayer with the kola nut thus:

Creator of the universe, chew kola nut. Our ancestral spirits, chew kola nut. He who brings kola nut brings life. Wherever a child may be, may it wake each dawn. We will all live. Forward jumps the male monkey; it never jumps backward. If a kite and an eagle perch, whichever says the other should not perch, may its wings break. Whatever one's occupation, may it provide for his old age. (p. 48).

The *oji* (kola nut) and *mmanya-oku* (hot drink) are also important during libations, the food and drink of the gods. It is through libation that the African tries to normalize or balance the relationship between the three worlds. This libation is made to God through the agency of the ancestors and other deities. The Igbo believe that through gifts, like the kola nut, they can gain God's favour.

b. **Divination and Prophecy**

The kola nut is an important element during divination and prophecy among the Igbo. Divination involves a process of inquiry. People who wish to know why certain things happen, how to solve certain problems, and so on, go to diviners. This is usually done through the agency of a particular deity. The Igbo would say *Onye amaghi ebe mmiri bidoro maba ya, anaghi ama ebe okwusiri* (He who does not know where rain started beating him cannot know where it stopped.). The kola nut in divination speaks the minds of the gods. When it is broken and thrown to the ground, the diviner or prophet interprets what the gods are saying to a particular situation or individual. This interpretation is shaped by the way the lobes fall, whether facing up or down.

For instance, if after the lobes are thrown to the ground or in a plate and they lie open on their backs, it is called *itu mnwiri enu* and is a sign of good things to come, but if they lie on their faces with their backs up, it is called *itu mnwiri ala*, and is a sign of bad omen. When it is a half face up, it is called *itu mnwiri nko enu*. When it is a half face down, it is called *itu mnwiri nko ala*. If the lobes forma circle, it is a sign of life. If they form a cross, it is sign of conflict or death.

c. **Festivals, Rites, Rituals and Ceremonies**

The kola nut is never absent in Igbo religious festivals, rituals, rites and ceremonies. The reason is simple; the gods cannot be invited for a ceremony without making provision for their food: the kola nut. Religious festivals and rituals, such as new yam festivals, harvest seasons, hunting seasons and planting season festivals, are activities that demonstrate and express belief and faith in *Chukwu* and the spirit world. During these ceremonies, what God or the spirits have done for human beings are commemorated and powers obtained from the spirit world. For instance, the Igbo's celebration of the new yam festival is connected to the month of *Ahiajioku*. It is a time when they give thanks to *Chukwu*, His deans and the ancestors for granting them a bountiful harvest for the year. Igbo traditional marriage ceremonies, etc., also provide an opportunity for communion with the ancestors, as the Igbo invoke their blessings upon the newly married couple.

d. **Sacrifice and Worship**

The kola nut occupies an important place in Igbo ritual home. For some, it is a crop grown in the forests and sold; but for the Igbo, it is an instrument for a holy communion. Its sacredness explains why it is used by human beings during sacrifices and worship. Through it, the human person is able to reach out to the gods.

e.   **Oath-taking, Covenants and Settlement of Disputes**
The five and six-lobed kola nuts are used during oath-taking (*Inu iyi*), covenants (*Igbo ndu* or *Igbo oriko*) and settlement of disputes (*Ikpe ikpe*) to invite the gods and ancestors to be witnesses to the covenant that is made or oath that is taken or agreement reached during dispute settlement. The five-lobed kola is used for the settlement of dispute. If after the dispute is settled and the kola nut is broken, shared and eaten, it is sign that peace must reign between the persons involved. If afterwards, a mischief maker arises from among the persons, he would be in trouble.

2. Symbol of Inter-human Relations

The Igbo kola nut symbolizes the unity and togetherness of the Igbo people. This understanding begins from the shape of the kola nut itself: it has the shape of the human heart, and so it is regarded as the heart of the Igbo people. It is in this regard that it is said that 'the kola nut is the heart of the Igbo people' (*Oji bu mkpuru obi ndi Igbo*). It does not just symbolize the Igbo people in an abstract sense, it is also a culture that holds the Igbo people together; wherever they meet, the kola nut carries the same meaning and power. Once it is presented, every Igbo person knows what it symbolizes and what should be done. It is within this context that the Igbo say that 'the kola nut is the culture that holds the Igbo together' (*Oji bu omenani jikotaru ndi Igbo*). It is at this level of understanding that it becomes easier to connect the Igbo kola nut with *Igwebuike* philosophy which means *otu obi* (one heart and one soul) – *cor unum et anima una*.

This philosophy of *otu obi* that the kola nut signifies is evident when it is presented to a visitor as a sign of reception and hospitality. To offer a visitor kola nut is to receive the visitor with one's life, and beyond that, it is also wishing the person life, because an Igbo proverb says that 'he that brings kola brings life' (*onye wetara oji wetara ndu*). According to Uchendu (1964), "Kola nut features in all aspects of Igbo life. It is the symbol of Igbo hospitality. To be presented with a kola nut is to be made welcome; and one is most welcome when the kola nut turns out white, whether this is by accident or by design" (p. 448).

The lobes of the kola point to the reality of complementarity in human relationships. When these lobes stay together they remain alive, but when they separate they die and dry off. Their togetherness is a symbol of life, and their separation, death. Life in Africa is about being in relation to the other. To be is to belong, and not to belong is to suffer alienation (Kanu, 2017d and 2016d). The kola nut also symbolizes the African worldview, which is characterized by a common origin, common worldview, common language, shared culture, shared race, colour and habits, common historical experience and a common destiny. The communal-individuality of the African is expressed in the Igbo proverb which says 'If a lizard stays off from the foot of a tree, it would be in danger' (*Ngwere ghara ukwu osisi, aka akpara ya*) (Kanu, 2014). Mbiti (1970) classically proverbialized the community-determining role of the individual when he writes, "I am because we are and since we are, therefore I am" (p. 108). The existence of others assures one of their solidarity and complementarity, without which I cannot be. Achebe (1958) brings the essential nature of the Igbo-African communal relationship to a higher and more fundamental focus when he writes:

> We do not ask for wealth because he that has health and children will also have wealth. We do not pray to have more money but to have more kinsmen. We are better than animals because we have kinsmen. An animal rubs its itching flank against a tree, a man asks his kinsman to scratch him. (p. 132).

The kola nut points to the fact that existence is not only meaningful, but also possible only in a community.

THE KOLA NUT AND *IGWEBUIKE* PHILOSOPHY OF SCIENCE

There might have been other sources of knowledge of African philosophy of science; however, the kola nut as a symbol inundated with multiple meanings among the African people must have contributed to or deepened the understanding of African philosophy of science. This is very important, especially as the kola nut is a gift from *Chukwu*, who is Himself the source of all science and knowledge.

1. The Kola Nut and *Igwebuike* Physics

The two-lobed kola nut has implications for an African physics. The two lobes signify actions and events within the African world. Umeogu (2019) refers to it as that force of impression that would move a body and stop a body in motion, and the kola produces cause and effect, action and reaction. It is through the movement and interaction of these forces of nature that reality comes into existence (Kanu, 2020). Instances include:

a. *Universal Gravitational Force*- Everything works towards the centre of the earth which points to the African concept of the Complementarity of reality. In spite of the multiplicity of reality, reality is one.

b. *Synthesis Theory of Urea*: This theory believes that the synthesis of inanimate things brings about the formation of animate realities. It points to the interconnected of reality.

c. *Neutralization Reaction*: It holds that the combination of elements brings about the formation of new ones. For instance, oxygen + hydrogen=water or Acid + Base= salt + water

If it is through the interaction of forces, and sometimes conflicting forces, that new realities come into existence. It then implies that in African physics, alterity is not a problem but a potentiality for the birth of new reality. It further presents the Igbo universe as one of conflicts of opposites: good and evil, light and darkness, hot and cold, wet and dry, male and female, etc. These conflicts do not spell the end of the universe but the hope of sustenance and remaining in being.

2. The Kola Nut and *Igwebuike* Astronomy and Theogenesis

The unity of the lobes of the kola nut, in spite of their divisibility, unrepeatability and uniqueness, registers the fact about the 'commonness' in the midst of alterity in the African universe. It manifests the fact that reality in the African universe is one. It does not just point to the oneness of reality but to the mysterious beginning of the universe (from the one-lobed kola - a symbol of *Chukwu*). It all began from the ONE, with whom there was no second. That ONE is *Chukwu* who alone, in Himself and by Himself, created the universe. We did not create it but found ourselves in it. We are because He does exist, and nothing would be in existence without Him, for everything was made through Him and in Him. The case of the one-lobed kola nut, *Oji Ogbi*, tells His story. It is the first kola from which other kola nuts emerged. It is neither a male nor female, just as *Chukwu* is neither male nor female.

The one-lobed kola nut points to the importance of numbers in the African universe, and how Igbo-Africans devoted much time and interest in mathematics. They did not only develop it, but used numbers to explain the reality of the universe. It is in this regard that 1,2,3,4,5,6,7 lobed kola nuts give profound explanations about the Igbo universe and how realities can be explained in relation to numbers. The one-lobed kola, being the beginning and source of other kola nuts, points to the important place that the number ONE occupies in Igbo astronomy. The number ONE is not only the central number but the centre of the universe and the heart of reality. Every reality began from the number ONE Its destiny is determined by the ONE and would end in the ONE. This One is *Chukwu*.

Since everything exists in and through the frame of the ONE, every reality finds its unity in Him. It is within this context that *Igwebuike* understands every individual reality as part of and the completion of the whole, and thus, there is a unity in the midst of diversity (Kanu, 2019).

3. The Kola Nut and *Igwebuike* Biology and Anthropogenesis

Focusing on the four-lobed kola nut, which is made of two female lobes and two male lobes, in which the male lobe faces the female lobe and the female lobe faces the male lobe, the source and foundation of the Igbo-African family is traced. It makes it clear that according to Igbo biology, it is from the union of the male and female that other males and females emerged. It is through the crossing of the male and female that every other thing was generated. The male and female speak of the positive and negative polar charges of being that must cross each other before a being of their kind can come into existence. Thus, the four-lobed kola nut speaks of the source of creative light and life. When the male and female lobes cross each other, light is ignited which further brings about life in the Igbo world.

4. The Kola Nut and *Igwebuike* Scientific Method

The multiplicity of the lobes, which does not in any way make the kola nut two or three or four kola, but united to form a whole, points to a holistic approach in science. Its 'holisticness' of the approach is anchored on the fact that all parts of reality are interconnected and find identity, meaning and purpose through relationships. Thus, *Igwebuike* emphasizes the importance of multidimentionality in research (Kanu, 2017g). An investigation of a particular situation or reality should imply several viewpoints or perspectives so as to arrive at a global, balanced and enriched position (Kanu, 2017h).

The implications of the lobes of the kola nut lying side by side as support to each other establish the importance of interdisciplinary approach in scientific investigations. The interdisciplinary approach is based on the interconnectivity of reality. By interdisciplinary approach, it is meant the combining of two or more established academic disciplines in a process of research (Kanu, 2019). Thus, an interdisciplinary research synthesizes perspectives, knowledge, skills, interconnections, epistemologies, etc. The interdisciplinary method draws knowledge from several other professions, technologies and fields (Kanu, 2016a). This further implies that science as a field of study is not independent of other fields of human endeavour. While it can give explanations for the causes of certain realities in the universe, it cannot alone give meaning or purposefulness to human existence.

CONCLUSION

Among the Igbo-Africans, the kola nut remains one of those symbols that have defied the blades of civilization. It is, therefore, not surprising that, in spite of the influx of modernity into the African society, the place of the kola nut remains undiminished, and may have even grown in stature. One of the reasons for its persistence through time is because of its sacredness and place in ceremonies and festivals. It is such that ceremonies like marriage, child birth, naming of a child, new yam festivals, etc., without the kola nut, may be considered incomplete. The kola nut does not only symbolize the essence of the African acclaimed hospitality, it manifests the goodwill employed to welcome a visitor. It is also used to settle interpersonal or inter-communal disputes. From the foregoing, Acholonu (2006) avers that "the kola nut functions at the heart of Igbo-African collective psyche and spirituality" (p. 1).

It is because of the centrality of the kola nut in the Igbo psyche and spirituality that its relationship with *Igwebuike* philosophy, which captures the Igbo-African worldview, becomes unavoidable. This work has unveiled the symbolic manifestation of *Igwebuike* philosophy in the kola nut. The kola nut manifests the reality of being human within the context of a web of relationships with persons and other inhabitants of the universe. The kola nut and *Igwebuike* philosophy understand the human person and other realities around him/her as a social being, rather than a solitary individual. Herein, being human involves an unfolding, evolving and developing dimension, one that has a cumulative experience and wisdom of one's community, locally and globally. It is within this context that the kola is understood as a symbolic expression of *Igwebuike* philosophy.

REFERENCES

Achebe, C. (1958). *The things fall apart*. England: Heinemann.

Acholonu, R. (2006). Women and the kola nut saga in Igbo culture: A human rights abuse. In Uchem, R. (Ed.). *Women and the kola nut* (pp. 1-8). Enugu: SNAAP Press.

Fairchild, H. P. (1965). Dictionary of sociology and related sciences. England: Little field Adams.

Kanu I. A. (2015b). *A Hermeneutic Approach to African Traditional Religion, Theology and Philosophy*. Nigeria: Augustinian Publications.

Kanu I. A. (2017a). *Igwebuikeconomics*: Towards an inclusive economy for economic development. *Igwebuike: An African Journal of Arts and Humanities. Vol. 3. No. 6.* 113-140.

Kanu I. A. (2017b). Sources of *Igwebuike* Philosophy. *International Journal of Religion and Human Relations. 9. 1.* pp. 1-23.

Kanu, A. I. (2016a). *Igwebuike* as a trend in African philosophy. *IGWEBUIKE: An African Journal of Arts and Humanities. 2. 1.* 97-101.

Kanu, A. I. (2016b). *Igwebuike* as an Igbo-African hermeneutic of globalization. *IGWEBUIKE: An African Journal of Arts and Humanities. 2. 1.* 1-7.

Kanu, A. I. (2016d). *Igwebuike* as a trend in African philosophy. *IGWEBUIKE: An African Journal of Arts and Humanities. 2. 1.* 97-101.

Kanu, I. A. (2014). *Igwebuikology* as an Igbo-African philosophy for Catholic-Pentecostal relations. *Jos Studies. 22. pp.87-98.*

Kanu, I. A. (2015a). *African philosophy: An ontologico-existential hermeneutic approach to classical and contemporary issues.* Nigeria: Augustinian Publications.

Kanu, I. A. (2016c). *Igwebuike* as an Igbo-African Hermeneutics of Globalisation. *IGWEBUIKE: An African Journal of Arts and Humanities,* Vol. 2 No.1. pp. 61-66.

Kanu, I. A. (2017c). *Igwebuike* and the logic (Nka) of African philosophy. *Igwebuike: An African Journal of Arts and Humanities. 3. 1. pp. 1-13.*

Kanu, I. A. (2017d). *Igwebuike* and Question of Superiority in the Scientific Community of Knowledge. *Igwebuike: An African Journal of Arts and Humanities.*Vol.3 No1. pp. 131-138.

Kanu, I. A. (2018a). *Igwe Bu Ike* as an Igbo-African Hermeneutics of National Development. *Igbo Studies Review. No. 6. pp. 59-83.*

Kanu, I. A. (2018b). *Igwebuike* as an African Integrative and Progressive Anthropology. *NAJOP: Nasara Journal of Philosophy.* Vol. 2. No. 1. pp. 151-161.

Kanu, I. A. (2019). Collaboration within the Ecology of Mission: An African Cultural Perspective. *The Catholic Voyage: African Journal of Consecrated Life.* Vol. 15. pp. 125-149.

Kanu, I. A. (2019). *Igwebuike* Research Methodology: A New Trend for Scientific and Wholistic Investigation. *IGWEBUIKE: An African Journal of Arts and Humanities (IAAJAH). 5. 4. pp. 95-105.*

Kanu, I. A. (2020). African Culture as an Ancient Landmark: Culture versus Identity. *Igwebuike: An African Journal of Arts and Humanities. Vol. 6. No. 3.* pp. 49-54.

Kanu, I. A. (2014a). Igbo proverbs as *depositum* of Igbo-African philosophy. *International Journal of Humanities and Social Sciences. Vol. 4. No. 1.* pp. 164-168.

Kanu, I. A. (2014a). Suicide in Igbo-African ontology. *Developing Countries Studies.* Vol. 4. No. 5. USA. pp. 27-38.

Kanu, I. A. (2014b). Suffering in Igbo-African Ontology. *Research on Humanities and Social Sciences.* Vol. 4. No. 5. pp. 8-13.

Kanu, I. A. (2014b). The place of Igbo myths in Igbo-African philosophy. *American Journal of Contemporary Research. Vol. 4. No. 2.* pp. 98-102.

Kanu, I. A. (2015). African traditional democracy with particular reference to the Yoruba and Igbo political systems. *International Journal of Philosophy and Public Affairs.* Vol. 2. No. 3. pp. 147-160.

Kanu, I. A. (2015). *Personal identity and punishment in John Locke* (A Dissertation for the Award of Master of Arts Degree in Philosophy- Metaphysics), University of Nigeria, Nsukka, Enugu State.

Kanu, I. A. (2015a). *African philosophy: An ontologico-existential hermeneutic approach to classical and contemporary issues.* Nigeria: Augustinian Publications.

Kanu, I. A. (Ed.) (2016a). *Complementary ontology: Provocative essays on Innocent Asouzu's African philosophy of integration for progressive transformation.* Germany: Lambert Academic Publishing.

Kanu, I. A. (Ed.) (2016b). *Ibuanyidanda: A complementary systematic inquiry. Reflections on Innocent Asouzu's African philosophy.* Germany: Lambert Academic Publishing.

Kanu, I. A. (2016). *Igbo-African Christology: A cultural Christological construct in Post-Missionary Africa.* Germany: Lambert Publications.

Kanu, I. A. (2016a). African traditional folk songs as dialogue between education and entertainment. *Cambridge International Journal of Contemporary Education Research.* 6. 6. pp. 53-64.

Madu, E. J. (2011). *Symbolism in African cosmology: The Igbo perspective.* Nnamdi Azikiwe University, Awka. Lecture Notes, 2011.

Mbiti, J. (1970). *African religions and philosophy.* Nairobi: East African Educational Publishers.

Nzekwu, O. (1966). Wand of noble wood. New York: Signet.

Osamugha, C. (2006). Women and the kola nut in Igbo culture: A theological reflection. In Uchem, R. (Ed.). *Women and the kola nut* (pp. 9-14). Enugu: SNAAP Press.

Pendergrast, M. (2000). For God, country and coca-cola. New York: Basic Books.

Uchendu, V. C. (1964). Kola hospitality and Igbo lineage structure, man. Vol. 64. Britain: Royal Authr Institute.

Uchendu, V. C. (1965). *The Igbo of South East Nigeria*. New York: Holt Rinehart and Winston.

Umeogu, B. U. (2019). *Kolanut in Igbo metpahysics: A phenomernalysical research into its symbolismic universe*. Inaugural Lecture delivered on 26th September at the Nnamdi Azikiwe University, Awka, Anambra State

'IGWEBUIKE' PHILOSOPHY AND THE MANAGEMENT OF COVID-19 IN NIGERIA

OMOJOLA Immaculata Olu, (SSMA), PhD
Department of Business Administration and Management
Villanova Polytechnic, Imesi Ile, Osun State
omojolassma@yahoo.co.uk

EXECUTIVE SUMMARY

This paper discussed 'Igwebuike' philosophy and the management of Corona virus pandemic (Covid-19) in Nigeria. It attempted to show the correlation between this philosophy and how Covid-19 is being managed in Nigeria. The development of the disease, its spread and preventions were deliberated upon, in the sense that it originated from China. It has spread into many countries, and can be contracted through droplets from the affected person(s). Avoidance of gatherings (both social and religious), use of face masks and sanitizers were presented to be some of the ways in which the spread of the pandemic could be curbed. To arrive at a lasting solution, the government introduced social lockdown, and foodstuffs were distributed to people to cushion its effects on them. The work revealed that 'Igwebuike' philosophy and Covid-19 are related in the sense that both deal with people and their affairs. It brought about solidarity on the part of government and the populace in finding solutions to the common problem of the pandemic in their ability to search for vaccines, while individuals were suggesting African herbs. Also, the Covid-19 period encouraged families to stay together in unity and harmony as 'Igwebuike' philosophy resonates. It was then recommended that there should be proper database for unbiased distribution of palliatives. The lockdown should be a nation-wide issue for proper supervision, and that other deadly deceases ravaging the country, like lasser fever, should be well-managed like the issue of Covid -19. In conclusion, leaders could embrace 'Igwebuike' philosophy of solidarity in decision making so as to avoid followers losing confidence in them as it happened at a point during the management of Covid-19 pandemic in Nigeria. Phenomenological method of inquiry was used for the purpose of this study.

Key Words: 'Igwebuike' Philosophy, Kanu Ikechukwu Anthony, Management, Covid-19, Palliatives, Social distancing, Isolation Centre and Face mask.

INTRODUCTION

The outbreak of Corona Virus disease, otherwise known as Covid-19, started in December 2019 in China. This is an infectious disease that has been presented to be caused by a newly discovered virus. According to the report of Matt and Sabrina (2020), it seems to have originated from Wuhan seafood market where all sorts of wild animals like marmots, birds, rabbits, bats and snakes are merchandized illegally. "Coronaviruses are known to jump from animals to humans, so it is thought that the first people infected with the disease – a group primarily made up of stallholders from the seafood market contracted it from contact with animals" (p.4). There are many contending views on the origin of the virus. Matt and Sabrina further said that virologist assessment shows that the infection is from bat, while some are of the opinion that the early cases of Covid-19, however, appeared to have inflicted people with no link to the Wuhan market at all, suggesting that the initial route of human infection may pre-date the market cases. By implication, it might be transmitted between human to human. Some also said it came from the laboratory investigations, whereas another opinion was that it was a recurring of pandemic of past centuries. With these competing views, the origin of this pandemic might not be known. The only fact is that it was invented from China.

Within the first week of April 2020, the following countries were the top ten that were affected by the Corona virus pandemic-USA, Italy, Spain, Germany, China, France, Iran, United Kingdom (UK), Switzerland and Turkey (Duddu, 2020). In the same vein, Matt and Sabrina (2020) reported that the disease had been detected in more than 200 countries and territories, with the US, Russia and the UK experiencing the most widespread outbreaks, followed by Brazil, Spain and Italy. With this information, a lot of awareness programme came up and how to control it became important. It was described in numerous alertness programmes that Covid-19 was majorly transmitted through droplets of the infected persons. When an infected person coughs or sneezes, the droplets from these actions hang in the air or surfaces. If anyone comes in contact with the droplets either by breathing it in or by touching the contaminated surfaces from there to the mouth, eyes or nose, the person has been infected. It is spread through socialization, therefore, avoidance of close contacts, social lockdown, including religious gatherings were used as means of controlling the spread of the sickness. The precautionary measures have created a lot of setbacks for virtually every individual and every one of the countries it touches. It is beyond health issues because if prolonged, it might have political, social and economic effects. The poor will suffer more in this regard and those who rely on their daily income for survival may not find it interesting.

As presented by the Nigeria Centre for Disease Control, The first Corona virus case was announced in Nigeria on the 27th of February 2020 in Lagos. The second one came up on the 9th of March, 2020 at Ewekoro, Ogun State. This pandemic kept spreading that as at the time of this research (14/5/2020), the total confirmed cases had risen to 5,162 - active cases, 3,815; recovered cases, 1,180 and number of diseased persons, 167 within 34 states in Nigeria, as analyzed below.

CONFIRMED CORONA VIRUS CASES BY STATES IN NIGERIA

STATE AFFECTED	NO OF CASES(LAB CONFIRMED)	NO OF CASES ON ADMISSION	NO DISCHARCHED	NO OF DEATH
Lagos	2,099	1,525	541	33
Kano	753	633	87	33
FCT	379	290	82	7
Katsina	224	183	29	12
Bauchi	207	179	25	3
Borno	191	151	20	20
Jigawa	176	169	4	3
Ogun	134	72	57	5
Gombe	124	36	87	1
Kaduna	114	94	17	3
Sokoto	112	59	40	13
Edo	92	60	27	5
Oyo	73	55	16	2
Zamfara	73	50	18	5
Kwara	56	43	12	1
Osun	42	8	30	4
Rivers	30	25	5	3
Yobe	32	28	3	1
Kebbi	31	16	11	4
Nasarawa	29	23	5	1
Plateau	25	21	4	0
Delta	22	9	9	4
Adamawa	21	14	7	0
Ondo	19	7	11	1
Taraba	17	16	1	0
Akwa Ibom	17	3	12	2
Ekiti	15	5	9	1
Enugu	12	10	2	0
Niger	10	8	2	0
Ebonyi	9	9	0	0
Imo	7	5	2	0
Bayelsa	6	6	3	3
Benue	4	4	0	0
Anambra	2	1	1	0
Abia	2	1	1	0

SOURCE: NCDC MICROSITE. As at 15/5/2020

MANAGEMENT OF COVID-19 IN NIGERIA

Covid-19 pandemic did not enter Nigeria as a surprise. Before the first case was announced, many countries had been experiencing it and it was proclaimed to be a pandemic. Therefore, apart from the fact that people heard about it themselves through the media, the government did some sensitization programmes to bring the issue of this pandemic to people's doorsteps for preparations. In the report given by Adepoju (2020), the following were done even a month before the spread of the pandemic in Nigeria: giving information on personal hygiene and cough etiquette, creating health workers network centers around the nation, gathering skilled workers for tracing and to treat infected cases, and five testing laboratories were developed.

In the 2014, during the Ebola epidemic, some of the public-health institutes created to help in curbing this infectious disease became useful now, and improvement on them came in preparation for Covid-19 pandemic. This was why Nigeria Centre for Disease Control (NCDC) was being signed into law in 2018, to give the legal backing to perform its functions, according to Adepoju (2020). All these efforts were put together in preparation for Covid-19 pandemic, and in the report of Adepoju, it seems the arrangements were not sufficient as he asserts "Nigeria's prevention efforts are limited to screening international travelers at its airports while promoting hand washing and hygiene among the general populace. The country is relying on temperature screening at the airport, travelers' travel history and promotion of self-isolation for people visiting Nigeria from countries with numerous confirmed cases of COVID-19" (p.4).

Apart from these initial and immediate preparations, Nigerians were encouraged to wash their hands with soap under running water, regular use of sanitizer was mandatory, use of face mask was made compulsory and social distancing became very important. Majority complied with these directives and people were using various kinds of masks, some even customized theirs. Covid-19 became real to Nigerians when the Federal Government declared total lockdown in March, 2020, in Federal Capital Territory, and Lagos and Ogun States. Other states within the country joined and it became a nationwide lockdown. Therefore, nothing seemed to function. There was no market, except for few hours in a day. Places of worship were under lock and key, businesses were not operative, schools at all levels could not continue and all recreational centers were closed in a bid to control the spread of Covid-19 pandemic. Only essential workers were allowed to move and work actively.

In this situation, Nigerians came together to fight this pandemic, and proposals on how to go about it became important. Many methods of solving it in an African way turned out to be necessary in the application of local herbs. The Benedictines Monks were prominent in this regard. Their research ended up in a solution, as announced by Adodo (2020) in this statement: "Paxherbals has developed a novel drug, called CVD PLUS specifically for the treatment of COVID-19," the Clinic's founder, Fr. Anslem Adodo announced in a press release dated April 29" (p.1). While government was looking for vaccines for cure, the idea to adopt Afghanistan drug became glaring.

When this practice was on, those tested positive were kept in the isolation centers for treatment and to prevent them from mingling with the people. Some victims lost their lives in the process and majority were discharged from the centers. Another effort made by the government was the distribution of palliatives in terms of food items to cushion the effects of this pandemic on the people. It was a difficult moment for many Nigerians, especially those who relied on their daily struggles for survival, like labourers, drivers and petty traders or traders generally. They were spending their savings, even their capitals could be used to feed families during this period. Those who work for private organizations did not receive salaries during the pandemic period, but federal and state workers were receiving salaries regularly. As this was in progress, the number of confirmed cases kept increasing.

The need to ease the social lockdown came up in May, 2020, and work resumed skeletally. Markets especially became very active. Movements within states were allowed and interstate movements were forbidden. The interesting part of the lockdown exercise was the reactions of people after a while. Majority lost confidence in the government and lost trust in the procedure of managing covid-19 because what was been presented on social media was not enough to prove that this pandemic was real or was prominent in Nigeria. A comedian at a time called it 'Covid-19 for business.' There were no sufficient evidences that people were dying of the pandemic in Nigeria and the media kept showing empty beds in the isolation centers, and the number of infected cases continued to rise, while death rate was increasing without revealing burial processes.

Since the Covid-19 has impacted religion in various ways, including the closure of churches, restriction on public worship of various faiths, as well as the cancellation of pilgrimages and religious festivals, religious leaders started reacting to why churches would not open and markets were operative. After all, the interactions in most churches are not as noticeable as that of markets. Onaiyekan, the Catholic Archbishop Emeritus of Abuja, in a write-up circulated through the social media said that "On a more practical level, if government finds reasons to relax measures for banks, markets and farms, there is no reason why churches and mosques should be excluded from the same special consideration" (p.2). This implies that the congestions in banks and markets, including farms, could also spread this pandemic.

IGWEBUIKE PHILOSOPHY

Igwebuike has been described by Professor Kanu Ikechukwu Anthony, who has systematized the thought over time "as an Igbo word that expresses the heart of African thought, logic and the modality of being in African philosophy" (Kanu 2017, p.17). He further says that "it means 'number is strength' or 'number is power', that is, when human beings come together in solidarity and complementarity, they are powerful and can constitute an insurmountable force"(p.17). By inference, therefore, this philosophy is people-oriented and establishes the fact that I am because we are.

In an attempt to describe *Igwebuike* philosophy, Ejem (2018) states that, "it establishes that there exists a common link between human persons and that it is through this relationship that every other person realizes himself/herself" (p.17). In another development, Kanu (2017) declares that the philosophy is highly connected with mutual association. This is related, according to him, to "a common origin, common world-view, common language, shared culture, shared race, colour and habits, common historical experience and a common destiny" (p.17). Therefore, as long as there is a unifying factor, we are meant for each other's good.

Igwebuike philosophy is significant in this regard because it moves away from an individualistic life to the communal life that Africans have always preached and lived. It emphasizes cooperation among a group of people, irrespective of their backgrounds, keeping in mind that what makes our coming together relevant is the fact that we are human beings. If this philosophy is ever considered by all members of a group, it will foster love and unity for the attainment of both individual and group purposes. The end result of *Igwebuike* philosophy is common benefit, in which members stand with themselves in times of good and bad; hence, it is a life of 'sharedness,' as Kanu (2014, 2015, 2016 & 2018) affirms.

IGWEBUIKE PHILOSOPHY AND THE MANAGEMENT OF COVID-19

Having analyzed what *Igwebuike* philosophy stands for, its relevance to the management of Covid-19 in Nigeria will be divided into three parts. The first is the fact that both *Igwebuike* philosophy and Covid-19 are about people. This philosophy centers on the affairs of others and having consideration for another person; so also are the issues of Covid-19. This was reflected in the management of the pandemic when isolations centers were built to separate affected people from others to avoid them being infected. The imposition of the use of face masks was for individual good and for the good of others as well.

Another common factor was the issue of joint efforts on the part of the government and the populace to find solution to this common problem, as we have in the search for local herbs on the part of the populace, and government was in search of vaccines. This problem was addressed in a common manner as *Igwebuike* philosophy pays attention to collective matters, in keeping with Kanu's declaration that it involves "a common origin, common world-view, common language, shared culture, shared race, colour and habits, common historical experience and a common destiny"(p.17). To Nigerians, the Corona Virus pandemic was a collective problem that needs collective efforts to resolve.

The third part of this relevance is about unity and oneness. The summary of *Igwebuike* philosophy is actually unity. This is what Kanu emphasises in his explanation of *Igwebuike* philosophy in people coming together in solidarity and complementarity to form an insurmountable force. The Corona Virus pandemic period has has seen families and the nation uniting in prayers. Many families that have ever lived apart can now use this phase to stay together and share memories of a lasting value. Children are at home with their parents, closely in prayers and sharing what they have together as they hope and yearn to have more years for family ties.

RECOMMENDATIONS

Based on the discussions above, the following recommendations are presented:

1. That in case of future occurrence, the government should be more proactive in closing the borders to prevent travelers who transport the diseases from entering the country. In a case like this, less attention should be paid to the immediate effects of it on the economy; after all, the economy was affected and many lives were lost as recorded.

2. The country needs a functional database in a time like this for the distribution of palliatives. Many people did not receive any food items as support from the government. This brought about their anxiety to return to their businesses, since their immediate needs could not be met. If there had been a well-designed database, palliatives would have been easy to distribute as other measures to curb the diseases were being put in place like fumigation of public places and building of isolation centers.

3. Any situation that may cause total lockdown needs to be adequately planned. Total lockdown should be general, that is, it should be a nationwide programme happening at the same time in all the states. The regulations on how to go about it must be left to the federal government, instead of individual state governments.

4. The efforts put into fighting the Corona virus pandemic on the part of the government were commendable. However, attention should be paid to other communicable diseases in Nigeria, if our interest is on saving lives. Lassa fever, malaria resulting from dirty environments, and diarrhea ensuing from regular climate change claiming lives every time can be addressed so that people will enjoy good living in peaceful environments.

CONCLUSION

This paper discussed *Igwebuike* philosophy and the management of Corona virus disease (Covid-19) pandemic in Nigeria. It was an epidemic in China that occurred in December, 2019 which suddenly turned to be a pandemic, throwing the whole world into panic. It came to Nigeria in 2020 February and it has been adequately managed by the government and the entire people of Nigeria, giving their support through compliance with the regulations of the government on how to go about it. This cooperative effort is actually laudable as it gave much hope for the future.

It is important to note that before the era of Covid -19 in Nigeria, there have been other issues confronting the populace in this country that are not on health basis, but are deadly. Therefore, attention should be given to lack of qualitative education, problem of insecurity, development matters in terms of amenities, job creation for youths and young school leavers, functional pension scheme for workers and the needs of retirees. Lack of robust plans for the above might lead to negative effects on the health of Nigerians. Consequently, they develop high blood pressure, depression, dementia and all sorts of health issues that result in untimely deaths of the concerned. Hence, consideration should be given to all areas of their lives to encourage better living.

Nigerians are known for struggles and stressful life style; hence, let everyone keep in mind that Covid-19 lockdown had given all the opportunity to rest and get refreshed. Finally, leaders at all levels need to adopt the 'Igwebuike' philosophy of solidarity in decision making so as to avoid followers losing confidence in them, as it happened at a point during the management of Covid-19 pandemic in Nigeria.

REFERENCES

Adepoju P. (2020). Nigeria responds to COVID-19; first case detected in sub- Saharan Africa. Retrieved (14/5/2020) from https://www.nature.com/articles/d41591-020-00004-2

Adodo A.G. (2020). How a Nigeria-Based Catholic Medical Centre is responding to COVID-19 Search for Cure. Retrieved (20/5/2020) from https://www.aciafrica.org/news/1266/how-a-nigeria-based-catholic-medical-centre-is-responding-to-covid-19-search-for-cure

Duddu P. (2020).COVID-19 coronavirus: Top ten most-affected countries. Retrieved (14/5/2020) from https://www.pharmaceutical-technology.com/features/covid-19-coronavirus-top-ten-most-affected-countries/.

Ejem P.S (2018). Comparative Study of *Igwebuike* Philosophy and Julius Nyerere's Philosophy of African Brotherhood. Retrieved (13/5/2020) from https://www.academia.edu/37608513/.

Kanu I.A (2017). Igwebuike Philosophy and the Issue of National Development *in African Journal of Arts and Humanities Vol. 3 No 6, September 2017. ISSN: 2488-9210(Online) 2504-9038.*

Kanu, I. A. (2017). *Igwebuike* as the hermeneutic of individuality and communality in African ontology. *NAJOP: Nasara Journal of Philosophy.* Vol. 2. No. 1. pp. 162-179.

Kanu, I. A. (2017a). *Igwebuike* and question of superiority in the scientific community of knowledge. *Igwebuike: An African Journal of Arts and Humanities.*Vol.3 No1. pp. 131-138.

Kanu, I. A. (2017a). *Igwebuike as a philosophical attribute of Africa in portraying the image of life.* A paper presented at the 2017 Oracle of Wisdom International Conference by the Department of Philosophy, Tansian University, Umunya, Anambra State, 27-29 April.

Kanu, I. A. (2017b). *Igwebuike* as a complementary approach to the issue of girl-child education. *Nightingale International Journal of Contemporary Education and Research.* Vol. 3. No. 6. pp. 11-17.

Kanu, I. A. (2017b). *Igwebuike* as a wholistic response to the problem of evil and human suffering. *Igwebuike: An African Journal of Arts and Humanities.* Vol. 3 No 2, March.

Kanu, I. A. (2017e). *Igwebuike* as an Igbo-African modality of peace and conflict resolution. *Journal of African Traditional Religion and Philosophy Scholars. Vol. 1. No. 1. pp. 31-40.*

Kanu, I. A. (2017g). *Igwebuike* and the logic (Nka) of African philosophy. *Igwebuike: An African Journal of Arts and Humanities. 3. 1. pp. 1-13.*

Kanu, I. A. (2017h). *Igwebuike* philosophy and human rights violation in Africa. *IGWEBUIKE: An African Journal of Arts and Humanities.* Vol. 3. No. 7. pp. 117-136.

Kanu, I. A. (2017i). *Igwebuike* as a hermeneutic of personal autonomy in African ontology. *Journal of African Traditional Religion and Philosophy Scholars. Vol. 2. No. 1. pp. 14-22.*

Kanu, I. A. (2018). African philosophy, globalization and the priority of 'otherness'. *Journal of African Studies and Sustainable Development.* Vol. 1. No. 1. pp. 40-57.

Kanu, I. A. (2018). *African traditional philosophy of education: Essays in Igwebuike philosophy.* Germany: Lambert Publications.

Kanu, I. A. (2018). *Igwe Bu Ike* as an Igbo-African hermeneutics of national development. *Igbo Studies Review. No. 6. pp. 59-83.*

Kanu, I. A. (2018). *Igwebuike* as an African integrative and progressive anthropology. *NAJOP: Nasara Journal of Philosophy.* Vol. 2. No. 1. pp. 151-161.

Kanu, I. A. (2018). New Africanism: *Igwebuike* as a philosophical Attribute of Africa in portraying the Image of Life. In Mahmoud Misaeli, Sanni Yaya and Rico Sneller (Eds.). *African Perspectives on Global on Global Development* (pp. 92-103). United Kingdom: Cambridge Scholars Publishing.

Kanu, I. A. (2019). Collaboration within the ecology of mission: An African cultural perspective. *The Catholic Voyage: African Journal of Consecrated Life.* Vol. 15. pp. 125-149.

Kanu, I. A. (2019). *Igwebuike* research methodology: A new trend for scientific and wholistic investigation. *IGWEBUIKE: An African Journal of Arts and Humanities (IAAJAH). 5. 4.* pp. *95-105.*

Kanu, I. A. (2019). *Igwebuikeconomics*: The Igbo apprenticeship for wealth creation. *IGWEBUIKE: An African Journal of Arts and Humanities (IAAJAH). 5. 4.* pp. *56-70.*

Kanu, I. A. (2019). *Igwebuikecracy*: The Igbo-African participatory cocio-political system of governance. *TOLLE LEGE: An Augustinian Journal of the Philosophy and Theology. 1. 1.* pp. 34-45.

Kanu, I. A. (2019). On the origin and principles of *Igwebuike* philosophy. *International Journal of Religion and Human Relations.* Vol. 11. No. 1. pp. 159-176.

Kanu, I. A. (2019b). An *Igwebuike* approach to the study of African traditional naming ceremony and baptism. *International Journal of Religion and Human Relations.* Vol. 11. No. 1. pp. 25-50.

Matt R and Sabrina W (2020). How Corona Virus Started; What happened next Explained. Retrieved (14/5/2020) from https://www.wired.co.uk/article/china-coronavirus.

Onaiyekan J. (2020). Covid-19: A Case for the Resumption of Controlled Worship Gatherings in Churches and Mosques. Catholic Archbishop Emeritus of Abuja. Write –up circulated on social Media.

The Nigeria Centre for Disease Control (NCDC). Retrieved (13/5/2020) from https://covid19.ncdc.gov.ng/

'IGWEBUIKE' PHILOSOPHY OF SCIENCE AND TECHNOLOGY

Ikechukwu Anthony KANU
Department of Philosophy and Religious Studies
Tansian University Umunya, Anambra State
ikee_mario@yahoo.com

EXECUTIVE SUMMARY

Contrary to the opinion of some scholars which holds that science is independent of particular worldviews in its presuppositions and method, this paper argues that although the presuppositions of science have no worldview content, science may provide evidence that has a bearing on a certain worldview. This dependence on a worldview is what gives science some level of political autonomy; that is, some kind of scientific citizenship in philosophy that gives credence to a form of local knowledge, and thus, gives voice to a group of people. This is very important as science and technology is not just about doing or making by hand; it involves not only human activities, but also the skills of the crafts-man or woman, which does not leave out the art of the human mind that does the manufacturing. It is on this basis that this paper studies Igwebuike as the basis for science and technology in Africa. Igwebuike falls within the parameters of the art of the African mind. It shapes the African thinking as it is the basis of the African logic. At this point, science and technology become a revelation of the Igwebuike framework. This piece, therefore, studied how Igwebuike impacts on science and technology through its determination of the logic (nka) employed in science and technology. It discovered that the African worldview conceptualized in Igwebuike is capable of a science that is anchored on the structure of the African world. For the purpose of this study, the Igwebuike complementary method of inquiry was employed.

Keywords: *Igwebuike*, Science, Technology, Pillar, Logic, Worldview, Complementarity

INTRODUCTION

Scholars like Cherry (1965) and Okonkwo (2012) observe the importance of a people's language and worldview in the shaping of their thoughts, including thoughts and developments in the areas of religion, philosophy, science, technology, among others. He writes:

The language of a people largely constrains their thoughts. Its words, concepts and syntax, out of all the signs that people use, are the most important determinant of what they are free and able to think. It makes their particular epistemology, their special view of the world, and what they notice or do not notice, (p. 73).

It is in this regard that Fuller (cited in Okonkwo, 2012) speaks of a scientific citizenship in philosophy that should be "designed to give credence to a form of local knowledge... to retain a certain level of political autonomy" (p. 73). The implication of this is that every language community has its own science and technology, which should be integrated into what is now known as technology. This, according to Okonkwo (2012), would deepen ordinary democratic franchise by giving voice to a group of people.

Moreover, if science is understood as "an organized, systematic enterprise that gathers knowledge about the world and condenses the knowledge into testable laws and principles" (Wilson 1998, p. 58), and in the perspective of Afisi (2016) "as the concerted human effort to have a clear understanding of the history of the natural world, and how the natural world works, with observable physical evidence as a basis for that understanding" (p. 59), it then implies that peoples and societies, both local and advanced rational and intellectually open societies, are capable of science, even if it might not be in full accord with what the West has developed as science. Beyond the reality of pluralism in the world, science has a social character that makes it part of social and cultural traditions, and it is at this point that we can speak of particular worldviews as characterising different sciences. It is also within this context that *Igwebuike* philosophy of science and technology is discussed.

An understanding of technology makes profound the idea of the social character of science and technology. Technology is not just about doing or making by hand, it involves the skills of the crafts-man or woman, which involves the art of the human mind. The art of the human mind is shaped by particular worldviews, and, therefore, the source of the influence of the worldview on science and technology. To understand the power of worldview on a particular science and technology, there is the need to go back to the definition of technology. Etymologically, it stems from the Greek *techné*, which designates "skill," "art," and "craft," a mode of doing or making. It is in this spirit that Plato understood politics as fundamentally belonging to the domain of *techné*, politics as first and foremost a political skill to be learned, an art or, better yet, a kind of technology of the *polis*. *Techné,* in the original Greek usage, refers to both the skill or power of doing/making and that which is performed, produced, or fabricated—in other words, *techné* designates both art and artifice. From this perspective, *techné* (art/artifice) is opposed to *physis* (nature), most fundamentally in terms of causality. Thus, *techné* implies a mediation by an external agent (Reason) to an object in order to bring about change in it, which means that the principle of change is here foreign to the object (Nadal 2012).

Technology is a product and performance of man's dealings with *physis* through *techné*, the bridge is the materialization or actualization of an intended, desired end (Jean-Luc 2000). Thus, Heidegger (1977) writes that: "The manufacture and utilization of equipment, tools, and machines, the manufactured and used things themselves, and the [social] needs and ends that they serve, all belong to what technology is" (p. 288). It can be, therefore, said that science and technology only become a revelation or the bringing forth of what the art of the mind conceals.

It is from the context of the dynamics of 'the art of man' and the 'artifice' that this work studies *Igwebuike* (which conceptualizes a worldview) as the basis for science and technology in Africa. *Igwebuike* falls within the parameters of the art of the African mind. It shapes the African thinking as it is the basis for African logic. From the forgoing, science and technology become a revelation of the *Igwebuike* framework. This piece would, therefore, study how *Igwebuike* impacts on science and technology through its determination of the logic (*nka*) of the scientific and technological. It argues that the African worldview conceptualized in *Igwebuike* is capable of a science, notwithstanding that it is a predominantly religious worldview. What a worldview provides is the framework capable of responding to several questions at the same time, be it in the area of science, religion, politics, economics, etc. It is in this regard that worldview would be understood as a world of possibilities.

WORLDVIEW AS A FRAMEWORK FOR SCIENCE/TECHNOLOGY

Gauch (2007) outlines seven pillars that define and hold science. These pillars include:

1. **Realism**: It holds that the world is real. If it were not real, then it cannot be studied or analyzed
2. **Presuppositions:** It holds that the world is orderly and comprehensible. If it were not comprehensible, then it wouldn't be studied by science.
3. **Evidence:** This means that science requires empirical, public evidence for its conclusions.
4. **Logic:** It holds that scientific thinking employs standard logic.
5. **Limits:** It holds that science has limits; it cannot explain everything.
6. **Universality:** This holds that science is open to all people from all cultures; in principle, anybody can engage in scientific activity.
7. **Worldview:** This states that science contributes to a meaningful worldview.

Developing his thesis further, Gauch (2007) argues that science is independent of particular worldviews in its presuppositions and method. This notwithstanding, he avers that science can have worldview import. Interpreting the position of Gauch, Irzik and Nola (2009) write:

> We understand this as follows. Gauch believes that although the presuppositions of science and scientific method/reasoning have no worldview content, science

> may provide evidence that has bearing on a certain worldview belief, say p. Such evidence can be employed as a premise in an argument. Then using scientific reasoning (that includes standard logic), p is reached as a conclusion. Gauch seems to think that this is the only way science is relevant to worldview beliefs—if, that is, they can be obtained as the conclusion of an argument that contains evidence as one of its premises. Let us call this the argument–argument. (p. 735).

Reacting to the position of Gauch, Irzik and Nola (2009) argue that science does have worldview content, even in its presuppositions and method. In other words, the scientific method is not worldview-independent. Thus, science, in the quite minimal sense, has worldview content in other respects as well.

> This content derives from its presuppositions that include its criticizability, logic, the orderliness and the comprehensibility of the world, from its method of inquiry and mode of explanation. Of course, science is also relevant to worldviews by also providing empirical evidence and then reaching conclusions that have worldview content. This is not to say that science can answer every worldview question, but it is a rich and powerful source of worldview beliefs. Furthermore, by challenging, confronting and conflicting with other worldviews, it forces their defendants to improve upon them. Natural theology, for instance, owes as much to science as it does to religion (p. 744).

This position is based on the fact that the history of science reveals how it emerged from mythological and religious worldviews; using a remarkable episodes in the history of human kind, they made reference to the Scientific Revolution in the 16th and 17th centuries, which was highly influenced by philosophical and religious beliefs. Thus, from the above perspectives, it can be said that science, as a universal enterprise, is independent of worldview; however, in relation to the person who does the science and the influence of his or her background, science can be said to have a worldview.

AFRICAN WORLDVIEW (LOGIC) AND SCIENCE IN AFRICA

Like the discussion on whether there is an African philosophy or not, there has been a debate on whether there is an African science or not. This section of this paper joins the position of scholars who have argued for an African science, and the basis which this piece provides for the possibility of an African science is the African logic. It is the African logic that shapes what Ezeabasili (1977) refers to as the "African account of nature and how it works" (p. xi), or what in the contention of Murfin (1992) is Africa's attempt to unfold the truth in nature. The idea of an African attempt to unfold the truth in nature or give an account of the workings of their universe points to the pluralism in science, involving the inquiries of systematic cultures.

One of the pillars on which science stands, as seen in the work of Gauch (2007), is logic. It is also logic that gives and directs the scientific process and findings. It is at the point of logic which is embedded in the African worldview that the African worldview makes its distinctive impact on science in Africa. Speaking of African logic, the focus is on the structure of African thought. Every culture or people have their own peculiar way of thinking or reasoning, and it is the African pattern of reasoning that has led to an investigation into the African logic. Speaking on the diversity of logic, Momoh (1989) relates logic to human language which differs from culture to culture:

> In everyday usage of natural language we talk of a person as being logical if he is reasonable, sensible and intelligent; if he can unemotionally and critically evaluate evidence or a situation; if he can avoid contradictions, inconsistency and incoherence, or if he can hold a point of view argue for and from it, summon counter-examples and answer objections. (p. 174).

The adjective 'African' attached to the word 'logic' speaks of the context or the *locus* of logicality. It is the application of reason to the world and culture of the African people (Kanu, 2017). There are two implications to this:

First, it sees logic as a universal phenomenon. This is very important, since logic is a fundamental ingredient of the human person whose thoughts and thinking are organized, analyzed and sustained by some intrinsic structures that make the way for a systematic conception of reality. This being the case, it can be said that logic is thus a necessary element of every culture. There is no culture that does not accommodate a good argument, especially as it concerns their conclusions. Whether in Africa or in Europe or in America or in Asia, if the assumption of an argument is true, the conclusion of the argument would always be true. For instance:

If Njoku is an African philosopher,
then Njoku is a great African thinker,
Njoku is an African philosopher,
Therefore, Njoku is a great African thinker

If Kanu is shorter than Emeka,
then Kanu should be taller than Usman
Kanu is taller than Emeka
Therefore, Kanu is taller than Usman

These are arguments that are logical and cannot be accepted in one culture and rejected in another culture. Their conclusions are all acceptable as their assumptions are true. Thus, the principles of logic are universal principles that could be generally applied to diverse situations, no matter where. They are, thus, topic-neutral and con-contingent, in the sense that they do not depend on any accidental features of the world.

Second, there is the particularity of logic, by which is meant the context in which logic is applied. It speaks of the worldview which differs from one place to another; this bears on the universal application of logic. While logic is universal, it is clear knowledge that the cultural experiences of people are meaningful within the context of an organized language that points to a logical ability- it is a people's language that communicates their logical world. It is in this regard that Kuhn (1962), in his incommensurability theory, speaks of competing paradigms without a common measure, and Feyerabend (1981) holds that there does not exist a single scientific method that we can agree on as the "events, procedures and results that constitute the sciences have no common structure" (p. 1).

Following from the construct of the African ontology which is complementary, African logic in general is complementary and integral in character, accepting the co-existence of opposing realities as complementary. It is based on its capacity for complementarity and openness to co-existence of opposing realities that it is described within the context of *Igwebuike*. *Igwebuike* is the modality of being in African philosophy. It is from the Igbo composite word and metaphor *Igwebuike*, a combination of three words. Therefore, it can be employed as a word or used as a sentence: as a word, it is written as *Igwebuike*, and as a sentence, it is written as, *Igwe bu ike*, with the component words enjoying some independence in terms of space (2018a). The three words involved are: *Igwe* is a noun which means 'number' or 'population,' usually a huge number or population. *Bu* is a verb, which means *is*. *Ike* is a noun, which means *strength* or *power* (Kanu, 2018b). Thus, put together, it literally means 'number is strength' or 'number is power'. Beyond the literal sense, it speaks of *otu obi* (one mind and one heart), asserting that when human beings come together in solidarity and complementarity, they are powerful or can constitute an insurmountable force or strength, and at this level, withstand the probabilities of life. *Igwebuike* is, therefore, an African philosophy of harmonization and complementation. It understands the world immanent realities to be related to one another in the most natural, mutual, harmonious and compatible ways possible (Kanu, 2016a&b). *Thus,* 'to be' is 'to be with the other', in a community of beings (Kanu, 2017a).

The African worldview, therefore, is ruled by the spirit of complementarity, which seeks the conglomeration, unification, summation of fragmented thoughts, opinions and other individualized and fragmented thoughts and ideas. It understands reality within the context of the whole being greater than the corresponding parts. It is also a view that maintains that by the coming together of the individuals or parts, a viable and sustainable whole will emerge (Kanu, 2017b). Because *Igwebuike* captures the dialectical character of African thought, it is referred to as African logic. And by dialectics, it is meant a method of philosophical argument that involves some sort of contradictory process between opposing sides. In African logic, there is the reliance on the contradictory process of opposing sides, though in a unique manner. For instance, day is vivified and complemented by night, and good by evil. The adage that *"Abasi obot mbat, abot udara ikpat,"* meaning "the God who creates mud made available something to wash off the mud", explains this fact of the complementarity of contradictory realities. The two realities – "mud" and "water" – are mutually opposed, but are two sides of the same coin. Anyanwu (1981) describes this contradictory dialectics as the "inner curve of reciprocity" (p. 87) that makes African epistemology to avoid the dualism of subjectivism and objectivism. The contradictory dialectics is not negative but affirms the functionality of differences as essential and incomplete dimensions of the whole.

THE OPENNESS OF AFRICAN SCIENCE

The Nri hegemony and its influence on Igbo history cannot be over-emphasized. Thus, Madubuko (1994) observes that the story of the Igbo, no matter how briefly considered, would be incomplete if one omits the Eri-Nri contribution. Afigbo (1981) shows Eri clan as originating from the regions of Anambra River, at Aguleri; from there they fanned eastward and established various communities. In a discourse of this kind on African science and technology, knowing full well the place that Nri myth occupies in Igbo history, religion and culture, it would not be out of place to search beyond the surface of the mythology of Nri to discover profound 'senses' of African science and technology.

The myth has it that Eri is the father of all Nri; and tradition says that he came from *Chukwu*. It is reported that the earth was not firm when he came to the world. To solve the problem of flood, he employed blacksmiths from Awka to use their bellows to dry the flooded land (Uzukwu, 1988). That Eri, the father of all Nri who came from *Chukwu*, needed blacksmiths from Awka to use their bellows to dry the earth already shows the dialogue between philosophy, religion and science. In spite of the fact that *Chukwu*, with all His wisdom and knowledge, would allow for his son to employ the help of these traditional scientists and technologists, the fact is established that science and technology are also part of His divine arrangement for the human person achieving his purpose in life, and thus, does not contradict the divine purpose, if employed in proper perspective. Within the context of *Igwebuike* philosophy of science, in spite of the fact that philosophy religion and science deal with different aspects of human life and the existence of the universe, these areas of study achieve their full potentials only when they collaborate with other areas of study.

This notwithstanding, there are two major implications that can be drawn from this myth in relation to the African concept of science.

1. *Science as an independent dependent Worldview*

There is a seeming categorization of worldviews into different types. Freud (1933) categorized worldview into religious or philosophical and rational or scientific worldviews and understands the categories are completely independent from each other. Irzik and Nola (2009) made categorization of worldviews into religious, philosophical, political, cultural, scientific, etc. These categorizations are done in a manner that poses that these worldviews are antagonistic to one another. Obviously, science is a special cognitive activity aimed at objective and systematic knowledge about reality, different from religion which is based on faith or mystical experience, and also different from philosophy which studies the fundamental characteristics and principles of reality. In spite of their uniqueness as areas of study with different interests, there is always a meeting point, where an aspect of one influences or flows from the other.

The categorization of religious worldview that is differentiated from others on the basis of the predominance of the belief in a universal spirit: God, deity or divine entity, in which the divine entity has established a moral order which is known to human beings, and human beings have a moral duty to obey it as it has future consequences in relation to life after death, with a comprehensive perception of the world. Under this categorization, you find the mythological worldview, especially when it uses myths, folklore or legends believed to be supernatural and true for the interpretation of nature, universe, events and humanity. The distinction between religious and mythological worldviews, not withstanding, a mythological worldview can also be a religious worldview. Non-religious worldviews also include the philosophical worldview, which uses logical reasoning, mathematics and speculation to interpret and provide answers to fundamental questions about reality. The third is the scientific worldview, which uses the premises and findings of science in explaining the meaning of life, morality, creation, etc. Although it is more exact and authentic, it does not provide meaning to existence as it is limited to the material realm.

The researcher's argument is that a scientific worldview can still have elements of religious beliefs. The fact that a person is a scientist does not necessarily mean that the person ceases to have a religion. One can be a Christian or a Muslim and still be a scientist. More so, science can still emerge from a worldview that is dominated by religious perspectives. This is very important because the African worldview is highly considered to be a religious worldview. If understood purely as a religious worldview, then it would be incapable of science and technology. And yet science emerges from the African worldview. It is on this basis that the researcher argues that worldviews are not independent but dependent. Science itself is not an independent field of human inquiry as it requires other perspectives in the search for the meaning of life. It is, therefore, understood as an independent dependent worldview. This explains why Eri, the son of *Chukwu,* in spite of his rich religious and philosophical background, implored the help of Awka traditional scientists; in this, he showed that science complements philosophy and religion, and vice versa.

2. *The Human Person is Central to Science*

What compelled Heidegger to write on technology lies in his observation that "everywhere, man remains un-free and chained to technology"(p.287), a situation in which the more technology advances, the more it "threatens to slip from human control" (p. 289). This adversely has affected the ordering of the world - in fact, disordering the world. As a result, a questioning of technology became necessary and urgent for Heidegger. Balancing his critique of technology further, Heidegger (1966) thinks that there is the possibility of the use of technology in such a way that it would further the being of man:

> We can use technical devices, and yet with the proper use also keep ourselves so free of them, that we may let go of them at any time.... We can affirm the unavoidable use of technical devices, and also deny them the right to dominate us, and so to warp, confuse, and lay waste our nature.... I would call this comportment toward technology which expresses "yes" and at the same time "no," by an old word, releasement toward things (p. 54).

From the myth of Nri, when Eri called the blacksmith to come and help him move the water away with their scientific and technological expertise, the myth only resounds that science and technology is relevant only to the extent that it helps the human person to advance and preserve his life. This is based on the fact that the *Igwebuike* worldview is anthropocentric. Man is at the centre of the universe. Mbiti (1970) asserts that "Man is at the very centre of existence and African people see everything else in its relation to this central position of man... it is as if God exists for the sake of man" (p. 92). Corroborating Mbiti's assertion, Metuh (1991), avers that "Everything else in African worldview seems to get its bearing and significance from the position, meaning and end of man" (p. 109). The idea of God, divinities, ancestors, rituals, sacrifices etc., is only useful to the extent that they serve the needs of the human person. Science is, therefore, meant for man and not man for science and technology.

Heidegger's argument against modern technology is that it looks at realities that do not conform to the standard of calculability and utility with suspicion, and addresses such as mere myth or superstition (Adorno and Horkheimer, 2002). Heidegger (1977) describes this as a challenge that "puts to nature an unreasonable demand that it supply energy, which can [then] be extracted and stored" (p. 296).

> The work of the peasant does not challenge the soil of the field. In the sowing of the grain it places the seed in the keeping of the forces of growth and watches over its increase. But meanwhile even the cultivation of the field has come under the grip of another kind of setting-in-order, which sets upon nature. It sets upon it in the sense of challenging it. Agriculture is now the mechanised food industry. Air is now set upon to yield nitrogen, the earth to yield ore, ore to yield uranium, for example; uranium is set upon to yield atomic energy, which can be released either for destruction or for peaceful use (p. 15).

He argues that modern technology 'enframes' nature only to capture it; that is, it sees nature merely as a valuable material resource to be extracted, expropriated, and used-up for whatever man desires or wills of it. Under conditions of modern technology, "the earth," as Heidegger (1977) notes, "reveals itself as [only] a coal mining district, [its] soil as a mineral deposit" (p.

296). He believes that modern technology sees the world as an energy resource, a thing to be used, what he describes as a "standing-reserve" (p. 309).

Taking from the African complementary perspective of reality, nature is not just as a thing to be exploited; nature is part of a whole to which we belong as human beings. The exploitation of nature by science and technology is the exploitation of oneself because one belongs to nature as one is a part of nature. Thus, to treat nature with respect is to treat oneself with respect, and to treat nature without respect is to treat oneself without consideration and respect. More so, science and technology is meant to advance the freedom and humanity of the human person, and not to bring about human slavery.

CONCLUSION

Ozumba (2004) observes that every society has its own stock of epistemological thoughts, methods and worldviews. This assertion is fundamental to epistemology as the quest for knowledge is part of human nature; and thus, it is the prerogative of every culture or tradition. Like every other people, the African has his/her own method or means of acquiring knowledge, which is based on what Bacon (1952) calls the alphabets or forms of the world around him/her . Nature consists of alphabets or forms, and the discovery of these alphabets or forms of nature helps us to understand the multifarious complexities of the universe in which we live. Beneath the surface, *Igwebuike* philosophy of science understands science and technology as a collective achievement of the 'art of the human mind' and the 'artifice' involved with the purpose of generating a new order upon nature. The understanding of the dynamics of the alphabets or forms of nature involved in the process equips us better in the transformation of bodies, as these forms (the art of the mind and the artifice) are the determinants of the fundamental structure of the world.

A basic form or alphabet within the parameters of science and technology is the 'art of the mind' which flows from the worldview of the scientist and the technologist. It is from the worldview that the artifice of the scientist or technologist emerges (that is, the pragmatic side of science and technology). The artifice, therefore, reveals the art of the mind. It is on the basis of the discovery of these forms that the discourse on *Igwebuike* philosophy of science and technology is possible. The understanding of the nature of the forms involved in science and technology in Africa would help us understand the secret motions in the scientific and technological enterprise in Africa. In this, we see science and technology in partnership with nature to provide human needs in an environment in which they must survive by sustaining the existential grid in a cooperative fashion.

In discovering the forms of nature and the utilization of these forms for the betterment of human life, *Igwebuike* philosophy of science understands this pursuit or enterprise as a collaborative effort tailored towards the needs of the human person in a challenging universe.

Since it is a collaborative effort, *Igwebuike* philosophy of science and technology does not in any way see science and technology as independent fields of human inquiry, but in a spirit of complementarity with other fields of human inquiry work towards the achievement of a balanced solution to human needs or problems. This is the complementarity that produces a scientific citizenship in philosophy, which gives credence to a form of local knowledge. It is only within this context that we are able to speak of an *Igwebuike* philosophy of science and technology.

REFERENCES

Afigbo, E. A. (1975). Towards a history of the Igbo-Speaking people of Nigeria. In Ogbalu, F. C. and Emenanjo, E. N. (Eds.). *Igbo language and culture* (pp. 11-27). Ibadan: Heineman.

Anyanwu, K. C. (1981). Pre-suppositions of African Socialism. *The Nigerian Journal of Philosophy.* 1.2.

Asouzu, I. (2011). *Ibuanyidanda and the philosophy of essence.* Calabar: University Press.

Cherry, C. (1975). *On human communication.* Cambridge Mass: MIT Press

Freud, Sigmund (1933). New introductory lectures on psycho-analysis. *SE,* 22: 1-182.

Gauch, H. G. (2007). Science, worldviews and education. *Science and Education.* Vol. 18. 729-745.

Heidegger M. (1966). *Discourse on Thinking.* Trans. John M. Anderson and E. Hans Freud. New York: Harper and Row.

Heidegger M. (1977). *The Question Concerning Technology.* Trans. William Lovitt, Basic Writings. New York: Harper and Row.

Irzik, G. and Nola, R. (2009). Worldviews and their relation to science. *Science and Education.* Vol. 18. 729-745.

Jean-Luc N. (2000). *Being Singular Plural.* Trans. Robert D. Richardson and Anne O'Byrne. Stanford: Stanford University Press.

Kanu I. A. (2017). *Igwebuikeconomics:* Towards an inclusive economy for economic development. *Igwebuike: An African Journal of Arts and Humanities.* Vol. 3. No. 6. 113-140.

Kanu I. A. (2017). Sources of *Igwebuike* Philosophy. *International Journal of Religion and Human Relations.* 9. 1. pp. 1-23.

Kanu, A. I. (2016a). *Igwebuike* as a trend in African philosophy. *IGWEBUIKE: An African Journal of Arts and Humanities. 2. 1.* 97-101.

Kanu, A. I. (2016b). *Igwebuike* as an Igbo-African hermeneutic of globalization. *IGWEBUIKE: An African Journal of Arts and Humanities. 2. 1.* 1-7.

Kanu, I. A. (2014). *Igwebuikology* as an Igbo-African philosophy for Catholic-Pentecostal relations. *Jos Studies. 22. pp.*87-98.

Kanu, I. A. (2016a). *Igwebuike* as an Igbo-African Hermeneutics of Globalisation. *IGWEBUIKE: An African Journal of Arts and Humanities*, Vol. 2 No.1. pp. 61-66.

Kanu, I. A. (2016a). *Igwebuike* as the consummate foundation of African Bioethical principles. *An African journal of Arts and Humanities* Vol.2 No1 June, pp.23-40.

Kanu, I. A. (2017g). *Igwebuike* and the logic (Nka) of African philosophy. *Igwebuike: An African Journal of Arts and Humanities. 3. 1.* pp. 1-13.

Kanu, I. A. (2018). *Igwe Bu Ike* as an Igbo-African Hermeneutics of National Development. *Igbo Studies Review. No. 6.* pp. 59-83.

Kanu, I. A. (2018). *Igwebuike* as an African Integrative and Progressive Anthropology. *NAJOP: Nasara Journal of Philosophy.* Vol. 2. No. 1. pp. 151-161.

Kanu, I. A. (2014a). Igbo proverbs as *depositum* of Igbo-African philosophy. *International Journal of Humanities and Social Sciences. Vol. 4. No. 1.* pp. 164-168.

Kanu, I. A. (2014a). Suicide in Igbo-African ontology. *Developing Countries Studies.* Vol. 4. No. 5. USA. pp. 27-38.

Kanu, I. A. (2014b). Suffering in Igbo-African Ontology. *Research on Humanities and Social Sciences.* Vol. 4. No. 5. pp. 8-13.

Kanu, I. A. (2014b). The place of Igbo myths in Igbo-African philosophy. *American Journal of Contemporary Research. Vol. 4. No. 2.* pp. 98-102.

Kanu, I. A. (2015). African traditional democracy with particular reference to the Yoruba and Igbo political systems. *International Journal of Philosophy and Public Affairs.* Vol. 2. No. 3. pp. 147-160.

Kanu, I. A. (2015). *Personal identity and punishment in John Locke* (A Dissertation for the Award of Master of Arts Degree in Philosophy- Metaphysics), University of Nigeria, Nsukka, Enugu State.

Kanu, I. A. (2015a). *African philosophy: An ontologico-existential hermeneutic approach to classical and contemporary issues.* Nigeria: Augustinian Publications.

Kanu, I. A. (Ed.) (2016a). *Complementary ontology: Provocative essays on Innocent Asouzu's African philosophy of integration for progressive transformation.* Germany: Lambert Academic Publishing.

Kanu, I. A. (Ed.) (2016b). *Ibuanyidanda: A complementary systematic inquiry. Reflections on Innocent Asouzu's African philosophy.* Germany: Lambert Academic Publishing.

Kanu, I. A. (2016). *Igbo-African Christology: A cultural Christological construct in Post-Missionary Africa.* Germany: Lambert Publications.

Kanu, I. A. (2016a). African traditional folk songs as dialogue between education and entertainment. *Cambridge International Journal of Contemporary Education Research.* 6. 6. pp. 53-64.

Madubuko, L. (1994). Igbo world-view. *Bigard Theological Studies. 14, 2.* 13.

Mbiti, J. (1970). *African religions and philosophy.* Nairobi: East African Educational Publishers.

Metuh, I. E. (1991). *African religions in western conceptual schemes.* Jos: Imico

Momoh, C. S. (ed.) (1989). *The Substance of African Philosophy.* Auchi: African Philosophy Projects Publications.

Okonkwo J. I. (2012). *Okwu Danahu onu: The Basic principle of Igbo philosophy of language.* Inaugural Lecture, Imo State University, Serial No. 6. Owerri: Imo State University Press.

Ozumba, G. O. (2001). *A Concise Introduction to Epistemology.* Calabar: Ebeneger Printing Press.

Nadal, P. (2010). *Heidegger's critique of modern technology: On "The question concerning technology".* Retrieved 27/4/17 from https://belate.wordpress.com/2010/07/12/heidegger-modern-technology.

Theodore Adorno and Max Horkheimer (2002). *Dialectic of Enlightenment.* Stanford: Stanford University Press.

Uzukwu, E. E. (1988). Nri myth of origin and its ritualization: An essay in interpretation. In E. E. Uzukwu (Ed.). *Religions and African culture, Inculturation: A Nigeria perspective* (pp. 56-80). Enugu: Spiritan Publications.

Afisi, O. T. (2016). Is African science true science: Reflections on the methods of African science. *Filosofia Theoretica: Journal of African Philosophy, Culture and Religion.* Vol. 5. No. 1. pp. 59-75

Wilson E. (1998). *Consilience: The Unity of Knowledge.* Knopf: New York

Ezeabasili, N. (1977). *African science: Myth or reality.* Vantage Press: New York.

Murfin, B. (1992). *African science, African and African-American scientists and the school science curriculum.* A paper presented at the NSTA national convention, Boston, Massachusetts on 26th March.

Kuhn, T. (1962). *The structure of scientific revolutions.* University of Chicago Press: Chicago.

Feyerabend, P. (1981). *Against method.* Verso of New Left Books: New York.

'IGWEBUIKE' AS THE KEY TO UNDERSTANDING AFRICAN PHILOSOPHY AND RELIGION

Ikechukwu Anthony KANU
Department of Philosophy and Religious Studies
Tansian University Umunya, Anambra State
ikee_mario@yahoo.com

EXECUTIVE SUMMARY

This work is a response to the questions within African philosophy and African traditional religion: the question of the underlying principle in both fields of study. It is a contribution to the ongoing investigations in the areas of African philosophy and African traditional religion in search for the keys to the understanding of both fields. This piece argued, contrary to the positions of Mbiti and Koech, that the key to understanding African traditional religion is Igwebuike. It also argued, in relation to African philosophy, that Igwebuike is the intricate web of African philosophy. It has remained constant in the midst of the changes in the history of African philosophy, and has continued to persist through changes. It argued that its sense of harmony, community, complementarity and solidarity have been expressed in virtually all the perspectives of African philosophers, from the time of Tempels to the contemporary era. This position was based on the fact that Igwebuike is based on or captures the African worldview which shapes African philosophy and religion. The method inquiry employed for the purpose of this investigation is the Igwebuike approach, which understands reality within the parameters of complementarity.

Keywords: African, Philosophy, Religion, *Igwebuike*, Complementarity

INTRODUCTION

The concept of a "key to understanding" introduces the image of a door that needs to be opened for the purpose of achieving a breakthrough. It places emphasis on both the result of understanding and the action of understanding. Within the context of this study, it is about discovering the interaction of underlying factors or assumptions that shape the course of African philosophy and religion, that is, a principle that runs through their multiplicities; thus, creating a unity in the midst of diversities.

69

In relation to African traditional religion, two major views will be studied and criticized. These views are the perspectives of Mbiti and Koech. While Mbiti argues that the key to understanding African traditional religion is an understanding of the African concept of time, Koech argues that mythology is at the heart of the understanding of African traditional religion and metaphysics. These views will be presented and studied within the context of their ability to enhance the understanding of African traditional religion.

Within the parameters of philosophy, the perspectives of African philosophers, dating from the time when the intellectual history of African philosophy attained significant level of systematization, beginning from the time of Tempels to the perspectives of contemporary African philosophers like Asouzu, will be studied to see the web or thread that holds these perspectives together, in spite of the diversities there in. The major question that this research will be responding to, therefore, is: what is the underlying principle or moving spirit of African traditional religion and philosophy?

THE KEY TO UNDERSTANDING AFRICAN TRADITIONAL RELIGION

Mbiti (1970) understands African ontology as a religious ontology, which is heavily anthropocentric. In this ontology are God, the spirits, animals and plants, and objects; however, at the centre is the human person. If this ontology would be understood, he argues that there is the need to penetrate its unity. Mbiti, therefore, avers that the African concept of time is the key to understanding the African religious ontology.

> The concept of time may help to explain beliefs, attitudes, practices and general way of life of African peoples not only in the traditional set up but also in the modern situation, whether of political, economic, educational or church life. (p. 16).

His idea of African time is built around his research on the Kikamba and Gikuyu languages, in which he analyzed three verbs that speak of the past and the future, covering only a period of six months and not beyond two years at most. He defines the African time as "a composition of events which have occurred, those that are taking place now and those which are immediately to occur" (p. 17). This would mean that Africans set their minds on things that have passed, rather than on the future. He describes the African time as concrete, epochal, and not mathematical. This would mean that when Africans are sitting down idle, they are not wasting time but waiting for time or producing time.

Mbiti's African time, in the perspective of Gbadegesin (1991), is only a communal worldview report which was never evaluated. Gyekye (1975), Kagame (1976) and Izu (2010) see Mbiti's African time as insulting and false, as it does not represent the general concept of time among Africans. Gyekye argues that contrary to Mbiti's African time, the Akan people of Ghana have a future time. From the foregoing, it is obvious that Mbiti's African time is not a consistent principle in African religious and cultural thoughts, and as such cannot be regarded as the unity or the key to understanding African traditional religion.

Koech (1977) speaks of African myths as the key to understanding African traditional religion and metaphysics. He writes that:

> Myth expresses the history, the culture and the inner experience of the African himself. The myth portrays the wishes and the fears of the African man as he gropes to understand the unknown by dissecting and remolding it to fit his frame of reference. In the myth, the African's metaphysics are created and his beliefs constructed. (p. 118).

Koech, thus, concludes that:

> The myth is the essence of the African himself in history. The modern African, if he is to find his real identity and to grasp the remnant of his culture, must look for it in myth... The African myth tarried to preserve the last drop of African-ness. It is the encyclopedia engraved in the chambers of the African mind to be passed from generation to generation. (p. 139).

Although myths articulate and preserve the outcome of investigations on the origin of the world, the national god, the origin of humanity, its place in creation, deity, the temple, the cult, etc., it cannot be regarded as the key to understanding African religion or metaphysics, for the simple reason that mythology is not an underlying principle in African traditional religion. Myths vary from one religious culture to another, and the religious meanings that mythological elements present in one culture might not be the same in another. Thus, rather than speak of unity, myths introduce the subject of polarity in African traditional religion.

The key to the understanding of African traditional religion should be based on the nature of the African cosmos or universe. Cosmology, etymologically, is from two Greek words: *cosmos* and *Logos*, meaning 'universe' and 'science' respectively. Put together, it is the 'science of the universe'. Scholars like Wambutda (1986), Ejizu (1986), Achebe (1986), Metuh (1987), Quarcoopome (1987), Arinze (1970), Madu (2004) and Kanu (2015a) hold that African cosmology is simply the way Africans perceive, conceive and contemplate their universe; the lens through which they see reality, which affects their value systems and attitudinal orientations. Cosmology is, therefore, the search for the meaning of life, and an unconscious but natural tendency to arrive at a unifying base that constitutes a frame of meaning often viewed as *terminus a quo* (origin), and as *terminus ad quem* (end) (Kanu, 2012).

African cosmology is essentially the underlying thought link that holds together the African value system, philosophy of life, social conduct, morality, folklores, myths, rites, rituals, norms, rules, ideas, cognitive mappings and theologies (Kanu, 2015b). *Igwebuike* as a concept captures the is-ness of the African cosmos; a universe of complementarity and sharedness. *Igwebuike* is, therefore, African cosmology, and African cosmology is *Igwebuike*. It is *Igwebuike* because, in spite of its departmentalization into the worlds of the spirits and human beings (Edeh, 1983; Abanuka, 2004 & Ijiomah, 2005; Kanu, 2017a), it is not a bifurcated world. The spiritual and physical dimensions overlap and harmoniously interact. In this interaction, human beings commune with God, the ancestors, etc., and vice versa. While the ancestors do for human beings what they cannot do for themselves, human beings do for the ancestors what they cannot achieve by themselves. This interactive capacity of the African universe has instilled a strong sense of community in every dimension of the African life, such that to be without belonging is to be annihilated (Kanu, 2017b). This has not only defined the social and political dimensions of the African life, but the spiritual or religious dimension as well. It is in this regard that *Igwebuike* is employed as the key to understanding African traditional religion. To understand the meaning that *Igwebuike* conveys is to understand the dynamics of African traditional religion.

THE KEY TO UNDERSTANDING AFRICAN PHILOSOPHY

This second section of this piece also argues that *Igwebuike* is the key to understanding African philosophy. Right from the philosophy of Tempels (1959), the *Igwebuike* spirit of complementarity, solidarity, etc., has permeated the perspectives of African philosophers. It is in this regard that Tempels argues that in Bantu Ontology:

> 'Beings forces' of the universe are not a multiple of independent forces placed in juxtaposition from being to being. All creatures are found in relationship according to the law of hierarchy... Nothing moves in this universe of forces without influencing other forces by its movement (p. 29).

Kagame (1951) and Jahn (1958) did establish the harmonious character of reality. They agree with Tempels that reality is force. It is not a force independent of other forces.

The nationalistic movements of the 20th century in Africa were linked by their emphasis on belongingness, familyhood, which was the basis for their socialisms. Thus, the social negritude of Senghor (1959, 1964 & 1975) places the family at the centre of the social structure. Nyerere (1968) bases his principle of Ujamaa on familyhood. The choice of socialism over capitalism by Awolowo (1969&1979) and the promotion of Pan-Africanism by Nkrumah (1963) were based on the distinctive complementary character of African ontology.

Edeh (1983), in his work on *Igbo Metaphysics,* continues with the perspective of Mbiti:

> Accordingly the Igbo way of life emphasizes 'closeness' but not closed-ness'. There is a closeness in living because each person 'belongs to' others and in turn, 'is belonged to' by others. By adopting this life of 'closeness' or 'belongingness', an Igbo becomes immersed in the culture's spiritual substance, love; and by love, he acquires a fulfillment as a person beyond mere individuality. (p. 105).

Gyekye (1987), writing on Akan philosophy, avers that the individual depends on the community:

> The individual's life depends on identifying oneself with the group. This identification is the basis of the reciprocal relationship between the individual and the group. It is also the ground of the overriding emphasis on the individual's obligation to the members of the group. (p. 156).

Iroegbu (1995) describes being in African ontology as belongingness. In response to the questions, 'what makes being, being?', 'what does it mean to be in the *uwa* (world - the true and valid *universum* along the possibilities of thinkables, experientials, perceivables and their commonness to all human beings. That is, the *worldhood* or universal *datum* that provides the "hood" for the perceivers and experiencing thinkers of this inescapable phenomenon)?' Iroegbu argues that it is belongingness, thus *Being is Belongingness*. What then is belongingness? He defines it as 'the synthesis of the reality and experience of belongingness' (p. 374).

Nkemnkia (1999) writes that in African ontology, the self is the other:

> The meaning of an individual's life is found in and through his relationship with the Other or Others. In fact it is meaningless to ask oneself "who am I" without having a complete knowledge of the Other, from whom, in the final analysis, one expects the answer. (pp. 111-112).

Wiredu (1995), focusing on the political dimension of the African life, sees complementarity and belongingness as characterizing political decision-making in Africa.

Asouzu (2004, 2007) and Njoku (2018) develop the notion of being within the new ontological horizon of *Ibuanyidanda*. Within the *Ibuanyidanda* context, Asouzu (2007) defines being as "that on account of which anything that exists serves a missing link of reality" (p. 103). Thus, being is located within the context of mutual complementarity of all possible relations in the sense of an existent reality (Kanu, 2016a&b).

From Tempels to Asouzu, the *Igwebuike* principles of harmony, community, solidarity and complementarity have never been lacking, therefore, positioning *Igwebuike* as the underlying principle of African philosophy.

CONCLUSION

This work is a contribution to the ongoing investigations in the areas of African philosophy and African traditional religion in search for the keys to the understanding of both areas of study. Contrary to the positions of Mbiti and Koech, this piece argues that the key to understanding African traditional religion is *Igwebuike*. It also argued, in relation to African philosophy, that *Igwebuike* is the intricate web of African philosophy. It has remained constant in the midst of the changes in the history of African philosophy, and has continued to persist through changes. Its sense of harmony, community, complementarity and solidarity has been expressed in virtually all the perspectives of African philosophers, from the time of Tempels to the contemporary era. This position is based on the fact that *Igwebuike* is based on or captures the African worldview which shapes African philosophy.

REFERENCE

Achebe, C. (1958). *The things fall apart*. England: Heinemann.

Asouzu, I. I. (2004). *Methods and principles of complementary reflection in and beyond African philosophy*. Nigeria: Chidal Global.

Asouzu, I. I. (2007). *Ibuanyidanda: New complementary ontology, beyond world immanentism, ethnocentric reduction and impositions*. Berlin: Transaction.

Asouzu, I. I. (2007a). *Ibuanyidanda: New complementary ontology, beyond world immanentism, ethnocentric reduction and impositions*. Berlin: Transaction.

Awolowo, O. (1968). *The People's Republic*. Ibadan: Oxford University Press.

Awolowo, O. (1979). *The problems of Africa: The need for ideological appraisal*. London: Macmillan.

Edeh, E. (1985). *Towards an Igbo Metaphysics*. USA: Loyola University Press

Ekwulu, B. I. (2010). Igbo concept of Ibe (the other) as a philosophical solution to the ethnic conflicts in African countries. In B. I. Ekwulu (Ed.). *philosophical reflections on African issues* (pp. 183-192). Enugu: Delta.

Gyekye, (1975). African religions and philosophy by J.S. Mbiti. *Second Order. 4. 1.* 86-94.

Gyekye, (1975). African religions and philosophy by J.S. Mbiti. *Second Order. 4. 1.* 86-94.

Gyekye, K. (1987). *An essay on African philosophical thought: The Akan conceptual scheme.* Cambridge: Cambridge University Press.

Ikemnkia, M. N. (1999). *African vitalogy: A step forward in African thinking.* Kenya: Paulines.

Iroegbu, P. (1994). *Metaphysics: The Kpim of Philosophy.* Owerri: International Universities Press.

Iroegbu, P. (1995). *Metaphysics: The kpim of philosophy.* Owerri: International Universities Press.

Iroegbu, P. (1995). *Metaphysics: The kpim of philosophy.* Owerri: International Universities Press.

Izu, M. O. (2010). The problematic of African time. *Uche: Journal of the Department of Philosophy, University of Nigeria, Nsukka. 16.* 19-38.

Jahn, J. (1958). *Muntu: An outline of the new African culture.* New York: Grove.

Kagame, A. (1951). *La philoosophie Bantu Rwandaise ae l' Etre.* Bruxelles: La Divine Pastorale.

Kagame, A. (1976). The empirical apperception of time and the conception of history in Bantu thought. *Culture and time* (pp. 101-102). The UNESCO Press.

Kagame, A. (1976). The Empirical Apperception of Time and the Conception of History in Bantu Thought. *Culture and Time* (pp. 101-102). UNESCO Press.

Kanu, I. A. (2016a). *Igwebuike* as the consummate foundation of African Bioethical principles. *An African journal of Arts and Humanities* Vol.2 No1 June, pp.23-40.

Kanu, I. A. (2016b) *Igwebuike* as an Expressive Modality of Being in African ontology. *Journal of Environmental and Construction Management. 6. 3.* pp.12-21.

Kanu, I. A. (2016a). African traditional folk songs as dialogue between education and entertainment. *Cambridge International Journal of Contemporary Education Research. 6. 6.* pp. 53-64.

Kanu, I. A. (2016a). *Igwebuike* as an Igbo-African hermeneutics of globalisation. *IGWEBUIKE: An African Journal of Arts and Humanities,* Vol. 2 No.1. pp. 61-66.

Kanu, I. A. (2016a). *Igwebuike* as the consummate foundation of African Bioethical principles. *An African journal of Arts and Humanities* Vol.2 No1 June, pp.23-40.

Kanu, I. A. (2016b) *Igwebuike* as an expressive modality of being in African ontology. *Journal of Environmental and Construction Management.* 6. 3. pp.12-21.

Kanu, I. A. (2016b). African traditional folktales as an integrated classroom. *Sub-Saharan African Journal of Contemporary Education Research.* Vol.3 No. 6. pp. 107-118.

Kanu, I. A. (2017). *Igwebuike* as an Igbo-African philosophy for Christian-Muslim relations in Northern Nigeria. In Mahmoud Misaeli (Ed.). *Spirituality and Global Ethics* (pp. 300-310). United Kingdom: Cambridge Scholars.

Kanu, I. A. (2017). *Igwebuike* as an Igbo-African philosophy for the protection of the environment. *Nightingale International Journal of Humanities and Social Sciences.* Vol. 3. No. 4. pp. 28-38.

Kanu, I. A. (2017). *Igwebuike* as the hermeneutic of individuality and communality in African ontology. *NAJOP: Nasara Journal of Philosophy.* Vol. 2. No. 1. pp. 162-179.

Kanu, I. A. (2017a). *Igwebuike* and question of superiority in the scientific community of knowledge. *Igwebuike: An African Journal of Arts and Humanities.*Vol.3 No1. pp. 131-138.

Kanu, I. A. (2017a). *Igwebuike as a philosophical attribute of Africa in portraying the image of life.* A paper presented at the 2017 Oracle of Wisdom International Conference by the Department of Philosophy, Tansian University, Umunya, Anambra State, 27-29 April.

Kanu, I. A. (2017b). *Igwebuike* as a complementary approach to the issue of girl-child education. *Nightingale International Journal of Contemporary Education and Research.* Vol. 3. No. 6. pp. 11-17.

Kanu, I. A. (2017b). *Igwebuike* as a wholistic response to the problem of evil and human suffering. *Igwebuike: An African Journal of Arts and Humanities.* Vol. 3 No 2, March.

Kanu, I. A. (2017e). *Igwebuike* as an Igbo-African modality of peace and conflict resolution. *Journal of African Traditional Religion and Philosophy Scholars. Vol. 1. No. 1. pp. 31-40.*

Kanu, I. A. (2017g). *Igwebuike* and the logic (Nka) of African philosophy. *Igwebuike: An African Journal of Arts and Humanities.* 3. 1. pp. 1-13.

Kanu, I. A. (2017h). *Igwebuike* philosophy and human rights violation in Africa. *IGWEBUIKE: An African Journal of Arts and Humanities.* Vol. 3. No. 7. pp. 117-136.

Kanu, I. A. (2017i). *Igwebuike* as a hermeneutic of personal autonomy in African ontology. *Journal of African Traditional Religion and Philosophy Scholars. Vol. 2. No. 1. pp. 14-22.*

Kanu, I. A. (2018). African philosophy, globalization and the priority of 'otherness'. *Journal of African Studies and Sustainable Development*. Vol. 1. No. 1. pp. 40-57.

Kanu, I. A. (2018). *African traditional philosophy of education: Essays in Igwebuike philosophy.* Germany: Lambert Publications.

Koech, K. (1977). African mythology: A key to understanding African religion. InN. S. Booth (Ed.). *African religions: A symposium* (pp. 117-139). London: Nok.

Mbiti, J. S. (1969). *African religions and philosophy.* Nairobi: East African Educational Publishers.

Njoku, F. O. C. (2015). *The philosophical grid of Igbo socio-political ontology: Ibu anyi danda.* 147th Inaugural Lecture of the University of Nigeria, Nsukka.

Nkrumah, K. (1963). *Africa must unite.* London: Oanaf.

Nyerere, J. (1968b). *Ujamaa: Essays on socialism.* Oxford: Oxford University.

Nyerere, J. (1968a). *Freedom and socialism.* Oxford: Oxford University.

Senghor, L. S. (1959). Elements of constructifs d'ume civilization d'inspiration negro-africaine. *Presence Africaine. February – May.*

Senghor, L. S. (1964). *On African socialism.* Trans. M. Cook. New York: F. A. Praeger.

Senghor, L. S. (1975). What is negritude? (Eds.) G. C. M. Mutiso and S. W. Rohio. *Readings in African Political Thought* (pp. 78-90). London: Heinemann.

Tempels, P. (1959). *Bantu Philosophy.* Paris: Presence Africaine.

Wiredu, K. (1995). Democracy and consensus in African traditional politics: A plea for a non-party polity. In O. Oladipo (Ed.). *conceptual decolonization in African philosophy: Four Essays* (pp. 53-63). Ibadan: Hope

IGWEBUIKE: A CONCEPTUAL TOOL FOR CHANGE IN THE LIBERATION OF AFRICAN WOMEN

Nnoruga James
Department of Religion and Human Relations
Nnamdi Azikiwe University, Awka
nnorugajames@gmail.com

EXECUTIVE SUMMARY

When women in their numbers find themselves socially, economically, politically deprived and progressively thrown further and further away from the centre of life and meaning, it is not a mere accident or effect of an unknown factor. Consciously or unconsciously, it shows that there is a big problem unattended to. The subjugation of women in the world remains one thing men do not consider seriously as something worth fighting for. Recently, the struggle has started toward the liberation of African women. Igwebuike principle is used here to show the way to the liberation of African women. The approach used here is reflective and theological approach.

Keywords: Liberation, Igwebuike, Kanu Ikechukwu Anthony, African, Women, Conceptual Tool

INTRODUCTION

Recently, liberation has been a cause of concern to the whole world, both from the point of men and women. For ages, liberation has been about men in Africa or community or village; nothing meaningful has been done or carried out about women liberation. According to Umeh (2004), the "Book of Exodus" is an account of God's liberation of the people of Israel. This means that liberation has been there for ages, about people who are dominated by other people stronger than they are. It is known that Israelite liberation happened because of injustice, slavery, social and economic exploitation found among the people of Israel by their stronger opposing nation, Egypt. This goes on to show that for liberation to take place, there must be underlying crisis or factors that necessitate liberation. It does not happen in a vacuum, for man always yearns to be free, yet always chained by one bad situation or the other.

Today, in the world of globalization, women suffer in different ways, which can stem from psychological, sociological, cultural, to political crisis or problem meted out to them by their male counterparts or society. Arinze-Umobi (2010) articulated it as thus:

> Violation of women's right is a global problem that affects third world countries and some developing countries …. Violence against women and girls is one of the most widespread violations of human rights. It can include physical, sexual, psychological and economic abuse, and it can include physical, sexual, psychological and economic abuse, and it cuts across boundaries of age, race, culture, wealth and geography. It takes place in the home, on the streets, in schools, the workplace, in farm fields during conflicts and crises. (P. 715).

From the above quotation, one recalls the prevalent rape going on everywhere in most places, or brutal killings of women in war or by terrorists. Objectively, liberation cut across all ages, races, continents, human right and status because sufferings or crises are seen or emanate virtually from these aspects and spheres of life or from any part of the world. So far, it is known that crisis or suffering is a monster bedeviling our society or African nations, especially for their backwardness or understanding of life in this contemporary age. Hence, there is need for the liberation of African women from all these shackles of devils reducing their meaningful and joyful life.

Sequel to this hopeless situation in Africa, this write-up views *Igwebuike* principles as a way of liberation for African women. This will ensure a balance and joyful life for African women. Though many principles or solutions for the liberation of African women have been given or suggested by many African scholars or theologians, from their own point of view, *Igwebuike* principles will ensure the development and advancement of African women because it is based on African world views primarily, rather than other world views. Though references may go beyond African women, but it measures more on African women and Igbo perspective.

AFRICAN SITUATION: WOMEN PREDICAMENT

African nations, as of today, are still suffering heavily from the burdens of their past invasion, exploitation and partition of African countries by the European countries. Under the evils of slave trade, millions of Africans, especially women, were taken into slavery and abused violently, and most of them died. Slave traders engaged in the exportation of able-bodied women for sexual activities outside Africa. This is one of the ways the rights of the African women were subdued, and violence enthroned into their lives. Today, slavery is being replaced by human trafficking in major parts of Africa, and this involves women and children mostly. It goes on to show that women are less valued in our society today. There may be other causes of women trafficking but the bottom line is that society does not value them as their male counterparts, and government in place does not protect its citizens. It is known that recently, African women are deceived for better jobs in other countries of the world, like Italy, Germany, Malaysia, China, and so on. Slavery or women trafficking, which may be caused by unemployment, poverty, greed, ignorance, will be controlled through quality education and self-sustenance, and this involves liberation.

Culturally, African women are subjugated in different ways. This hampers them from living the fullness of their lives as normal human beings. According to Oborji (2005), there are some cultural hardships that African women are experiencing. These range from aspects of African customs and traditions that oppress women and put them in the state of inferiority complex, when they compare themselves with other women in the world. This, of course, prevents them from participating fully and elegantly in the development of the African society. There are some cultures that restrict African women from coming out at certain times of the day or at festivals. Most of the African cultures place more value on the male child in the society.

With this, women or girls in the African society or family are valued less than their male counterparts. Sometimes, this leads the head of the family to marry another wife, thereby putting the woman or the wife in perpetual agony. Here, Ezeigbo (1966) is of the opinion that the losing or changing of names upon marriage by African women subdues them all the more, though marriage is seen as one of the hallmarks of a complete woman. Ezenwanebe (2010) agrees strongly that being an African woman in the family has a lot of demands like pregnancy, house work, child care, and so on, which is a burden to womanhood and a serious threat to self-realization and freedom. Yet, marriage is seen or perceived as the major perspective from which one can better access a woman's other life aspirations. According to Muonwe (2016), a woman is, so to speak, a nobody outside of marriage" (P. 3).

From the social point of view, African women are subjugated in different ways. They are being discriminated against in so many ways in favour of their fellow Africans or male counterparts in the family circle. Muonwe (2016) relates that:

> In the traditional Igbo society, during her menstruation, the wife is not allowed
> to cook for her husband, especially if he is a titled man (though this practice is
> no longer wide spread today), because she is believed to be impure…. She is not
> only forbidden to cook for her husband during this period, but is also required
> to avoid coming near him. In certain cases, she lives in a separate house and
> is forbidden to touch ceremonial objects, else they become defiled. (pp. 14-15).

Poverty also has helped to reduce African women to a mere human whose task cannot be more than that of man or just bearing children. Unemployment finally gave a deadly blow to our economy, and consequently our women are affected adversely. Traditionally, it is believed that there are certain tasks or employments or jobs women will not do. This hampers greatly the actualization of their dreams in life. Some African men believe that the task of women begins and ends in the kitchen and "the other room". Through this way, abuses and violence are done to African women, and their rights constantly denied. According to Arinze-Umeobi (2010):

> Violence affects the lives of millions of women worldwide, in all socio economic and educational classes. It cuts across cultural and religious banners, impeding the right of women to participate fully in a society. Violence against women takes a dismaying variety of forms, from domestic abuse and rape to child marriages and female circumcision. (P. 716).

Some ideologies believe in the reality of inequality. This shows that women, generally, in the family and society are oppressed. Marxists claim that gender inequality originated from man's desire to own property in herding and agricultural economy of pre-industrial society. Engels (cited by Ezenwanebe, (2010)) points out that certain historical conditions led to women's subjugation and this started when man's desire to ensure the paternity of the children, who would become heirs to his properties, led to an increased restriction of the women; a mere instrument for breeding children. Zaretsky (1976) agrees with the Marxists that it is the capitalists who benefit most from women's subjugation and oppression. In private life, women dominate, but in public life, it is believed to be the area of men; that is why Zaretsky agrees with Marxists that capitalism benefits more from domestic labour of housewives who reproduce future generation of workers at no cost to the capitalist. Male domination or chauvinism has been traced again as the source or the problem of women's subjugation in most places. This is seen most often in patriarchal societies. This ideology or society favours male issues and sees women as not equal to men.

It is known that Africans accepted this ideology or cultural system without making any effort to deconstruct the system. The deconstruction of patriarchal ideology is necessary for the growth of African women. This is a social system in which men hold primary power and pre-dominate in roles of political leadership, moral authority, social privilege and control of property. Some patriarchal societies are also patrilineal, meaning that property and title are inherited by the male lineage. This patriarchal ideology is attributed to inherent natural differences between men and women. But sociologists tend to see patriarchy as a social product and not as an outcome of innate difference between the sexes, and they focus attention on the way that gender roles in a society affect power differentials between men and women. In fact, most societies are patriarchal in practice.

Again, feminist theorists see it as a primary cause of women's oppression and subjugation. So many feminists have called for culture repositioning as a method for deconstructing patriarchy. This culture repositioning relates to culture change and it involves the construction of the cultural concept of a society. Layli (cited by Ezenwanebe, 2010)) defines feminism as the "critical perspective and social movement that revolves around the eradication of sexism, the dismantling of patriarchy and elimination of violence against women" (p. 6). This is a view that women are oppressed and subdued by many obstacles limiting the actualization of their potentials. It calls for women to challenge and transgress the obstacles to free themselves.

Most feminist theorists believe that it is an unjust social system that is harmful to both men and women. It involves any social, political or economic mechanism that evokes male dominance over women. Again, some feminists believe that it is man and his society, not capitalists, who benefit most from women oppression, and only a change in the status of women in society can bring an end to their subservient oppression. But Firestone (1970) argues that gender inequality and women operation are3 biologically determined, producing what is referred to as sexual class system. The above thought refers to the burden of family lives on women. Some scholars objected strongly to the view that it is not the family task or biological make up of women that devalues them but the way African society interprets their world view, and the interpretation that ties them to reproduction and family care.

This in a great way hampers African women from the business of governance in Africa. In fact, women in politics are sometimes seen as wayward women; it is only recently that the mentality is changing. Sequel to this and other factors, women are not seen much elected in political offices in the African political arena. Even in the process of appointment into political offices, African women are neglected because of mindset . But women can lead when elected and can manage authority more than men. It is on record that during this Corona virus pandemic that most countries of the world ruled by women are low in the number of people affected and number of people that died. But most countries in the world ruled by men recorded more suffering and death during this Corona virus pandemic. This means that women govern well and care very much.

African women are highly subjugated or oppressed in the world today. There are many accusing fingers pointing at the ugly situation of African women. The solution is yet farfetched; where it is found or suggested, it is hard to be implemented. The worst is that even the women themselves seem to accept and enjoy the situation. *Igwebuike* principle will help to enhance the freedom of African women because it is African worldview-oriented and it is going to be achieved by collective and individual efforts.

IGWEBUIKE AND ITS PRINCIPLES

Having seen the condition of African women, which needs liberation urgently, we proffer and analyze the principles to ameliorate the conditions of African women. For it is known that most African women migrate to other continents of the world for better living and balanced life. Recently, the rate of rape against African women reported in the internally displaced peoples' camp was alarming. Sequel to all these, the principles of *Igwebuike* developed by Professor Kanu Ikechukwu Anthony need to be analyzed for the liberation of African women. According to Kanu (2015), *Igwebuike* is the modality of being, and being in Igbo ontology is 'idi', that is 'to be'. *Igwebuike* is an Igbo word which is a combination of three words. According to him:

> It can be understood as a word and as a sentence: as a word, it is written thus *Igwebuike*, and as a sentence, it is written thus, *Igwe bu ike,* with the component words enjoying some independence in terms of space and [meaning]. (p. 67).

He goes further to explain the three words that make up the word, *Igwebuike. Igwe* is a noun which means 'number' or 'population', usually a large number or population; *Bu* is a verb which means 'is'; *Ike* is a noun, which means 'strength' or 'power.' When these words are put together, it means 'number is strength' or 'number is power' (Kanu, 2016, 2017, 2018, 2019). This, in effect, means when a good number, group or society of human beings comes together in solidarity, they are powerful. Again, solidarity combines with complementarity because everybody needs each other to make a complete whole. It constitutes a powerful group and an insurmountable force. At this level, Kanu asserts that no task is beyond their collective capability. Again this analysis provides or proves an African ontology that presents being as that which possesses a relational character of mutual relations. Mbiti (1960) also asserts that "man is at the very centre of existence, and African people see everything else in its relation to this central position of man… it is as if God exists for the sake of man" (p. 92). Metuh (1991) affirms that "everything else in African worldview seems to get its bearing and significance from the position, meaning and end of man" (p. 109).

The above analysis shows that for man to achieve his aims or objectives in this world, he has to be in relational character with the other people around him. This will ensure a formidable force. The human person, following the African worldview, is understood in his relation with God and his fellow human beings. Ideologically, Kanu (2015) argues that 'to be' is to live in solidarity and complementarity, and to live outside the parameters of solidarity and complementarity is to suffer alienation. 'To be' is to be with the other in a community of being. Onwubiko (1991) expresses this sense of community rightly with Lozi proverb which says: "Go the way that many people go, if you go alone you will have reason to lament" (p. 13).

Anchoring on or explaining Igwebuike on the basis of African worldview, Iroegbu (1994) describes it as being characterized by a common origin, common worldview, common language, common historical experiences and common destiny. Determining the role of community to individual or human beings, Mbiti (1969) asserts that "I am because we are and since we are, therefore I am" (p. 108). The sense of community here portrays family-hood or brotherhood, which means collaboration in existence. Achebe (cited by Kanu, 2015), in order to bring out the essential nature of the Igbo African communal relationship, asserts that:

> We do not ask for wealth because he that has wealth and children will also have wealth. We do not pray to have more money but to have more kinsmen. We

are better than animals because we have kinsmen. An animal rubs its itching flank against a tree, a man asks his kinsmen to scratch him. (p. 68).

The above shows that life is shared in African worldview which makes life meaningful. So, it is in relationship or coming together that each completes a whole. Thus, every being has a missing part and is at the same time a missing part. Ekwulu (cited by Kanu, 2015) confirms the above view that "if the other is my part or a piece of me, it means that I need him for me to be complete, for me to be what I really am. The other completes rather than diminishes me" (p. 189).

This rightly explains why Igbo-African worldview would refer to the other as *'ibe'*, which means a piece of or a part of, as in *'ibe ji'* (a piece of yam), or *'ibe ede'* (a piece of cocoyam). Kanu (2015) asserts that the Igbo-African refers to the other person as *'ibe'* which means 'my piece', or *'mmadu ibe m'* (my fellow human being). This is a concept also employed in relation to relationships and reciprocity: love one another *(hunu ibe unu n'anya)*, help one another *(nyere nu ibe unu aka)*, respect one another *(sopuru nu ibe unu)*. From the above, we see that *Igwebuike* portrays the African sense of commonality, solidarity, brotherhood, familyhood and complementality as the root of African world view, thought and ontological quality of real the African which is needed to liberate African people from the state of subjugation seen in all aspects of their lives (Kanu, 2016 & 2018).

IGWEBUIKE AND ITS POWERS TOWARDS LIBERATION

We have seen the ugly situation of African women which needs liberation to have a full life. We noticed again that the feminist writers, more than any set of people, increasingly and strongly call attention to an end to the oppression of women which has been there since human history. Sequel to the above, Tutu (1979) posits that liberation is the objective task of contemporary African scholars. African theologians have sought this liberation in the light of the gospel message. *Igwebuike* principles, on its own, combine gospel message and African world view in seeking a way of liberation for African women.

The liberation of African women entails eliminating all forces that hinder African women from living fully as human beings. The above assertion on the principles of *Igwebuike* are the same with Murray's (1979) principles of liberation which assert that the term liberation has three distinct levels of meaning:

a. Socio-political liberation,
b. A historical process of humanization and self-realization, and
c. Liberation from sin and admission to communion with God.

The *Igwebuike* principle is rooted in the African world view, and this can be linked to the inculturation used by theologians today (Kanu, 2017). It involves removal of bad traditional cultures. Oborji (2005) relates that these are those cultural hardships that African women experience; that is, those aspects of African customs and traditions which oppress women, put them in the state of inferiority complex and subjugation with the men folk, and deny them the right to participate fully as equal partners in the development of Africa. This entails that Africans can, on their own, stop all customs and traditions which they see that is oppressing their womenfolk. It coincides with the saying that man is meant for Sabbath and not Sabbath for man. This implies also replacing those customs and traditions with good ones that will make African women to be proud of themselves.

One of the principles of *Igwebuike* includes complementarities and shared experiences. It is true that men and women differ in some significant ways, but it equally shows that they are not different as day and night or light and darkness (Kanu, 2017 & 2019). Hence, Udebunu (2010) asserts that:

> From the stand point of nature, men and women are much closer to each other than either anything else and an exclusive gender identity is a suppression of these natural similarities. Men and women have the human "species characteristics" of capacity for language, intellect and imagination, upright stance, thumb opposition and manipulation, tool-making and tool-using and extended childhood and parenting that mark us off from other species and are constituents of the evolutionary jump to human society. These characteristics are shared between the sexes and there is no good reason to doubt that the shift from biological evolution to history should also be shared accomplishment. (P. 158).

This shows that human beings generally are almost the same in everything. Since men and women share the same capacity, ability and skill, there is no reason to suppress the other on the basis of gender.

Igwebuike is endowed with the principle of complementarity (Kanu, 2014). We know that no tree can make a forest. So, instead of amplifying the differences in men and women by virtue of their biological or body difference which leads to subjugation and exclusion of women from the vital activities in the African society, Africans should decide or develop how best to harmonize or complement the great qualities or skills found in men and women's biological nature to achieve great living and advancement in the society. However, Udebunu (2010) rejects the efforts of those who, in an attempt to achieve the above complementarity and advocated for both sexes, that is encouraging women to become more like men, dropping their womanly qualities, as if they succeed only to the extent they achieve masculine status or vice versa. Hence, *Igwebuike*, as a principle, is projecting a means whereby both male and female come together in a new synthesis or synergy and achieve a difficult task in a holistic manner.

Using *Igwebuike* as a conceptual tool for change, the issue of mental attitude towards certain areas of life has to be changed or reconstructed to accommodate womens' life in the society. For example, in terms of political life, family life is seen by certain feminists as the tyranny of family or criticized as barrier to political equality and a source of psychological, economic and political oppression. Here, the principle of relation in *Igwebuike* comes in because family must be part of the political life. Udebunu (2010) hints also that gone is the time when political institution exists exclusively of its own, independent of the family life. Bottomore (1964), on the above stand, says that "the institutions which exist in the differing spheres of society are not merely co-existent but are connected with each other by relations of coincidence or contradiction and mutually affect each other" (pp. 121-122).

This implies that there is a significant relationship that exists between the structure or formation of nuclear family and the structure of the wide political society of which it is a part and parcel . Eckstein (cited by Udebunu, 2010) supports the above when he points out that the stability of any political order is dependent upon the congruence between governmental authority structures and other such structures in the society, including those of work places, pressure groups, schools and, most significantly, the family. With this, the above family life, through the principles of *Igwebuike*, can never be a barrier to political life, but indeed can bring fullness of life for African women.

The principle of solidarity in *Igwebuike* again brings in the effort of women themselves to recognize the power in them and to rise up against oppression meted out to them by the menfolk. The coming together of women to have one voice and strength etymologically depicts *Igwebuike* (strength in number). This has been done in most countries of Africa where women liberate themselves from the oppression they found themselves in. Muonwe (2016) expresses the efforts of Igbo women through their organized women revolts as thus:

> Because of the weakened position Igbo women found themselves in, as a result of colonial policies and administrative strategies, the staged quite a good number of demonstrations, "wars", protests and riots. They did these to press home their demand for a better treatment and to register their displeasure with what they saw as injustice, deprivation of their basic rights, and bastardization of Igbo culture. (P. 97).

Some of these revolts by Igbo women include:

a. 1916 Onitsha Women Market Demonstrations.
b. 1925 Women Movement.
c. Oil Mill Demonstration 1940-1950.

There are revolts, especially those bordering on rape in the recent times, by which young women in Nigeria and other African countries protest openly against rape and other oppressive actions. Finally, the situation of African women needs liberation. The principles of *Igwebuike*, as a tool for change, when properly applied within Africa, will definitely help in liberating the African women.

CONCLUSION

The write-up has shown the possibility of liberating African women using the liberating principles of *Igwebuike*. It does not involve dismantling of any institution, but transforming our world view which involves change of attitude, empowerment, and proper education of African women. This will ensure that every woman can say no to subjugation and exploitation or oppression of any kind. Mbefo (2009) supports and enumerates strategies for winning the battle or the struggle for African women liberation from male hegemony and subjugation. Firstly, he proposes that we must look into the contemporary situation of women in the wider world in order to insert African women into broader global picture. African women must see themselves as modern women of twenty-first century. Secondly, in order not to be alienated from African roots and, therefore, to highlight their identity as African women, women must look deeper into their African history to effect a genuine update of African values. All these affirm the principles of *Igwebuike* discussed above. However, this involves strong will and effort, for liberation struggle entails much.

REFERENCES

Achebe, C, (1958). *Things fall apart*. London. Heinemann.

Arinze-umeobi, S. O. (2010). Women and Globalization in the Nigerian FilmIndustry: An Appraisal of Selected Nigerian films. In *A. B. C.* Chiegboka, T. U. Utuh, Ezeajuh and G. I. Udechukwu (Eds.). *The Humanities and Globalization in the Third Millennius* (pp. 715-720). Nimo: Rex Charles and Patrick.

Bottomore, T. B. (1964). *Elites and society*. England: Harmondsworth.

Ezeigbo, A. T. (1996). *Gender issues in Nigeria: A feminist perspective*. Lagos: Vista.

Ezenwannebe, O. C. (2010). Issues in women's liberation struggles in contemporary Nigeria: A study of Ezeigbo's hands that crush stone. *Journal of International Women's Studies*. 16,3, 262-276.

Firestone, S. (1992). *The dialects of sex*. London: Paladin.

Iroegbu, P. (1995). *Metaphysics: The kpim of philosophy*. Owerri: International University Press.

Kanu I. A. (2015b). *A hermeneutic approach to African traditional religion, theology and philosophy*. Nigeria: Augustinian Publications.

Kanu I. A. (2017). *Igwebuikeconomics*: Towards an inclusive economy for economic development. *Igwebuike: An African Journal of Arts and Humanities. Vol. 3. No. 6.* 113-140.

Kanu I. A. (2017). Sources of *Igwebuike* philosophy. *International Journal of Religion and Human Relations. 9. 1. pp.* 1-23.

Kanu, A. I. (2016a). *Igwebuike* as a trend in African philosophy. *IGWEBUIKE: An African Journal of Arts and Humanities. 2. 1.* 97-101.

Kanu, A. I. (2017c). *Igwebuike* as an Igbo-African philosophy of inclusive leadership. *Igwebuike: An African Journal of Arts and Humanities.* Vol. 3 No 7. pp. 165-183.

Kanu, A. I. (2017d). *Igwebuike* philosophy and the issue of national development. *Igwebuike: An African Journal of Arts and Humanities.* Vol. 3 No 6. pp. 16-50.

Kanu, A. I. (2017f). *Igwebuike* as an Igbo-African ethic of reciprocity. *IGWEBUIKE: An African Journal of Arts and Humanities. 3. 2. pp.* 153-160.

Kanu, I. A. (2010). Towards an African cultural renaissance. *Professor Bassey Andah Journal of Cultural Studies. Volume 3*, pp. 146-155.

Kanu, I. A. (2012). A metaphysical epistemological study of African Medical practitioners. In O. E. Ezenweke and I. A. Kanu (2012). *Issues in African traditional religion and philosophy (pp. 227-240)*. Nigeria: Augustinian Publications.

Kanu, I. A. (2012). Being qua belongingness: The Provenance and Implications of Pantaleon's redefinition of being. *Uche: Journal of the Department of Philosophy, University of Nigeria, Nsukka.* Vol. 17. pp. 57-58.

Kanu, I. A. (2012). From 'Onye' to 'Ife' hypothesis: The contribution of Edeh to the development of the concept of being. *Lwati: A Journal of Contemporary Research. 9, 4.* 218-223.

Kanu, I. A. (2012). Inculturation and Christianity in Africa. *International Journal of Humanities and Social Science.* Vol. 2. No. 17. pp. 236-244.

Kanu, I. A. (2012). The functionality of being in Pantaleon's operative metaphysics vis-a-vis the Niger Delta conflict. *African Research Review: An International Multi-Disciplinary Journal.* Vol.6. No.1. pp. 212-222.

Kanu. I. A. (2012). Towards an Igbo Christology, In Ezenweke, E.O and Kanu, A.I. (Eds) *Issues in African traditional religion and philosophy*, Jos: Augustinian Publications.

Kanu, I. A. (2012). The problem of being in metaphysics. *African Research Review: An International Multi-Disciplinary Journal*. Vol.6. No.2. April. pp. 113-122.

Kanu, I. A. (2012). The problem of personal identity in metaphysics. *International Journal of Arts and Humanities*. Vol.1. No.2. pp.1-13.

Kanu, I. A. (2012a). The concept of life and person in African anthropology. In E. Ezenweke and I. A. Kanu (Eds.). *Issues in African traditional religion and philosophy* (pp. 61-71). Nigeria: Augustinian.

Kanu, I. A. (2012b). Towards an Igbo Christology. In E. Ezenweke and I. A. Kanu (Eds.). *Issues in African traditional religion and philosophy* (pp. 75-98). Nigeria: Augustinian.

Kanu, I. A. (2013). African identity and the emergence of globalization. *American International Journal of Contemporary Research*. Vol. 3. No. 6. pp. 34-42.

Kanu, I. A. (2013). Globalisation, globalism and African philosophy. C. Umezinwa (Ed.). *African philosophy: A pragmatic approach to African probems* (pp. 151-165). Germany: Lambert.

Kanu, I. A. (2013). On the sources of African philosophy. *Filosofia Theoretica: Journal of African Philosophy, Culture and Religion, Vol. 2. No. 1.* pp. 337-356.

Kanu, I. A. (2013). The dimensions of African cosmology. *Filosofia Theoretica: Journal of African Philosophy, Culture and Religion, Vol. 2. No. 2.* pp. 533-555.

Kanu, I. A. (2014). A historiography of African philosophy. *Global Journal for Research Analysis. Volume. 3. Issue. 8.* pp. 188-190.

Mbefo, L. N. (2005). African women and the challenges of modernity. *Bigard*

Theological Studies. 29, 2. 51-63.

Mbiti, J. S. (1969). *African religions and philosophy.* London: Heinemann.

Metuh, I. E. (1991). African religions in western conceptual schemes. Jos: Imico.

Muonwe, M. (2016). *New dawn for African women; Igbo perspective.*

Bloomington: Xlibris.

Murray, P. (1979). Black theology and feminist theory: A comparative view. *In*

G. S. Wilmore & J. H. Cone (Eds*.). Black theology: a documentary history.*

1966-1979 (pp. 398-417). New York: Orbis Book.

Onwubiko, O. A. (1991*). The christian mission and culture in Africa. African thought, religion and culture.* Enugu: Snapp Press.

Tutu, D. M. (1979). Black theology/ African theology- soul mates or antagonists? *In G.S. Wilmore & J. H. Cone (Eds.). Black theology: A documentary history, 1966-1979* (pp. 483-491). New York: Orbis Book.

Udebunu, C. (2010). From nuclear to global family: Plato's feminism and the politics of identity. In A. B. C. Chiegboka, T. C. Utoh-Ezeajuh & G. I. Udechukwu (Eds.) In *The humanities and globalisation in the third millennium* (pp. 152-163). *Nimo: Rex Charles & Patrick.*

Umeh, E. C. (2004). *Option for the poor. An African liberation theology.* Enugu: Snaap Press.

Zaretsky, E. (1976). *Capitalism: the family and personal life.* London: Pluto Press.

IGWBUIKE PHILOSOPHY: A VEHICLE FOR PEACE AND CONFLICT RESOLUTION AMONG THE IGBOS OF SOUTH EAST NIGERIA

Onyeakazi Jude Chukwuma, PhD
Philosophy Unit, Directorate of General Studies
Federal University of Technology Owerri.
jude.Onyeakazi@futo.edu.ng; judefuto@gmail.com

EXECUTIVE SUMMARY

The concept of socialism and communalism has been an age-long problem in the history of philosophy. Philosophers, over the years, have tried to mediate in this age-long problem through their various theories: Nyerere's theory of 'Ujamaa' (togetherness as oneness), the collective consciousness of Emile Durkhiem, the Ibuanyindanda ideology of Innocent Asouzu and Kwame Nkrumah's philosophical consciencism, just to mention but a few. In all these socio-political ideologies, none has been properly exhausted to meet the desired result in the reduction and prevention of conflicts and man's cruelties against man, in terms of communal clashes, assorted forms of oppression, suppression, domination and discriminations. It is against this background that this research work titled 'Igwebuike philosophy: A vehicle for peace and conflict resolution among the Igbos of South East Nigeria' was chosen as a template to contribute to the prevention and reduction of violence and terrorism in the Nigerian state. It is a philosophical inquiry that attempts to interrogate the dynamics of our social environment, using Igwebuike (strength in unity) ideology, which was developed by Kanu Ikechukwu Anthony, depicting the Marcelian theory of intersubjectivity. Despite the fact that our own country is plagued with insecurity, communal violence, and anxiety from various terrorist attacks, this paper is optimistic that the scourge can be reduced to a reasonable limit via "Igwebuike" which is a call and an awakening to mutual complementary relationships. Furthermore, it aims at unraveling how this consciousness can be used as an essential tool for lasting peace and reconciliation, with the sole aim of restoring the meaning of life in our meaninglessness situation. Lastly, it recommends certain strategies for peace and conflict resolution among the various ethnic groups in Nigeria. The method of this paper is essentially analytical, expository and evaluative.

Keywords: Igbos, Igwebuike, Kanu Ikechukwu Anthony, conflict resolution.

INTRODUCTION: METAPHYSICAL DIMENSION OF *IGWEBUIKE* PHILOSOPHY

The fundamental principle which describes the core African spirit is harmony; although reality exists as individuals, they converge at the point of reasonableness.[1] *Igwebuike,* as an ideology developed by Professor Kanu Ikechukwu Anthony, rests on the African principle of solidarity and complementarity.[2] It provides an ontological horizon that presents being as that which possesses a rational character of mutual relation. To live outside the parameters of solidarity and complementarity is to suffer alienation. "To be" is "to be" with the other in a community of beings. [3] This is also captured in the philosophical assertion of Panteleon Iroegbu that "To be is to belong and to belong is to be"[4] and in Mbiti's "I am because we are and because we are, therefore, I am. Kanu, quoting Asouzu, opines: "Complementarity is a philosophy that seeks to consider things in the significance of their singularity and not in the exclusiveness of their otherness in view of the joy that gives completion of all missing link of reality."[5]

SOCIO-ANTHROPOLOGICAL ANALYSIS OF *IGWEBUIKE* PHILOSOPHY

Man is a socio-cultural being that always shares a relational affinity with other members of his community. Human beings and societies exist only in relation.[6] The intercultural philosophy of *Igwebuike* captures the socio-anthropological nature of man, especially the Igbo people. The Igbo people of southern Nigeria exhibit their social characteristics in their interactions with their fellow human beings, both within their ethnic nationality and outside of it.[7] *Igwebuike* is anchored on Igbo-African worldview which is characterized by a common origin, common worldview, common language, shared culture, shared race, colour, habit, common historical experience and a common destiny.[8] Thus, *Igwebuike* celebrates in deep cultural and philosophical modality our common humanity, interconnectedness and our common responsibility towards ones another. This is in line with the famous proverbial assertion of Mbiti, "I am because we are and since we are, therefore, I am". [9]

---

[1] Kanu, Ikechukwu Anthony. *Igwebuike as a Trend in African Philosophy, 84.*

[2] Kanu, Ikechukwu Anthony. *Igwebuike as a Trend in African Philosophy, 84.*

[3] Kanu, Ikechukwu Anthony. *Igwebuike as a Trend in African Philosophy, 84-85.*

[4] Panteleon, Iroegbu. *Metaphysics: The Kpim of Philosophy, 374.*

[5] Kanu, Ikechukwu Anthony. "*Igwebuike* and the Logic (Nka) of African Philosophy",in *IGWEBUIKE: An African Journal of Arts and Humanities,* Vol. 3, No. 1, January 2007, 14.

[6] Kanu, Ikechukwu Anthony. *Igwebuike as a Trend in African Philosophy, 74.*

[7] Christian, O. Ele. *Conflict Resolution Strategies in Igbo Religion: The Oath Taking and Covenant Making Perspective, 35.*

[8] Panteleon, Iroegbu. *Metaphysics: The Kpim of Philosophy, 108.*

[9] John, Mbiti. *African Religions and Philosophy,* Nairobi: East African Edu. Publishers, 1970, 108.

In the Igbo-African view, it is the community which defines the person as person.[10] Individualism is alien to Igbo experience of reality; hence, "Reality as a communal world takes precedence over the reality of individual life histories".[11] As a summary of this idea, Nwoko opines:

> An African Traditional Society is a society where the individual is always considered a free, integrated member of his community, a communion person. It is a society where individualism is considered a taboo, where each member takes the interest of the community as his own. His pride is community is power. The more united he is to the community, the more he sees the community as a mere extension of the family.[12]

The need to live together in community is seen as part of Igbo-African existential status. The individual has meaning only in the context of the community.[13] The Igbo-African society has been based on an extended family system, which in turn expanded to kinship groups which further extended to clan system and this is the theoretical basis of African communalism.[14] Therefore, the Igbo community denotes first and foremost ontological quality of human relation. It is ontological in so far as all the members of the community are believed to descend from a common ancestor.[15]

CAUSES OF CONFLICTS AMONG THE IGBOS

There are many causes of conflict within the Igbo societal setting; this can result either from land or boundary disputes, bad leadership, etc. Meanwhile, A major pivotal factor of conflicts in the South East zone of Nigeria is still the ownership of land[16] and kingship tussles. This is because land is a serious issue among the Igbos, since it touches both the material and the spiritual essence of Igbo ontology. Thus, land is something worth fighting and dying for.[17] Meanwhile, other sources of conflict in Igbo land, apart from land disputes, are chieftaincy titles tussles, political differences and search for dominance and hegemony, and matrimonial fallouts. On the other hand, social deviance, which contravenes norms of the society, such

---

[10] Ifeanyi, A. Menkiti. "Person and Community in African Traditional Thought," in *African Philosophy: An Introduction*, 3rd ed., (ed.) Richard A. wright. Lanham: University Press of America, 1984, 172.

[11] Ifeanyi, A. Menkiti. *Person and Community in African Traditional Thought*, 171.

[12] Nwoko, M. I. *The Rationality of African Socialism,* Rome: 1985, 71-72.

[13] Ikegbu, Ephraim. "African Communalism", in *A Colloquium on African Philosophy*, Vol. 1, G.O. Ozumba (ed.). Calabar: Prospper Ventures, 2003, 32.

[14] Uduigwomen, A. F. "African Communalism: Individual Freedom Versus Communal Demands," in *Sophism and African Journal of Philosophy*, Vol. 4, No. 1. Calabar: Pyramid Publications, 2002, 27.

[15] Nzomiwu, J. P. C. *The Moral Concept of Justice Among the Igbos*, Rome: AC. Alfonsiana, 1977, 38.

[16] Charles, C. Mezie-Okoye. "Tiv and Igbo Conflict Management Mechanism: A Comparative Study", in *International Research Journal of Social Science, Vol. 5 (7), 2016*, 25.

[17] Oguntola- Laguda, D. "The Role of Traditional Rulers and Religious Leaders in Conflict Management in Nigeria", in *The Practice of Religion in Nigeria*, Ilorin: Decency Press, 25.

as incest, stealing of yam or cattle, murder of fellow kinsman, adultery, insubordination to elders, are also causes of social disputes among the Igbos. These social deviances range from the minor deviant acts that require sanctions for their controls to heinous offences, *Nso-ala*.[18]

IGWEBUIKE AND CONFLICT RESOLUTION: A PHILOSOPHY OF SOCIAL INCLUSION

The Igbos organized their society to integrate the needs of the individuals, family, village, town and clan. Individuals benefit socially and psychologically from the support and protection of the community. Individual survival and safety is protected within the walls of the community. Every member of the community is responsible for the other.[19] The success of an individual increases the overall well-being of the entire community. The community which adopts communalism as a standard of operation delves into rights and freedom in order to protect the individual from harm and undue molestation.[20] Central to the idea of community is unity which is linked to peace and progress in the society.[21] Harmonious and friendly relationships facilitate progress and overall well-being in the human community.[22] Harmony within the community is a moral obligation ordained by God for the protection and promotion of life.[23] *Igwebuike* philosophy avers that development be holistic, and emphasizes the centrality of the human person in such a development. It calls for a collaborative approach in the search for better means of livelihood; this means that everyone must play a complementary role. *Igwebuike* is anchored on the thinking that the community has a moral responsibility in the face of human suffering. Everyone must do something to alleviate the suffering of the other.[24] The community spirit is very strong among the Igbos. Almost from the first, the individual is

---

[18] Nwankwo, Ignatius Uche. *"Traditional Multiple Level Conflict Resolution and The Appeal System of the Igbo Group of Southeast Nigeria and the Challenges of Social Change"*, 36.

[19] Kanu, Ikechukwu Anthony. "Igwebuike as a wholistic Response to the Problem of Evil and Human Suffering", in *Igwebuike: An African Journal of Arts and Humanities*, Vol. 3, No.2, March 2017, 72. Kanu I. A. (2015b). *A hermeneutic approach to African traditional religion, theology and philosophy*. Nigeria: Augustinian Publications. Kanu I. A. (2017). Igwebuikeconomics: Towards an inclusive economy for economic development. *Igwebuike: An African Journal of Arts and Humanities. Vol. 3. No. 6*. 113-140. Kanu I. A. (2017). Sources of *Igwebuike* philosophy. *International Journal of Religion and Human Relations. 9. 1*. pp. 1-23. Kanu, A. I. (2016a). *Igwebuike* as a trend in African philosophy. *IGWEBUIKE: An African Journal of Arts and Humanities. 2. 1*. 97-101. Kanu, A. I. (2017c). *Igwebuike* as an Igbo-African philosophy of inclusive leadership. *Igwebuike: An African Journal of Arts and Humanities*. Vol. 3 No 7. pp. 165-183. Kanu, A. I. (2017d). *Igwebuike* philosophy and the issue of national development. *Igwebuike: An African Journal of Arts and Humanities*. Vol. 3 No 6. pp. 16-50.

[20] Ikegbu, Ephraim. *African Communalism*, 32.

[21] Anthony, Kwakporo Nwogu. *The Christian Eucharist and Oriko: A Study in Conflict Resolution*, 14.

[22] Anthony, Kwakporo Nwogu. *The Christian Eucharist and Oriko*, 38.

[23] Anthony, Kwakporo Nwogu. *The Christian Eucharist and Oriko*, 40.

[24] Kanu, Ikechukwu Anthony. *Igwebuike as a wholistic Response to the Problem*, 72.

aware of his dependence on his kin group and his community. He also realizes the necessity of making his own contribution to the group to which he owes so much.[25]

As a principle of sustainable development, *Igwebuike* philosophy invites everyone to accept "community involvement". As committed members of the society, it implies a mutual involvement of individuals and society in the destiny of each other; a common social destiny. Therefore, it makes every member of the society responsible for the welfare of one another.[26] The community will definitely become better if everyone plays his/her own part very well. To this, Asouzu asserts:

> The African (Igbo) worldview, therefore is ruled by the spirit of complementarity which seeks the conglomeration, the unification, the summation of fragmented thoughts, opinions and other individualized fragmented thoughts and ideas. It believes essentially that the whole is greater than the corresponding parts, a viable and sustainable whole will emerge and by this, the part will get to the brim purpose of their existence. [27]

IGWEBUIKE PHILOSOPHY: A VEHICLE FOR CONFLICT RESOLUTION

The Igbo race took adequate measures to handle confrontations of social powers in their possibilities and actualities by evolving strategies that would prevent them, and at *conflictual*

---

[25] Uchendu, V. C. *The Igbo of Southeast Nigeria,* London: R and Wiston, 1965, 34.

[26] Edmund, Aku. *Solidarity, Subsidiarity and Common Good: Fundamental Principles for Community and Social Cohesion*, USA: Xlibris Corporation, 2011, 15.

[27] Kanu, Ikechukwu Anthony. *Igwebuike and the Logic (Nka) of African Philosophy*, 14. Kanu, I. A. (2018). *Igwe Bu Ike* as an Igbo-African hermeneutics of national development. *Igbo Studies Review. No. 6.* pp. 59-83. Kanu, I. A. (2018). *Igwebuike* as an African integrative and progressive anthropology. *NAJOP: Nasara Journal of Philosophy.* Vol. 2. No. 1. pp. 151-161. Kanu, I. A. (2018). New Africanism: *Igwebuike* as a philosophical Attribute of Africa in portraying the Image of Life. In Mahmoud Misaeli, Sanni Yaya and Rico Sneller (Eds.). *African Perspectives on Global on Global Development* (pp. 92-103). United Kingdom: Cambridge Scholars Publishing. Kanu, I. A. (2019). Collaboration within the ecology of mission: An African cultural perspective. *The Catholic Voyage: African Journal of Consecrated Life.* Vol. 15. pp. 125-149. Kanu, I. A. (2019). *Igwebuike* research methodology: A new trend for scientific and wholistic investigation. *IGWEBUIKE: An African Journal of Arts and Humanities* (IAAJAH). *5. 4.* pp. *95-105.* Kanu, I. A. (2019). *Igwebuikeconomics*: The Igbo apprenticeship for wealth creation. *IGWEBUIKE: An African Journal of Arts and Humanities* (IAAJAH). *5. 4.* pp. *56-70.* Kanu, I. A. (2019). *Igwebuikecracy*: The Igbo-African participatory cocio-political system of governance. *TOLLE LEGE: An Augustinian Journal of the Philosophy and Theology. 1. 1.* pp. 34-45. Kanu, I. A. (2019). On the origin and principles of *Igwebuike* philosophy. *International Journal of Religion and Human Relations.* Vol. 11. No. 1. pp. 159-176. Kanu, I. A. (2019b). An *Igwebuike* approach to the study of African traditional naming ceremony and baptism. *International Journal of Religion and Human Relations.* Vol. 11. No. 1. pp. 25-50.

situations, resolve them.[28] Conflict resolution in the Igbo society is rooted in their social structures and religion.[29] This is well- expressed by Christian Ele as thus:

> "In Igbo land, conflict Resolution strategies are embedded in their socio-cultural structures such as the family, kindred, village or clan and the entire town or community. In Igbo society, the family heads (*Ndi Okpara*), *Umunna* (the entire family of patriarchical roots), the council of elders (*ndi ichie*), the eldest in the kindred (*onyishi*), Traditional ruler (*Igwe or Eze*), the women groups (*umuada, umu nwunye Di*), youth groups (the age grade system, the *ogbo oha*), the maternal family (*ndi ikwu nne*), the grand child by a sister (*nwa di ana, oke nwa nwunye*), are all agents of Peace and stakeholders in conflict Resolution."[30]

Whenever there is an issue within the family or clan, it is often settled in the presence of everyone in an acclaimed open court through mediation and negotiations. The very aim of conflict resolution within the Igbo traditional setting is the reconstruction of social bridges and a reenactment of a supposed broken social order with a huge prospect of peaceful co-existence. It is not about justifying one and condemning the other, it works towards a compromise for the reconciliation of the both parties and the restoration of balance or the harmony of reality.[31] This very idea is simply an enactment of what *Igwebuike* (complementary and solidarity) philosophy stands for. It is, thus, a method of conflict resolution built upon the culture of the people.

TRADITIONAL MEANS OF CONFLICT RESOLUTION

Before the advent of white men, Igbos have already put into place mechanisms for adjudicating matters and for controlling the suppression of the weaker person by the stronger.[32] The basic unit for ensuring peace and preventing conflict was the family. However, there are many conflict resolution structures in traditional Igbo society. These are in forms of institutions, social groups and extra-mundane (metaphysical) beliefs or orientations that resolve matters between disputants, and prevent or counteract individual tendencies to deviance. They negotiate, mediate and arbitrate in dispute situations. They use tools like fines, banishment, food commensality, ostracism, oath-taking, to punish or resocialize persons whose behaviours violate role expectations, to preserve the society from disruption. The *Igwebuike* ideology and the communalistic nature of the Igbo people necessitate that there are established groups for

---

[28] Christian, O. Ele. *Conflict Resolution Strategies in Igbo Religion: The Oath Taking and Covenant Making Perspectives*, 35.

[29] Christian, O. Ele. *Conflict Resolution Strategies in Igbo Religion*, 35.

[30] Christian, O. Ele. *Conflict Resolution Strategies in Igbo Religion*, 38.

[31] Kanu, Ikechukwu Anthony. *Igwebuike as an Igbo-African Modality of Peace*, 37.

[32] Charles, C. Mezie-Okoye. *"Tiv and Igbo Conflict Management Mechanism: A Comparative Study"*, 27.

socio-cultural and socio-economic affairs. There are numerous religious and social groups for conflict resolution in Igbo land.

These conflict resolution structures, according to Nwankwo, include "Nuclear family structure, extended family assembly, age grades (Otu Ogbo), women association (Umuada), village assembly, festivals, Ozo title holders[33]". We shall explain only but a few of these structures.

NUCLEAR FAMILY STRUCTURE

The family is the foremost socialization and social control agent to which the individual is exposed. It controls the quality and quantity of new members of the society by educating the child on the rules, norms, mores and folkways that govern the society. In the society under study, the functions of socialization, social control and conflict resolution were executed by the nuclear as well as extended families. Nuclear family attends to disputes within the nuclear family setting between siblings, and spouses. It is usually presided over by the father and the elders of such families.[34]

EXTENDED FAMILY ASSEMBLY (IZU UMUNNA)

The extended family is a grouping into one functional unit of three or more generations of people linked by marriage, descent or adoption. They share a putative father and cannot inter-marry. In the Igbo society, the training was achieved by educating the child in the code of manners, conventions, customs, morals and laws of his society. At times, stories of heroes, or of tragedies that befell disputants or defaulters, are used to illustrate the essence of good behaviour.

The family restrains the child by meting out punishment as need arises. The kindred or members of the extended families form what is known as *umunna* assembly in Igbo tradition. They are represented by the *opara/okpala* – the most elderly male person. By virtue of his age and position, the *opara* acts as spokesman in conflict-related matters.[35] He performs socio-juridical functions and distributive justice is adjudicated by him. Any case which cannot be resolved by the opara is brought to the general assembly of the umunna. Every adult male has the right to contribute to the general deliberations at the assembly. The elders reserve the right to take the final decision after private consultations among themselves (*Igba izu*). The disputants or deviant members are customarily expected to comply with whatever punishment

---

[33] Nwankwo, Ignatius Uche. *"Traditional Multiple Level Conflict Resolution and The Appeal System of the Igbo Group of Southeast Nigeria and the Challenges of Social Change"*, 38-42.

[34] Nwankwo, Ignatius Uche. *"Traditional Multiple Level Conflict Resolution and The Appeal System of the Igbo Group of Southeast Nigeria and the Challenges of Social Change"*, 38.

[35] Anthony, Kwakporo Nwogu. *The Christian Eucharist and Oriko: A Study in Conflict Resolution*, Umuahia: Lumen Press, 2018, 18.

is prescribed, or face stiffer measures. In the Igbo society, a person who falls out of line with his extended family is likened to a bastard. For this reason, individuals carefully avoid violating the norms, thus, controlling their social behaviour and effectively resolving most conflicts. [36]

WOMEN ASSOCIATION (UMUADA)

The *umuada* is an association of women married outside their natal home. At birth, every female in the community is an ada and qualifies as a member of the *umuada* association. But she plays no practical role in the association until adult age, especially after she is married. In traditional Igbo society, the *umuada* association was a formidable conflict resolution structure and agent for the control of social behaviour of their members and of the larger public. Their influence was felt both in their lineage of procreation and in their husband's lineage.[37] Since pre-colonial era, Igbo women have imbibed the concept of *Igwebuike* in their diverse means of resolving conflicts and promoting peace. *Umuada* and *nwunye di* are the foremost women group and organization in Igbo land built on the truism of *Igwebuike* philosophy. These are organizations of daughters or wives of the clan who meet on several occasions to foster peaceful coexistence within the extended family, town or community. The *umuada* refers to the natal organization of daughters of the clan who are married either within or outside the community, while the *nwunye di* (co-wives) refers to the organization of women married within a family, kindred, clan or community in their maternal homes. *Umuada* exercises remarkable powers in their natal homes due to their status as daughters of the soil. The fundamental background of this very group is that their strength lies in their union and complemenatarity. No single person makes up the "*umu ada*". The Prefix "*umu*" already signifies plurality, and *umuada* work with communal strength. In performing the above social control functions, the *umuada* often adopt mechanisms like fine, demonstrations, gossip, praise and blame or expulsion of members as ways of expressing disapproval and to secure their demands. In sum, the *Uumuada* association was crucial in conflict resolution and social control in traditional Igbo society. They enjoy profound respect, even in contemporary times, and their verdict in all matters is taken seriously. Appeals may, however, be taken to council of elders, and Ozo title-holders group.[38]

EVALUATION AND CONCLUSION

It must be noted that despite the fact that *Igwebuike* philosophy has an Igbo semantic and cultural undertone, it is of universal relevance. It is not a philosophy specifically viable for the Igbo people alone, despite its uniqueness to the Igbo people. Despite its intrinsic worth, there

---

[36] Nwankwo, Ignatius Uche. *"Traditional Multiple Level Conflict Resolution and The Appeal System of the Igbo Group of Southeast Nigeria and the Challenges of Social Change"*, 39.

[37] Nwankwo, Ignatius Uche. *"Traditional Multiple Level Conflict Resolution"*, 40.

[38] Nwankwo, Ignatius Uche. *"Traditional Multiple Level Conflict Resolution"*, 41.

are also certain areas of consideration which must be critically evaluated so as to make the best use of *Igwebuike* philosophy. These shortcomings highlight the potential misconceptions, misappropriation or misapplications of *Igwebuike* philosophy.

It is often assumed by critics of *Igwebuike* Philosophy that communality kills the autonomy of an individual. This assumption may not necessarily be true, but if care is not taken, freedom and rights of individuals might be submerged and possibly suppressed in the strong tides of the community. More so, *Igwebuike* philosophy runs the risk of collectivism. Most times, in collectivism, the individual disappears.[39] It is similar to a democratic worldview which considers the opinion of the greater majority, since all the members of the community must not necessarily agree. In cases of misjudgment, compromise, bias, prejudice and conspiracy, popular opinion might not correspond to right judgments and decisions. The rich and influential people might also impose their thoughts on others.

The *Igwebuike* ideology is also established on the commonalities of interest and socio-political or socio-cultural background. Its emphasis on numerical strength might actually breed an undue hegemony as those with higher numerical strength can intimidate others and issue undue treatments to the less numerically privileged few based on this ideology. The *Igwebuike* philosophy, when wrongly conceived, will breed a problem of paucity of integration. There is also a tendency to consider those outside one's circle as enemies, strangers, and treated as second class citizens. This is because humans can be consigned into believing that reality is genuine only within their individual circles. There will, hence, be a tendency to trust only those who are closer to us, like kinsmen and family members.

EVALUATION AND RECOMMENDATIONS

In the face of ever-increasing complexities, the Igbo people have continued to employ Igbo categories in search for a solution to their many problems. This work, thus, employs the holistic, inclusive and complementary category of *Igwebuike* as a model for both conflict resolution and sustainable development. Peace and progress are the hallmarks of every developing society, and they are both realities derived from mutual relational affinities between individuals. Hence, they are products of unity; unity is synonymous with peace and progress. In the Igbo worldview, peace is not merely an abstract construct; it is a reality which links with the life lived in the human community.[40] This idea is best captured in the complementary philosophy of *Igwebuike* which stresses that solidarity and supplementary relationship built upon common background are very vital for social cohesion and advancement. It does not abrogate the importance of individual autonomy, but stresses an interdependent relationship whereby everyone assumes a social responsibility for the welfare of one another in the society. Hence, the intercultural philosophy of *Igwebuike* calls for a global action in conflict resolution and

---

[39] Ozioma, J. Nwachukwu. *Communalism in African Traditional Worldview*, Lagos: Change Pub, 2017, 71.
[40] Anthony, Kwakporo Nwogu. *The Christian Eucharist and Oriko*, 40.

a socio-anthropological communal involvement in a bid to create an enabling environment for development. The Igbos should concentrate on the fact that "together in peculiarities, the Igbos can make a formidable whole."

Hence, as a sort of recommendation, Igbos should appreciate more the philosophical heritage of their founding patrimony, since the conventional Western courts are now dominated by injustice and nepotism. The high cost of litigation in these courts is quite alarming, while the traditional means of conflict resolution does not charge fees for services rendered. Therefore, in issues of dispute resolution, the adoption of the *Igwebuike* philosophy should be taken with utmost priority.

CONCLUSION

Conflict resolution and sustainable development imply the ability of a society to improve the relational affinity and socio-economic standards of its citizens through various measures. From the *Igwebuike* perspective, the adopted approach must be complementary and balanced[41] – built upon the principle of solidarity. This work, thus, concludes by affirming that despite the alarming rate of conflicts and violence in our society today, a change of approach and employment of dialogue through *Igwebuike* consciousness will help to reduce tension in the society. It will help in building mutual understanding and respect in the society and, by so doing, enhancing sustainable development among the Igbo people of Nigeria. This research aims to re-awaken the spirit of participation in the life of others in the Igbo community, a call to a mutual service for common good.

---

[41] Kanu, I. A. (2017). *Igwebuike* as an Igbo-African philosophy for Christian-Muslim relations in Northern Nigeria. In Mahmoud Misaeli (Ed.). *Spirituality and Global Ethics* (pp. 300-310). United Kingdom: Cambridge Scholars. Kanu, I. A. (2017). *Igwebuike* as an Igbo-African philosophy for the protection of the environment. *Nightingale International Journal of Humanities and Social Sciences*. Vol. 3. No. 4. pp. 28-38. Kanu, I. A. (2017). *Igwebuike* as the hermeneutic of individuality and communality in African ontology. *NAJOP: Nasara Journal of Philosophy*. Vol. 2. No. 1. pp. 162-179. Kanu, I. A. (2017a). *Igwebuike* and question of superiority in the scientific community of knowledge. *Igwebuike: An African Journal of Arts and Humanities*.Vol.3 No1. pp. 131-138. Kanu, I. A. (2017a). *Igwebuike as a philosophical attribute of Africa in portraying the image of life*. A paper presented at the 2017 Oracle of Wisdom International Conference by the Department of Philosophy, Tansian University, Umunya, Anambra State, 27-29 April. Kanu, I. A. (2017b). *Igwebuike* as a complementary approach to the issue of girl-child education. *Nightingale International Journal of Contemporary Education and Research*. Vol. 3. No. 6. pp. 11-17. Kanu, I. A. (2017b). *Igwebuike* as a wholistic response to the problem of evil and human suffering. *Igwebuike: An African Journal of Arts and Humanities*. Vol. 3 No 2, March. Kanu, I. A. (2017e). *Igwebuike* as an Igbo-African modality of peace and conflict resolution. *Journal of African Traditional Religion and Philosophy Scholars*. Vol. 1. No. 1. pp. 31-40. Kanu, I. A. (2017g). *Igwebuike* and the logic (Nka) of African philosophy. *Igwebuike: An African Journal of Arts and Humanities*. 3. 1. pp. 1-13. Kanu, I. A. (2017h). *Igwebuike* philosophy and human rights violation in Africa. *IGWEBUIKE: An African Journal of Arts and Humanities*. Vol. 3. No. 7. pp. 117-136. Kanu, I. A. (2017i). *Igwebuike* as a hermeneutic of personal autonomy in African ontology. *Journal of African Traditional Religion and Philosophy Scholars. Vol. 2. No. 1. pp. 14-22.*

BELONGINGNESS AS IGWEBUIKE AND AFRICAN PHILOSOPHY A CRITICAL RELATIONSHIP

Jude I. Onebunne, PhD
Department of Philosophy
Nnamdi Azikiwe University, Awka
Anambra Sate, Nigeria
juno.anyi@gmail.com

EXECUTIVE SUMMARY

To be is to belong. That is to say being fundamentally belongs. Being is belonging. Belonging is being. To be, therefore, is to belong in one way or the other. By being and consequently belonging, human beings and realities are identified as such. Being foundationally relates to belongingness and belongingness to being. Belongingness, therefore, is an essential and indispensable character and intrinsic way of being. Hence, belongingness defines and describes a being, thereby justifying the conclusion thus: to be is to belong; not to be is not to belong. Until a being belongs, there is no identifying possibility with regard to what it can become or do amidst other realities. So, there is unity in strength by and in belonging. This is belongingness as Igwebuike. Belongingness guarantees the expression of relational unity as Igwebuike, which literally translates to unity is strength and guarantees pragmatic relationship that is symbiotic. These concepts, belongingness and Igwebuike, nevertheless are critically examined and philosophically contemplated within the paradigm of African philosophy amidst doubts of possibility and questions of existence with regard to nature, method, scholarship and history, which are genuinely part of world philosophical heritage.

Keywords: Belongingness, Kanu Ikechukwu Anthony, Igwebuike, African Philosophy

INTRODUCTION

Philosophy, *philosophia*, is love (philos) of wisdom (sophia). At the dawn of philosophy in the chequered history of man as rational animal, *being question* is very prominent and at the centre of philosophical discourse. Different philosophical traditions as well as philosophical epochs and periods had different problems to tackle philosophically. Contemporary period engaged more the reality as it confronts individual philosophy, demanding proper explanation and

103

response. At this point, many Western philosophico-traditional concepts are being replaced with complementary African philosophic-traditional concepts like *Igwebuike*, among others. These are individual philosophers' attempt at articulating reality as it relates to them, solving their problems and explaining their immediate environment.

BELONGINGNESS

Belongingness is a definitive principle in African communalism. It is a kind of societal bonding and genuine relationship within a community that stipulates that a thing belongs as it identifies with the environmental realities. Onebunne (2019a:) reiterates that, "belogingness is nevertheless expressed in few meta-theoretical concepts as: *Ibuanyidanda, Ubuntu* and *Ohazurume*" as well as in *Njikoka, Ezumezu* and more in *Igwebuike*. Belongingness, therefore, is the conceptual African metaphysics of being.

Belongingness has been identified as an ontological abstract term that specifies that a thing is because it belongs to one reality or the other. The idea of being as belongingness is nevertheless articulated on this understanding. Being, therefore, expresses itself in belongingness. Nothing actually is inactive or in its own unidentified with the other. It is only by implication that something can be thought to be inactive. Belongingness is the propulsive move of being to perfect itself and operates within an environment. Belongingness, as the African metaphysics of *To Be,* tries to locate by concretely defining and determining a being. Belongingness concretizes a being in existence. Hence, whatever is, as a being, must belong to something and/or somewhere. This is why being fundamentally belongs within the locus of spatial temporality. Onebunne (2018:429) notes that the typological interconnectedness of belongingness is that it connects to every being and every reality is networked. Being realizes its potentialities in belongingness. This is so because being fundamentally belongs within the spatial reality of *space-time.*

IGWEBUIKE PHILOSOPHY

Igwebuike is a modal action of a being in African worldview and understanding. It is an Igbo word, which is a combination of three Igbo words. Kanu (2017:23) in systematizing Igwe-bu-ike writes thus.

> 'To be' in Igbo ontology is *idi*. However, the modality of being is Igwebuike. It is an Igbo word, which is a combination of three words. Thus, it can be understood as a word and as a sentence: as a word, it is written thus, *Igwebuike*, and as a sentence, it is written as, *Igwe bu ike*, with the component words enjoying some independence in terms of space. Let us try to understand the three words involved: *Igwe* is a noun which means number or population,

usually a large number or population. Bu is a verb, which means is. *Ike* is a noun, which means strength or power. Put together, it means 'number is strength' or 'number is power', that is, when human beings come together in solidarity and complementarity, they are powerful or can constitute an insurmountable force. At this level, no task is beyond their collective capability.

The three words involved are: *Igwe* is a noun which means 'number' or 'population,' usually a huge number or population. It nevertheless means 'sky' or 'king,' depending on the pronunciation and the syllable stressed. *Bu* is a verb, which means *is* or *that which is*. *Ike* is another noun, which means 'strength' or 'power,' and as a noun it means 'buttocks,' or even as a verb, it means 'to create' or 'to share' (Kanu, 2014). Thus, put together, *Igwebuike* literally means *number is power* or *strength is power*. Put it the other way round, it means 'number is strength'. Number here refers to a group of beings, population of persons or people or reality. It refers to a congregation or multitude of human beings, animals or any reality that is capable of activity. You cannot gather for nothing. The *igwe* (in the sense of masses or assemblage) gathers for action to be replicated or exerted (Kanu, 2016). It is presupposed that the crowd or cluster of persons or any reality will exert enough might or vigour as well as force and supremacy or control for an end or activity to be achieved. Onebunne (2018:65) explains that *Igwebuike* "as employed by Igbo traditional philosophers as a theory based on an illustrative statement to teach that when human beings come together in solidarity and complementarity, they are powerful or can constitute an insurmountable force, and more so, to express their world of relationship, harmony, continuality and complementarity." At this level, no task is beyond collective capability. This provides an ontological horizon that presents being as that which possesses a relational character of mutual relations. As an ideology, *Igwebuike* argues that 'to be' is to live in solidarity and complementarity, and to live outside the parameters of solidarity and complementarity is to suffer alienation. *'To be'* is 'to be with the other' in a community of beings. This is based on the African sense of community, which is the underlying principle and unity of African philosophy (Kanu, 2019).

This work suggests that *Igwebuike* is the key to understanding African philosophy. While being in Igbo philosophy is 'Idi', that is, to be, *Igwebuike* is the modality of being. It is an Igbo word, which is a combination of three words. Therefore, it can be employed as a word or used as a sentence: as a word, it is written as *Igwebuike*, and as a sentence, it is written as *Igwebuike*, with the component words enjoying some independence in terms of space. As an ideology, *Igwebuike* postulates that 'to be' is to live in solidarity and complementarity, and to live outside the parameters of solidarity and complementarity is to suffer alienation. 'To be' is 'to be with the other', in a community of beings (Kanu, 2018). Such being with others is guaranteed by such others. That means one belongs with others, strengthening their existence. This is based on the African sense of community, which is the underlying principle and unity of African philosophy

BELONGINGNESS AS *IGWEBUIKE*

Igwebuike literally means *number is power* or *strength is power*. Kanu (2017), the apostle of *Igwebuike*, defines it as "the expressive modality of being in Igbo Ontology." For him, *Igwebuike*, which, according to Asouzu (2007:11), is literally *strength in togetherness,* is the locus of meeting of beings in Igbo communalist metaphysic, with special reference to existentialism and leadership. Kanu (2017:34), however, opines strongly on the concept of *Igwebuike* thus:

> Igwebuike provides an ontological horizon that presents being as that which possesses a relational character of mutual relations. As an ideology, Igwebuike rests on the African principles of solidarity and complementarity. It argues that 'to be' is to live in solidarity and complementarity and to live outside the parameters of solidarity and complementarity is to suffer alienation. 'To be' is 'to be with the other', in a community of beings. This is based on the African philosophy of community, which is the underlying principle and unity of African Traditional Religious and philosophical experience.

In developing this fundamental character of being as belongingness, Iroegbu (1998:45) initially defines belongingness as *a definitive principle in African communalism.* He uses belongingness in a technical sense. It is, thus, for him, a principle of membership applied to a given community. This membership is not mere identification but a kind of belonging that is security-assured. This belongingness implies the basic commonness that makes a community a community, in our context, what makes a given African community as such. Iroegbu shows that communalism makes belongingness an indispensible conceptual starting point for communal existence. Accordingly, Iroegbu explains thus: one native expression of belongingness is the term, *umunna.* In this sense, *umunna,* a basic community, transcends the nuclear family to mean, by extension, people of common lineage as well as commonness of origin. Belonging, however, is the human need to be an accepted member of a group. Abraham Maslow suggested that the need to belong was a major source of human motivation. And since *no man is an island,* the need to belong to and with one another becomes a basic demand for man's existence and co-existence. In belonging, people form a community of togetherness, and strengthened by such togetherness, many activities are possible. Some theories in life have also focused on the need to belong as a fundamental psychological motivation. We belong to a group with which we have commonalities. This feeling of belonging is a basic need and a unique term in the dynamics of living and existence.

Hence, Iroegbu (1995:19) asserts that "belongingness makes sure that all belong and none is marginalized, both contributively (duties and responsibilities) and distributively (sharing of communal cake)." This is the locus of *Igwebuike* at play. One does not necessarily belong. One is ever conscious of where one is putting oneself or belonging. The importance of communal existence is a rational provision aimed at a better understanding and appreciation of man, not as a discrete individual but as a being - properly expressed in belongingness as Igwebuike

This understanding has provided an enduring manner of attending to man as being with an inalienable interconnectivity with the rest of men. And so, the idea of coexistence as bedrock of caring and concern (sympathy) is highly significant in Africa as a whole. Hence, the Igbo people normally talk of power as belong to the multitude (*Igwe-bu-Ike*), especially when they cohabit or live together as in extended family system, a form of *onyeaghana nwanneya!*. In fact, the very concept of the multitude is in itself understood as a source of power and authority.

UNDERSTANDING OF AFRICAN PHILOSOPHY

African philosophy is philosophy as it is done in and for Africa and others. It is a philosophical tradition that is African within the mainstream of philosophy as a systematic study. African philosophy is the critical and universalizing interpretation of the culture and worldview of African people by philosophers within and outside the African continent. It is philosophy done within African philosophical tradition, designating the corpus of African philosophical writings. However, African philosophy, like other philosophical traditions, has a historical development along the path of human consciousness, critically encountering their realities (Kanu, 2015). This is against some philosophers' views and philosophical currents trying to demean and oppose the existence of African philosophy. African philosophy, therefore, is a systematic study within the limits of the *Africanity* of philosophy and *philosophicality* of African realities and heritage.

THE PHILOSOPHICALITY AND AFRICANITY OF AFRICAN PHILOSOPHY

Osuagwu (1999:28), in his criteria for the scientific philosophicality and scientific Africanity of African Philosophy, was apt to note thus:

> African philosophy is at the same time African and philosophical. In and by these terms, we are searching, on the one hand, for the genuine philosophicality, i.e., formal scientific philosophy, of the said African enterprise, and on the other hand, for the authentic scientific Africanity of that scientific philosophy. These two basic scientific criteria make African philosophy to bear the characteristics marks of its particularity and universality.

Philosophicality simply places African philosophy at par with *philosophia*, which is love of wisdom. To this extent, African philosophy remains part of the *world philosophical heritage*, with one philosophical monoculture, though from African *weltannchaunng*. Philosophicality, nevertheless, prunes African philosophy of the old socio-cultural bias of existence, and mere skeptical influence with pseudo-philosophical orientation. However, by this singular application of philosophicality, African philosophy is philosophy *qua* philosophy, irrespective of the philosophical traditions and/or philosophers' postulations, as long as it expresses the needed *love for wisdom* and maintains the search for knowledge with an unaided reason as the most basic instrument. African philosophy, in this perspective, is philosophy *per excellence,* considering its contribution to world philosophical heritage and even to Western ancient philosophers, like Socrates and other known philosophical figures, periodisation and traditions. If Socrates was regarded as a philosopher per se alongside Western philosophical tradition, then the tradition that produced him, which is the Egyptian African philosophical tradition, must have elements of such uncompromising philosophical innuendoes. Onebunne (2019d:3) summarily opines thus:

> *Philosophicality* is another principal criterion for determining African metaphysics. African philosophy is at the same time African, philosophical and metaphysical. By these terms, we are searching for the genuine understanding of philosophy. *Philosophicality,* as a basic scientific criterion makes African philosophy to bear the characteristic mark of its universality. Hence, echoing Osuagwu, I.M., therefore, in line with this understanding, African philosophy is, therefore, a universalization, a universal vocation, ordination, destination and determination of and in the African particular. To this extent African philosophy or metaphysics is carried on at the same time according to philosophy's general scientific norms, exigencies and African particular, traditional and natural factors. In this co-operation and mutual integration.

African philosophy has been very much neglected, rejected and denied on the purported grounds of its lack of genuine *scientificity,* authentic *Africanity* and systematic *philosophicality.* Through continued studies and sustained researches, African philosophy finds stability with its *Africanity* and more by its *philosophicality.* It is no more a question of, *Is there an African philosophy? Can there be African metaphysics?* Today, the emphasis of the question shifts rather from *can there be African philosophy?* to the issues of the *possibility* and how contemporaneously African philosophy is dealing with facts of historicity and method in African philosophy, principles, issues and special areas in African philosophy and her branches.

Equally, the *Africanity* of African philosophy is worth the salt. Scientific *Africanity* is a complementary principle in the definition of African philosophy. *Africanity* is a criterion that defines African philosophy properly with some parameters. According to Osuagwu (2001:24), "by its *africanity,* it is a particular, that is to say, a particular reflection, concentration, concretization, contextualization, experience, identification and differentiation of the philosophic, scientific universal." *Africanity* tries to solve the controversy and the project of African philosophy by going beyond the boundaries of the geographical Africa. Within the geographical context, *Africanity* expresses what it takes for any philosophy to be qualified, identified and differentiated as specifically and typically African. It contextualizes African experiences, life and reality within the realm of philosophy. For Osuagwu (2001:26). therefore:

Scientific *Africanity* refers to a set of African parameters or factors which include nature and culture, persons, places, times, events, doctrine, text and methods involved in philosophic enterprises so designated. These factors and many more constitute the common requirements by which a given subject matter is said to be African.

Borrowing an impressive idea from Kinyongo, Osuagwu (1999: 28) writes that "African philosophy is carried on at the same time according to philosophy's general scientific exigencies and Africa's particular natural and cultural factors. In this cooperation, and mutual integration, philosophy and *Africanity* look into each other to detect, engage and determine the scientifically valid and available in themselves."

BELONGINGNESS AND *IGWEBUIKE* AS PRODUCTS OF AFRICAN PHILOSOPHY

African philosophy, having come to stay, gave room for philosophical concepts that ordinarily would not attract any serious attention. But as long as philosophers of African origin and background are concerned, many of our concepts, having received the needed critical attention, can be projected naturally to the realm of rigorous discourse. It is no more: can there be African philosophy? Instead, it is dealing with African philosophy in a very sublime way, amidst given possibilities. The debate is over. What we are in now is *doing* African philosophy. Oblivious of Hegel's doubts on the possibility of the existence of African continent and the known facts with regard to Black Pharoahs of the Ancient Egypt, contemporary history is saddened with facts that Western philosophy is African philosophy in display as one doubts the authenticity of the burnt Alexandria Library.

African philosophy has made it possible for the emergence of African concepts that can comfortably challenge her contemporaries. Whatever it is like, Placid Tempels was bold enough to initiate then the debate on the possible existence of African philosophy with his publication of *Bantu Philosophy*. Amidst every known criticism, one must note that African philosophy is a viable philosophical option. This is because, philosophy, like African philosophy, has been rooted in the culture and worldview of the people. These socio-cultural data and worldviews of people's realities remain *the given* for critical appraisal in the quest or search for knowledge or wisdom which is philosophy. This is philosophizing *per se*. Okere (1983:15) opines strongly for the possibility of African philosophy based on this opinion, thus: "It is only within the context of hermeneutics that African culture can give birth to African philosophy." Why then do some philosophers refuse to accept and acknowledge that African culture has been reflected on and interpreted as such over the century amidst great scholarship and authorship, even as its methodological moments and scientific historicity are readily available? To this extent, any reference to African philosophy as mere derogatory ethno-philosophy than its foundation or fundamental root is a mark of great lack of scholarly ingenuity and serious disfavour to knowledge. Instead, one is inclined to accept that African philosophy is part and parcel of world philosophical inheritance.

DEFINITIONAL UNIVERSALITY OF AFRICAN PHILOSOPHY IN RELATION TO RAW MATERIALS FOR PHILOSOPHICAL REFLECTION

The definition and universality of African philosophy, against oddities of credibility and doubts of existence per chance, is resolved in the *philosophicality* and *Africanity* of African philosophy. African philosophy, therefore, has a share in the mainstream of philosophical traditions growing as a human enterprise as a result of critical interpretation of tradition and cultural realities. Okere (1983:38) asserts that "all philosophy is essentially an historical and time bound interpretation of being." In this line of thought, however, there are ethno-philosophical foundations to philosophy as critical engagement and philosophical traditions of which African philosophy or Chinese philosophy is no exception. This is far beyond referring to African philosophy as *Sage* or mere *Cultural* philosophy. Amidst all sorts of bizarre and false ideas on the capability of African man to philosophize, questioning the depth of his philosophy, one can boast of African philosophical scholarship as well as African authorship. However, Iroegbu (1994:116), an optimistic contemporary philosopher, was very apt in defining African philosophy as:

> The reflective inquiry into the marvels and problematics that confront one in African world, in view of producing systematic explanation and sustained responses to them. It is an inquiry with two aspects: *philosophical* and *African*.

Iroegbu was very *premier* in giving this succinct definition. In this definition, one can read a *kind* defense of African philosophy against being labeled mere folk, cultural or *ethno*-philosophy. The background at the time of this definition has to do with questioning and giving the possibility of African philosophy with regard to historicity and methodology. This is why for Iroegbu, African philosophy *is a philo-sophia, a quest for African wisdom*. However, Iroegbu was academically astute enough to reiterate that "African philosophy is philosophy done in an African context…the different aspects and complexities of existence that challenge him as an African person. In this respect, every philosophy is contextual philosophy." By this very act, I strongly add that every philosophy worth the salt is ethno-philosophical, relatively cultural and appropriately traditional to the philosopher. Alluding to this, Iroegbu (1994: 122) was vehemently bent on this general understanding of philosophy as: the global participation of all realities and entities in the general fact and understanding of being as being whether in African, Asian or Western philosophy. Summarily, Iroegbu (1994:122) gave ten areas of any contextual or ethno-philosophical basic foundation for genuine philosophical enterprise thus: *Geo-environmental, Socio-cultural, Episteme, Mythico-religious, political-moral, Historic, Ethnic –linguistic, Existential, Phenomenologico-pragmatical and ontological.* For Iroegbu, therefore, these philosophical concepts alone "are what we generally call the

African philosophical *philosophemena*: raw materials for philosophical reflection, questioning, responses, analysis and eventual synthesis." In this statement of fact, Iroegbu, continued to echo his teacher Okere Theophilus, who had earlier conceived the idea of *philosophemes* as deposit of conceptual data or realities for philosophical enterprise.

CONCLUSION

A definitive thoughtful interpretation and critical analysis of the symbols of African cultures would be African philosophy *qua tale*. That is to say, Igbo philosophy would, nevertheless, consist in the interpretation at a certain level of the various symbols and institutions or traditions of Igbo culture. The concept: belongingness or *Igwebuike*, for instance, stands for a kind of relationship or unity in strength respectively in Igbo philosophy. However, all those institutions, concepts and symbols in Igbo world that are ever-pregnant with sense and meaning are critically meaningful. Therefore, a reflection with profound application of criticality, analyticity and originality on most African thoughts, concepts and culture gives credence to philosophy and, rightly put, African philosophy. Such profundity in the critical appreciation of African or Igbo worldview makes of them veritable moments for African or even Igbo philosophy based on categories that are native to Igbo culture and worldview. Based on proper hermeneutics, one can dependably and realistically infer that African philosophy is a philosophy within the limits of African source and is nourished from African culture, as its cultural reservoir and primary critical nourishment as belongingness and Igwebuike have done in African philosophy.

REFERENCE

Asouzu, I.I (2007) Ibuanyidanda: New Complementary Ontology, Zurich: lit, Verlag GmbH & Co; Wien

Iroegbu, P., (2004). Kpim of time. Ibadan: Hope Publication.

Iroegbu, P., (1995). Metaphysics: Kpim of philosophy. Owerri: International University Press.

Iroegbu, P (1996b) Kpim of politics: Communalism, Owerri International Press

Kanu I. A. (2017). Sources of Igwebuike Philosophy. Towards A Socio-Cultural Foundation. *International Journal of Religion and Human Relations* Vol. 9 No 1 June.

Kanu, I. A. (2017). Igwebuike and Being in Igbo ontology: *Igwebuike: An African Journal of Arts and Humanities*. Vol. 4 No 5. [12-21].

Kanu, I. A. (2018). *Igwe Bu Ike* as an Igbo-African hermeneutics of national development. *Igbo Studies Review. No. 6.* pp. 59-83.

Kanu, I. A. (2018). *Igwebuike* as an African integrative and progressive anthropology. *NAJOP: Nasara Journal of Philosophy.* Vol. 2. No. 1. pp. 151-161.

Kanu, I. A. (2018). New Africanism: *Igwebuike* as a philosophical Attribute of Africa in portraying the Image of Life. In Mahmoud Misaeli, Sanni Yaya and Rico Sneller (Eds.). *African Perspectives on Global on Global Development* (pp. 92-103). United Kingdom: Cambridge Scholars Publishing.

Kanu, I. A. (2019). Collaboration within the ecology of mission: An African cultural perspective. *The Catholic Voyage: African Journal of Consecrated Life.* Vol. 15. pp. 125-149.

Kanu, I. A. (2019). *Igwebuike* research methodology: A new trend for scientific and wholistic investigation. *IGWEBUIKE: An African Journal of Arts and Humanities (IAAJAH). 5. 4.* pp. *95-105.*

Kanu, I. A. (2019). *Igwebuikeconomics*: The Igbo apprenticeship for wealth creation. *IGWEBUIKE: An African Journal of Arts and Humanities (IAAJAH). 5. 4.* pp. *56-70.*

Kanu, I. A. (2019). *Igwebuikecracy*: The Igbo-African participatory cocio-political system of governance. *TOLLE LEGE: An Augustinian Journal of the Philosophy and Theology. 1. 1.* pp. 34-45.

Kanu, I. A. (2019). On the origin and principles of *Igwebuike* philosophy. *International Journal of Religion and Human Relations.* Vol. 11. No. 1. pp. 159-176.

Kanu, I. A. (2019b). An *Igwebuike* approach to the study of African traditional naming ceremony and baptism. *International Journal of Religion and Human Relations.* Vol. 11. No. 1. pp. 25-50.

Kanu, I. A. (2017). *Igwebuike* as an Igbo-African philosophy for Christian-Muslim relations in Northern Nigeria. In Mahmoud Misaeli (Ed.). *Spirituality and Global Ethics* (pp. 300-310). United Kingdom: Cambridge Scholars.

Kanu, I. A. (2017). *Igwebuike* as an Igbo-African philosophy for the protection of the environment. *Nightingale International Journal of Humanities and Social Sciences.* Vol. 3. No. 4. pp. 28-38.

Kanu, I. A. (2017). *Igwebuike* as the hermeneutic of individuality and communality in African ontology. *NAJOP: Nasara Journal of Philosophy.* Vol. 2. No. 1. pp. 162-179.

Kanu, I. A. (2017a). *Igwebuike* and question of superiority in the scientific community of knowledge. *Igwebuike: An African Journal of Arts and Humanities.*Vol.3 No1. pp. 131-138.

Kanu, I. A. (2017a). *Igwebuike as a philosophical attribute of Africa in portraying the image of life*. A paper presented at the 2017 Oracle of Wisdom International Conference by the Department of Philosophy, Tansian University, Umunya, Anambra State, 27-29 April.

Kanu, I. A. (2017b). *Igwebuike* as a complementary approach to the issue of girl-child education. *Nightingale International Journal of Contemporary Education and Research*. Vol. 3. No. 6. pp. 11-17.

Kanu, I. A. (2017b). *Igwebuike* as a wholistic response to the problem of evil and human suffering. *Igwebuike: An African Journal of Arts and Humanities*. Vol. 3 No 2, March.

Kanu, I. A. (2017e). *Igwebuike* as an Igbo-African modality of peace and conflict resolution. *Journal of African Traditional Religion and Philosophy Scholars. Vol. 1. No. 1. pp. 31-40.*

Kanu, I. A. (2017g). *Igwebuike* and the logic (Nka) of African philosophy. *Igwebuike: An African Journal of Arts and Humanities*. 3. 1. pp. 1-13.

Kanu, I. A. (2017h). *Igwebuike* philosophy and human rights violation in Africa. *IGWEBUIKE: An African Journal of Arts and Humanities*. Vol. 3. No. 7. pp. 117-136.

Kanu, I. A. (2017i). *Igwebuike* as a hermeneutic of personal autonomy in African ontology. *Journal of African Traditional Religion and Philosophy Scholars. Vol. 2. No. 1. pp. 14-22.*

Osuagwu, M. I., (2001). Early medieval history of African philosophy. Enugu: Snaap Press.

Osuagwu, M. I., (1999). African historical construction. Owerri: Assumpta Press.

Okere,T. I., *African Philosophy: A historico – hermeneutical investigation of the conditions of its possibility,* (Lanham: University of American Press), 1983.

Onebunne, J., *Being as belongingness; Expanding the hermeneutics of African metaphysics of to be,* Awka: Fab Anieh Nig. Ltd., 2019a

Onebunne, J., *Belongingness: A definitive metaphysical principle in African communalism,* Awka: Fab Anieh Nig. Ltd., 2019b

Onebunne, J. in Kanu,,I,A., & Chabi, K., (eds), *A critical review of St. Augustine's concept of time.* Augustine Through the Ages: Echoes of Faith and Reason, Mauritius: Lambert Publishing C., 2018

Onebunne, J.I., *Method: A definitive demand in African hhilosophy,* Awka: Fab Anieh Nig. Ltd., 2019d

Onebunne, J. in Onebunne, J. Haaga, P & Ndubisi (eds), *Igwebuike: An African Metaphysics Of Communal Strength,* Igwebuike Ontology: An African Philosophy Of Humanity Towards The Other -Papers In Honour Of Professor Kanu, Ikechukwu Anthony, O.S.A,

THE DISSIPATIVE QUANTUM MODEL OF THE BRAIN: HOW CONSCIOUSNESS (OF THE OTHER) ARISES FROM THE INTERACTIVE PROCESS OF THE BODY-BRAIN AND ENVIRONMENT. OUR IGWEBUIKE-NESS IS QUANTUM

Dozie Iwuh, OSA
Department of Philosophy
Augustinian Institute Makurdi
Benue State
registered501@gmail.com

EXECUTIVE SUMMARY

It was Boethius who defined person as an individual substance with a rational nature, pointing out three important aspects of the nature of the human person, namely his individuality, his rationality and his being a substance. The rational nature of man is not just limited to the use of logic in his dealings, it is not merely reduced to the fact that man thinks or reasons before and even after undergoing an action. It also comprises the fact that man is conscious of all that he does, he is aware of his rationality. The human person is not the only substance in the animal kingdom with consciousness, for all animals have a certain level of consciousness, but the human person is the only animal whose consciousness comes with an awareness; that is to say that the human person is conscious of his awareness or is aware of his consciousness (to put in tautological terms, he is conscious of his consciousness and aware of his awareness). The issue of consciousness only gained momentum in the 19th/20th century, although some put it in the mid 20th century. The debate as to how man is conscious and as to how this power arises in him has awed greatly the scientific world, with some holding that the validly accepted explanation to this resides in the homunculus, which is original dated to the 16th century alchemist Paracelsus. This theory is presently rejected, using the infinite regress argument. With the dawn of the quantum field theory, which is relativity applied to quantum mechanics, applied to the field of Neuroscience, the issue of how consciousness arises from the brain has resurfaced. Applying Quantum Field Theory (QFT) to the thought about the brain and consciousness has paved the way for the quantum model of the brain. How much can we know of our conscious state using QFT? Is it even possible to dabble into the matter of consciousness whose matter is absent, yet whose effect is seen, using scientific theories that depends on the availability of matter? The Igwebuike ideology speaks of two strong tenets, solidarity and complementarity (and even togetherness). What this paper will address is that these two main tenets of Igwebuike depend on consciousness, for it is the consciousness of the other, that is the foundation of Igwebuike's trends of solidarity and complementarity. With this being said, can it be proposed that the Igwebuike gospel has not just macroscopic underpinnings but it also has quantum?

Keywords: Consciousness, QFT, Kanu Ikechukwu Anthony, Brain, Neuroscience, Igwebuike, Other (Environment)

WHAT IS CONSCIOUSNESS?

Consciousness is a scientific problem that is unlike any other. Our own consciousness, as Descartes noted, is the most indubitable feature of our existence. It is the most precious one, as well: consciousness is life itself, and for most people having their bodies kept alive in a vegetative state is no better than dying. The major religions are defined by their theories of consciousness: whether a person's essence consists of his consciousness (his soul) or his body; how that consciousness ultimately fares as the result of its choices in life (whether it goes to a special place, or melds into a global mind); and whether the world contains forms of pure, disembodied consciousness in the form of gods, demons, angels and spirits. And the conviction that other people can suffer and flourish as each of us does is the essence of empathy and the foundation of morality.[42] Consciousness consists of inner, qualitative, subjective states and processes of sentience or awareness. Consciousness, so defined, begins when we wake in the morning from a dreamless sleep - and continues until we fall asleep again, die, go into a coma or otherwise become "unconscious." It includes all of the enormous variety of the awareness that we think of as characteristic of our waking life. It includes everything from feeling a pain, to perceiving objects visually, to states of anxiety and depression, to working out cross word puzzles, playing chess, trying to remember your aunt's phone number, arguing about politics, or to just wishing you were somewhere else. Dreams, from this definition, are a form of consciousness, though of course they are in many respects quite different from waking consciousness.[43] This definition is not universally accepted, and the word consciousness is used in a variety of other ways. Some authors use the word only to refer to states of self-consciousness, i.e. the consciousness that humans and some primates have of themselves as agents. Some use it to refer to the second-order mental *states about other mental states;* so according to this definition, a pain would not be a conscious state, but worrying about a pain would be a conscious state. Some use "consciousness" behaviouristically to refer to any form of complex intelligent behaviour.[44] The term 'conscious' is used most frequently to refer to the condition of people and other creatures when they are awake and responsive to sensory

---

[42] D.M. Rosenthal, *Concepts and Definitions of Consciousness,* in The Encyclopedia of Consciousness, W.P. Banks ed, Academic Press, Elsevier Inc, Oxford, 2009, v.

[43] J.R. Searle, *Consciousness,* Originally published October 8, 1999 as an academic paper at the University of California at Berkeley, Posted on KurzweilAI.net August 13, 2001.

[44] Ibid.

stimulation. A creature lacks consciousness in this first sense when it is asleep, anaesthetized, in a coma, and so forth. The main concern with this kind of consciousness is to explain in biological terms the difference between creatures' conscious and unconscious conditions. Because consciousness of this sort is a property of creatures, it is convenient to refer to it as creature consciousness.[45] This pertains to all sentient and animate creatures. A second important phenomenon we call consciousness is a creature's being conscious, or aware, of something. There are two ways creatures are conscious of things. A person or other animal is conscious of an object by seeing, hearing, or touching it, or sensing it in some other way. But one is also conscious of something, even without sensing that thing, if one has a thought about it as being present to one, that is, a thought that represents that thing as being in one's immediate environment. Because we describe this phenomenon by reference to a grammatical object, we may call it transitive consciousness. Explaining transitive consciousness consists in explaining what it is for a thought to be about something and what it is for a perception or sensation to be of something. A third phenomenon is more controversial in nature, and is the subject of much recent scientific and philosophical literature. We are conscious of various things by virtue of our having perceptions of them or thoughts about them. But those perceptions and thoughts can themselves be conscious or not conscious. Subliminal perception is an example of nonconscious perceiving, and it is widely accepted that many thoughts occur nonconsciously as well, that is, outside our stream of consciousness. Since this phenomenon is a property of mental states, rather than of creatures that are in those states, it is convenient to call it state consciousness.[46] Consciousness refers to individual thoughts, memories, feelings, sensations and environment. One's consciousness is one's awareness of yourself and the world around you. This awareness is subjective and unique.[47] Consciousness, thus, refers to experience itself. Rather than being exemplified by a particular thing that we observe or experience, it is exemplified by *all* the things that we observe or experience. Something *happens* when we are conscious that does not happen when we are not conscious—and something happens when we are conscious *of something* that does not happen when we are not conscious of that thing. We know what it is like to be conscious when we are awake, as opposed to not being conscious when in dreamless sleep. We also know what it is like to be conscious *of* something (when awake or dreaming) as opposed to not being conscious of that thing.[48]

---

[45] D.M. Rosenthal, *Concepts and Definitions of Consciousness*, in The Encyclopedia of Consciousness, W.P. Banks ed, Academic Press, Elsevier Inc, Oxford, 2009, 157

[46] Ibid.

[47] K. Cherry, *Consiousness is the Psychology of Awareness*, in VeryWellMind online journal, February 24th, 2020, https://www.verywellmind.com/what-is-consciousness-2795922, Received 12th May, 2020.

[48] M. Velmans, *How to Define Consciousness and How not to Define Consciousness*, in Journal of Consciousness Studies, 16(5), 2009, pp 139-156

THE QUANTUM MODEL OF THE BRAIN

The quantum model of the brain makes use of excerpts from QFT. So, it would be better to let a little about QFT before delving into the quantum model of the brain.

Why QFT? QFT is physics,[49] as it seeks to uncover that which is fundamental to existence, and it owes a lot to classical physics. Classical physics is physics that does not make use of quantum mechanics or the theory of relativity. Newtonian mechanics, thermodynamics, and Maxwell's theory of electromagnetism are all examples of classical physics. Many theories in classical physics break down when applied to extremely small objects such as atoms or to objects moving near the speed of light. In spite of all its achievements, classical physics proved itself to be incapable of handling further fundamental issue of reality, like the photoelectric effect, the Compton effect, to name a few.

- The photoelectric effect: This is the emission of electrons by a metal when light falls on it. According to classical physics, electrons require some energy to escape from the surface of the metal. This amount of energy is called the work function and is given the symbol, ϕ. According to the wave theory of light, the energy of the incident light is spread over the whole surface. Electrons should, therefore, only be emitted if the intensity of the light, given by:

Intensity = Power absorbed by surface/Area of the surface.

The maximum kinetic energy of the electrons and the number of electrons emitted are also predicted to depend on the intensity of the light. The frequency of the light should not matter, apart from being included in the intensity of the light:

Intensity $\propto$ Frequency

These predictions are clearly at odds with the experimental evidence seen.

It was Einstein who assumed that 'light consists of quanta of energy, called photons.' In fact, Planck had introduced the concept of material resonators possessing quanta of energy nhv, where n is an integer, while Einstein assumed that each quantum of light possesses the energy hv. The absorption of a single photon by an electron increases the energy of the electron by hv. Part of this energy is used to remove the electron from the metal. This is called the work function. The remaining part of the energy imparted to the electron increases its velocity - and consequently its kinetic energy. Thus if hv, the energy of a photon incident on a metal, is greater than the energy E required to separate the electron from the metal, and v is the velocity of the emitted electron, then the following relation must hold:

---

[49] Physics deals with the behavior and composition of matter and its interactions at the most fundamental level

$$hv = E + 0.5mv^2$$

The above formula shows that if the energy of the incident photon is less than the work function, the electrons cannot be separated from the surface of the metal and, therefore, will not be emitted. For a particular metal, the work function E being constant, the relationship between the energy of the incident photon and the kinetic energy of the emitted electron is linear. It is also clear that a more intense source of light will cause photons to be emitted at a greater speed, and this will produce a stronger electron current. Thus, Einstein was able to provide a completely satisfactory picture of the photoelectric effect by using the concept of the quantum nature of light.[50]

- The Compton Effect: This is also referred to as Compton scattering. The **Compton Effect** is the term used for an unusual result observed when X-rays are scattered on some materials. By classical theory, when an electromagnetic wave is scattered off atoms, the wavelength of the scattered radiation is expected to be the same as the wavelength of the incident radiation. Contrary to this prediction of classical physics, observations show that when X-rays are scattered off some materials, such as graphite, the scattered X-rays have different wavelengths from the wavelength of the incident X-rays. This classically unexplainable phenomenon was studied experimentally by Arthur H. Compton and his collaborators, and Compton gave its explanation in 1923. The experiment exhibits that the change in the frequency of incident radiation is independent of its initial frequency and depends only upon the angle of scattering. This can be satisfactorily explained by the quantum theory of light by making use of

---

[50] M. Saleem, *Quantum Mechanics*, IOP Publishing Ltd, 2015, 3. Einstein saw that the experimental evidence was explainable if it was assumed that light comes in discrete 'quanta' or packets of energy, which became known as photons.

Each photon has a specific energy ($E=hf$), and only collides with one electron. The probability of two photons colliding with one electron is very low. Thus an electron can only absorb a specified amount of energy for light of a specific frequen*cy.

If this energy is insufficient to allow an electron to escape the surface of the metal, no electrons will be emitted. This creates a threshold frequency, above which a photon will provide an electron with enough energy to leave the surface, and below which the electrons cannot escape. The minimum energy required to remove an electron from the metal is the work function, Φ. If a photon provides more energy to the electron than this, the rest will be seen as kinetic energy.

Thus:

$K.E_{max} = hf- \Phi = hf-hf_o = h(f-f_o)$

$K.E_{max} \propto (f-f_o)$

where $K.E_{max}$ is the maximum kinetic energy of the electrons, Φ is the work function of the surface, h is Planck's constant, and f_o is the threshold frequency.

Increasing the intensity only affects the rate of electrons being emitted, but does not affect their maximum kinetic energy. This is because increasing the intensity while keeping frequency constant increases the number of photons hitting the metal per second, and so increases the number of electrons which absorb them. It has no effect below the threshold frequency, because even if a huge number of electrons absorb photons, none of them have the energy to escape the surface.

relativistic expressions for various quantities.[51] To explain the shift in wavelengths measured in the experiment, Compton used Einstein's idea of light as a particle. The Compton Effect has a very important place in the history of physics because it shows that electromagnetic radiation cannot be explained as a purely wave phenomenon. The explanation of the Compton Effect gave a convincing argument to the physics community that electromagnetic waves can indeed behave like a stream of photons, which placed the concept of a photon on firm ground.

Other areas in which classical physics failed to give explanation to included the Heisenberg Uncertainty Principle, the correspondence principle, Schrodinger's wave equation etc.

The advent of the quantum theory gave better explanation to these happenings, as science could further understand that what was earlier considered as the fundamental element of all that is, yet had others more fundamental, and that these resided in a world known as the quantum world. From the above failures of classical physics, it is apparent that what led to such failure was the deterministic way in which classical physics conceived of reality, and reality proved itself again and again to not be as deterministic as classical physics claimed it to be.

To add to the above-mentioned, the course of this write-up is aimed at arriving at richer insights when it comes to the study of the brain. QFT and its elements of study provide the basic work tools to undergo this study. According to Jibu and Yasue:

> ...physicist H. Umezawa in the early 1960's (wrote for, *addition mine*) the necessity of emergence of quantum field theory in describing and investigating the typical physical aspect of living matter, because complex systems of atomic ingredients with strong mutual correlation like living matter cannot be treated by quantum statistical mechanics but only by quantum field theory.[52]

What Is QFT? There is no rigidly acceptable definition of QFT, it can thus only be described. It is the mathematical and conceptual framework for contemporary elementary particle physics. It can also be considered as an extension of Quantum Mechanics (QM), which deals with particles, over to fields.[53] QFT deals with and seeks answer to the most fundamental questions to life and to the origin of all that is. If we were to account taxonomically for the organism known as the human being, using him as a means of questions and answers we would say:

What are people made of? People are made of muscles, bones, and organs.

---

[51] M. Saleem, *Quantum Mechanics*, IOP Publishing Ltd, 2015, 3.

[52] M. Jibu-K. Yasue, *Quantum Brain Dynamics and Quantum Field Theory*, in Brain and Being: At the Boundary Between Science, Philosophy, Language and Arts, G.G. Globus, K.H. Pribram and G. Vitiello eds., John Benjamins Publishing Company, Amsterdam/Philadelphia, 2004, 273.

[53] M. Kuhlmann, *Quantum Field Theory*, in the Stanford Encyclopedia of Philosophy, Sept 27th, 2012, https://plato.stanford.edu/entries/quantum-field-theory/ retrieved 12th May, 2020.

Then what are the organs made of? Organs are made of cells.

What are cells made of? Cells are made of organelles.

What are organelles made of? Organelles are made of proteins.

What are proteins made of? Proteins are made of amino acids.

What are amino acids made of? Amino acids are made of atoms.

What are atoms made of? Atoms are made of protons, neutron, and electrons.

What are electrons made of? Electrons are made from the electron field.

What is the electron field made of?...

To the best of our present ability to perceive and to reason, the universe is made from <u>fields and nothing else</u>, and these fields are not made from any smaller components.[54] At the fundamental physical level, this is expressed by the quantum foundation of the notion of extended mind in QFT (Quantum Field Theory). It was formerly held that matter and particles are the fundamental building blocks. Yet, the deeper truth is that the basic building blocks of Nature are not discrete particles at all; rather, they are continuous fluid-like substances that spread throughout all of space, and they are called fields. A very good example of fields are the electric and the magnetic fields. These fields, nonetheless, like other areas of nature, have laws that they must obey and these laws are inquired by quantum mechanics (QM). Quantum field theory (QFT) is the current paradigm of fundamental physics. It emerges from the convolution of quantum physics and relativity, the two major theoretical revolutions of the 20th-century physics.[55] While quantum field theory reverts back to quantum mechanics for its mathematical representation, it nonetheless admits of relativism in reality than does QM. Quantum field theory deals with systems with infinitely many degrees of freedom. For such systems, the algebra of observables that results from imposing canonical commutation relations admits multiple Hilbert-space representations that are not unitarily equivalent to one another. This differs from the case of standard quantum mechanics, which deals with systems with finitely many degrees of freedom. For such systems, the corresponding algebra of observables admits unitarily equivalent Hilbert-space representations.[56] One thing that makes QFT so special is that it provides a unified framework where the quantum theory and the theory of relativity become consistently integrated out. Sometimes, field theory is

---

[54] B. Skinner, *A Children's Picture-Book Introduction to Quantum Field Theory*, in Ribbonfarm Online Journal, 20th August, 2015, <u>https://www.ribbonfarm.com/2015/08/20/qft/</u> retrieved 12th May, 2020.

[55] M. Asorey, *A Concise Introduction to Quantum Field Theory*, in International Journal of Geometric Methods in Modern Physics, October 2018, 1-45.

[56] M. Kuhlmann, *Quantum Field Theory*, in the Stanford Encyclopedia of Philosophy, Sept 27th, 2012, <u>https://plato.stanford.edu/entries/quantum-field-theory/</u> retrieved 13th May, 2020.

identified as the theory of particle physics. This is not completely correct. Field theory is a framework which goes beyond particle physics. In fact, there are field theories where there is no particle interpretation of the states of the theory. But it is also true that most of the successful field theories admit a particle interpretation. That means that there are states which can be correctly interpreted as particle states and in those cases field theory provides a causal framework for particle interactions where action at a distance is replaced by local field interactions. Although this can also achieved by classical field theory, the difference between the classical and quantum theories resides in the fact that in the quantum theory, the interaction between the particles can be interpreted as a creation and destruction (also known as creators and annihilators) of messenger particles process. The association of forces and interactions with particle exchange is one of the most interesting features of QFT. The particles that appear in field theory are very special: they are all identical. This means that the electrons in the earth are the same as the electrons in Alpha Centauri because all of them are excitations of the same electron field in quantum electro dynamics (QED). Another essential characteristic of relativistic field theories is that when the field theory admits particle states, they are accompanied by antiparticle states; that is, the theory requires the existence of antiparticles.[57]

Areas To Note When Representing QFT: A quantum field theory is a quantum theory which is relativistic invariant, and exists where there is a special type of quantum operators which are associated with the classical fields. In the case of a real scalar field $\emptyset$, a consistent theory should satisfy the following principles.

- P1 Quantum principle: The space of quantum states is the space of rays in a separable Hilbert space H.[58]

- P2 Unitarity: There is a (anti)unitary representation $U(\Lambda; a)$ of the Poincare group in H, where time reversal T is represented as an antiunitary operator U(T).

- P3 Spectral condition: The spectrum of generators of space-time translations P_u is contained in the forward like cone:

$$v_+ = \{P_u; P^2 \geq 0; P_0 \geq 0\}$$

- P4 Vacuum state: There is a unique state $\Psi \epsilon \mathcal{H}$, satisfying that $P_u \Psi_0 = 0$.[59]

- P5 Field Theory (real boson): For any classical field f in the space $S(\mathbb{R}^3)$ of fast decreasing smooth $C^\infty(\mathbb{R}^3)$ functions there is field operator $\emptyset(f)$ in $\mathcal{H}$ which

---

[57] Ibid.

[58] A Hilbert space is an abstract vector space that possesses the structure of an inner product which allows length and angle to be measured.

[59] The vacuum state also known as the ground state is that at which the quantum energy level is at its lowest.

satisfies that $\emptyset(f) = \emptyset(f)$. The field operator can be considered as the smearing by f of a fundamental field operator $\emptyset(x)$

$\emptyset(f) =$

$$\int d3xf(x)\emptyset(x)$$

The subspace spanned by the vectors $\emptyset(f_1)\emptyset(f_2)\ldots\ldots \emptyset\ (f_n)|0\}$ for arbitrary test functions $f_1; f_2; \ldots\ldots f_n \epsilon S(\mathbb{R}^3)$ is a dense subspace of $\mathcal{H}$.

- P6 Poincare covariance: Let $f\epsilon S(\mathbb{R}^4)$ be a test function defined in Minkowski space-time[60] and $\emptyset(\dot{f}) =\int_{R4}d^4x\emptyset(x)\dot{f}(x)$;

    Where $\emptyset(x) = \emptyset(x; t) = e^{itP0}\ \emptyset(x)e^{-itP0}$.

Then

$$U(\Lambda;a)\ \emptyset(\dot{f})U(\Lambda;a)^i = \emptyset(\dot{f}_{(\Lambda;a)}),$$

with

$$(\dot{f}_{(\Lambda;a)})(x) = \dot{f}(\Lambda^{-1}(x-a))$$

- P7 (Bosonic) Local Causality: For any f, $g\epsilon S(\mathbb{R}^3)$ the corresponding field operators $\emptyset(f); \emptyset(g)$ commute

$$[\emptyset(f); \emptyset(g)] = 0.^{61}$$

Commutators pertains to Bosonic particles, while Anticommutators pertains to fermonic particles.

---

[60] Minkowski Space-time, is a combination of 3-dimensional Euclidean Space and time into a 4-dimensional manifold, where the interval of spacetime that exists between any two events is independent of the inertial frame of reference. The Minkowski spacetime coordinate system has axes given as (x, y, z, ct). It can also be written as (x_1, x_2, x_3, x_4). The differential for arc length in spacetime is given by the equation: $ds^2 = -c^2dt^2 + dx^2 + dy^2 + dz^2$.

[61] When it is said that operators in the quantum realm commute, what is implied is that they are identically zero. As seen above. Let us consider that we have a state Ψ and two observables (operators) A, B. when these operators are simultaneously diagonalised in a given representation, they act on the state Ψ just by multiplication with a real number either a or b, or an eigen value of the operator ($A\ \Psi = a\ \Psi$, $B\ \Psi = b\ \Psi$). Imagine that this were real numbers, a and b, this will hold like $ab - ba = 0$ (signifying identicality) or in the operator form $(AB-BA)\ \Psi = 0$ or $((A,B)\ \Psi = 0)$. Thus the expression AB-BA= [A,B] indicate that they commute. Commutators are used for Bose particles (bosons). There is also the expression anticommutators, and these are used for fermion particles. When talking about fermions, the commutators have to be adjusted accordingly (as in the case $\{\theta_1\theta_2 = -\theta_2\theta_1\}$). To ensure that identicality is recorded so that it sums up to zero, it needs to be adjusted to $(\{\theta_1\theta_2 = -\theta_2\theta_1 \rightarrow \theta_1\theta_2 + \theta_2\theta_1 = 0\})$.

QUANTUM BRAIN DYNAMICS

QFT is all about gaining a fundamental understanding to matter. Matter can either be macroscopic or microscopic, and even quantum. What is being considered here is brain matter. The use of QFT, in what concerns matter, has proven insightful in blazing new trails as pertaining to the understanding of matter in its fundamentality. Quantum Brain Dynamics is used to describe long range ordered dynamics of the quantum system of electromagnetic field, and water dipole field in the brain is proposed as a revival of the original idea developed by Umezawa in the early 1960s.[62] QBD is nothing else but Quantum Electrodynamics (QED) of the electric dipole field of dipolar solitons and water molecules with a symmetry property under the dipole rotation. The highly systematized functioning of the brain is found to be realized by the spontaneous symmetry-breaking phenomena. Memory printing, recall and decay processes are represented by the fundamental physical processes standing for the phase transition process, the symmetry-restoring process and the quantum-tunneling process, respectively.[63] The brain, as already noted, is a typical macroscopic object extraordinary in its functioning as it gives rise to highly advanced mental "objects" such as consciousness (plus unconscious), mind, memory and will. It is the custom and cognitive sciences to regard the brain as a tissue made of a huge of brain cells, and many phenomenological theories of brain functioning based on the macroscopic picture of electric and chemical circuits of cells take into account various mesoscopic aspects of the brain cell revealed by molecular biological studies.[64] Of all living matter, the brain is considered as the highest example. Thus, investigating the brain and its functionality thus pertains to the Quantum field. QBD is a completely new theoretical framework to describe the fundamental physical process of the brain dynamics that makes man human on the basis of quantum field theoretical analysis of the fundamental system of brain tissue.[65]

The Fundamental System of Living Matter: The brain is a living matter. Thus, it will be best to investigate the essential characteristic of the fundamental system of living matter. In living matter, there is specifically two degrees of freedom to which QFT ponders; the first is the dipolar soliton (also known as the Davydov soliton), localized in each protein filament of the background three-dimensional network structure and the water molecules surrounding them. In the words of Jibu and Yasue, the first degree of freedom we are looking for in the fundamental system of living matter may be found as an internal degree of freedom of the background three dimensional network structures of protein filaments free from

---

[62] M. Jibu-K. Yasue, *Magic without Magic. Meaning of Quantum Brain Dynamics* in the Journal of Mind and Behaviour, Vol 18, No2/3, 205-227

[63] M. Jibu-K. Yasue, *Quantum Brain Dynamics and Quantum Field Theory, in Brain and Being. At the Boundary Between Science, Philosophy, Language and Arts,* 269.

[64] M. Jibu-K. Yasue, *Magic without Magic. Meaning of Quantum Brain Dynamics.*

[65] M. Jibu-K. Yasue, *Quantum Brain Dynamics and Quantum Field Theory, in Brain and Being. At the Boundary Between Science, Philosophy, Language and Arts,* 279.

thermalization.[66] This degree of freedom was found by Davydov in 1979 as a coherent dipolar solitary wave propagation along the one-dimensional chain of protein molecules such as the protein filament.[67] In quantum field theory, a coherent solitary wave propagation is considered as a localized degree of freedom maintaining and carrying energy, without loss due to thermalization, and it is called the "Davydov soliton" or "dipolar soliton."[68] Namely, energy in coming from the metabolizing system of living matter through the ATP cyclic process to the fundamental system of living matter induces first dipolar solitons localized in each protein filament. As a specific character of soliton in quantum field theory, energy stored in soliton form is kept free from thermalization and belongs to the fundamental system of living matter, though creation of soliton is triggered by incoherent and disordered interaction with the metabolizing system. In other words, the creation and annihilation process of dipolar solitons plays the role of a gateway between metabolizing and fundamental systems.

These dipolar solitons in the human brain are referred to as Corticons,[69] but "In the general case of cell assembly, we call it simply 'dipolar soliton'".[70] The second degree of freedom of the fundamental system of living matter is the water molecule. Jibu and Yasue capture this better as they note:

> The water molecule, H_2O, is a typical molecule simple in its form but rich in its physical characteristics. The origin of richness can be found, however, in simpleness of its form. Namely, due to the spatial geometric configuration of two hydrogen atoms relative to one oxygen atom, the water molecule manifests nonvanishing electric dipole moment. Thus, the totality of enormously large number of water molecules can be well described from a physical point of view by a quantum mechanical degree of freedom of electric dipole moment moving and rotating freely. This is the second degree of freedom of the fundamental system of living matter. We call it the "water dipole moment."[71]

Finally, we have obtained a physical picture of the fundamental system of living matter. It is essentially a quantum mechanical many-body system described by two different degrees of

---

[66] Ibid. Thermalization is the process of physical bodies reaching thermal equilibrium through mutual interaction.

[67] A.S. Davydov, *Solitons in molecular systems*, in Physica Scripta, *20*, 1979, 387–394.

[68] The dipolar soliton is a collective mode of many dipolar oscillations maintained by nonlocalized electrons trapped in the one-dimensional chain of protein molecules and may be regarded as the first degree of freedom of the fundamental system of living matter. It is a quantum mechanical degree of freedom representing electric dipole moment localized in each background protein filament. the dipolar soliton arises from a coherent solitary wave propagation of nonlocalized electron along each protein filament. The dipolar soliton is created at the end of each protein filament by energy gain from the metabolizing system through, for example, the ATP cyclic process.

[69] C.I.J.M. Stuart., Y. Takahashi, H. Umezawa, *On the stability and non-local properties of memory*, in Journal of Theoretical Biology, 71, 1978, 605–618.

[70] M. Jibu-K. Yasue, *Quantum Brain Dynamics and Quantum Field Theory*, in Brain and Being, 278.

[71] Ibid.

freedom interacting with each other, that is, dipolar solitons localized in the background three-dimensional network structure of protein filaments and water dipole moments surrounding them.[72] As earlier stated, the brain is a living matter; thus, there are two major components (in the words of Jibu and Yasue, degrees of freedom) that are vital in the computing of the QBD, namely; the dipolar solitons and the water dipole moment.[73] Yet, in the brain, these solitons are referred to as Corticons, and these protein filaments are immersed in water molecules, leading to a somewhat superimposition of states. Thus, instead of having two degrees of freedom acting in the brain, as in other living matter, we have one superimposed degree of freedom known as corticons. These corticons can be described as "the fundamental system of brain tissue described by a single degree of freedom of electric dipole field spanning the spatial volume of the brain tissue."[74] According to Jibu and Yasue,

> The corticon in QBD is now fully described by the electric dipole field (of both dipolar solitons and water dipole moments) spanning the spatial volume of the brain tissue. In this sense, we may call the fundamental system of brain tissue simply as the "system of corticons," hereafter. Considering the physical background of the electric dipole field as those of dipolar solitons and water dipole moments, we may assume that the electric dipole field manifests symmetry under rotation. Namely, even if the electric dipole field on each position is rotated by any spatial angle, the total energy of the system of corticons is kept invariant. In quantum field theory, the total energy of the system of any field quantity plays an important role in specifying dynamics of the field, and it is usually called the "Hamiltonian." So, we refer to the total energy of the system of corticons as the Hamiltonian of the system of corticons or equivalently the Hamiltonian of QBD. Then, we obtain the following invariant or symmetry property: The system of corticons in QBD manifests a symmetry under the rotation of the electric dipole field in a sense that the Hamiltonian of QBD is invariant.[75]

Thus, we can define QBD as nothing but Quantum Electro Dynamics (QED) of the electric dipole field with symmetry under the dipole rotation.

---

[72] Ibid, 279.

[73] Permanent dipoles are found in water molecules and these occur when two atoms in a molecule have substantially different electronegativity. A molecule with a permanent dipole moment is called a polar molecule. In electromagnetism, there are two kinds of dipoles: An electric dipole is a separation of positive and negative charges. The simplest example of this is a pair of electric charges of equal magnitude but opposite sign, separated by some (usually small) distance. A permanent electric dipole is called an electret. A magnetic dipole is a closed circulation of electric current. A simple example of this is a single loop of wire with some constant current through.

[74] M. Jibu-K. Yasue, *Quantum Brain Dynamics and Quantum Field Theory, in Brain and Being*, 280.

[75] Ibid.

The Spontaneous Breaking of Symmetry: Symmetry plays a big role in physics. It often greatly simplifies the solution to a problem. Suppose we have an object shaped like the base of a wine bottle, and a marble is placed on the hump at the base of the wine bottle, even though the floor of the wine bottle after the hump is yet perfectly symmetric, the marble will not end up in the centre, where it would be sitting on a hump; it will come to rest somewhere on the circle of lowest points. This is precisely what *spontaneous symmetry breaking* is about; for the ground or lowest-energy state does not share the symmetry of the underlying physics. Instead, there is a whole family of ground states, the different points on the circle.[76] The symmetry breaking is *spontaneous* in the sense that (unless we have extra information) we cannot predict which of these ground states will be chosen. Spontaneous symmetry breaking is ubiquitous in condensed matter physics. It often occurs when there is a phase transition between a high-temperature, symmetric phase and a low-temperature one in which the symmetry is spontaneously broken. The simplest example is freezing. If we have a round bowl of water sitting on a table, it looks the same from every direction; it has rotational symmetry. But when it freezes, the ice crystals form in specific orientations, breaking the symmetry.[77] Symmetry is said to be spontaneously broken when the Lagrangian of a system is invariant under a certain group of continuous symmetry, say G, and the vacuum or ground state of the system is not invariant under G, but under one of its subgroups, say G'. The ground state then exhibits observable ordered patterns corresponding to the breakdown of G into G'. The possibility of having different vacua with different symmetry properties is provided by the mathematical structure of QFT, where infinitely many representations of the canonical commutation relations (CCR) exist, which are unitarily inequivalent with respect to each other, i.e. there is no unitary operator transforming one representation into another one, and thus they are physically inequivalent as well, that is they describe different physical phases of the system.[78] In SBS theories, the Goldstone theorem predicts the existence of massless bosons called Nambu-Goldstone (NG) particles. The spin-wave quanta, called magnons in ferromagnets, the elastic wave quanta called phonons in crystals, the Cooper pair quanta in superconductors, etc., are examples of NG particles. NG bosons condensed in the ground state of the system, according to the Bose-Einstein condensation, are the carriers of ordering information out of which ordered patterns (space ordering or time ordering as, e.g., "in phase" oscillations) are generated. The condensation density of the NG boson quanta determines the macroscopic field which is called *order parameter*, e.g. the magnetization in ferromagnets.[79] The order parameter is a classical macroscopic field in the sense that it is not affected by quantum fluctuations. Its value may be considered to be the *code* or *label,* specifying the physical phase of the system. In the absence of gauge fields, the NG quanta are observed as realistic physical quanta, and

---

[76] T.W.B. Kibble, *Spontaneous Breaking of Symmetry In Gauge Theories,* in Phil. Trans. R. Soc. A 373: 2015 http://dx.doi.org/10.1098/rsta.2014.0033, 1-12.

[77] Ibid.

[78] W.J. Freeman-G. Vitiello, *Dissipation and spontaneous symmetry breaking in brain dynamics,* in Escholarship. org, 2008, https://escholarship.org/uc/item/5c43n596, 1-16. By contrast, in Quantum Mechanics all representations are unitarily (and therefore physically) equivalent.

[79] Ibid.

excitations of the system ground state extend over the whole system (*collective modes* or *long range correlations*). They may scatter with other particles of the system or with observational probes. If a gauge field is present, the NG bosons still control the ground state condensation in the ordered domain, and the gauge field propagation is confined into regions where the order is absent. Through the generation of NG collective modes, SBS is responsible for the change from microscopic to macroscopic scale: crystals, ferromagnets, superconductors, etc., are *macroscopic quantum systems*. They are quantum systems, not in the sense that they are constituted by quantum components (like any physical system), but in the sense that their macroscopic properties, accounted for by the order parameter field, cannot be explained without recourse to the underlying quantum dynamics.[80]

In the words of Vitiello, symmetry "corresponds to indistinguishable points."[81] But the symmetry which gets broken in the creation of observable ordered patterns is the symmetry of the dynamical equations; symmetry is said to be spontaneously broken when the symmetry of the ground state is not the symmetry of the dynamical equations.[82] This means that the symmetry is said to be broken since the vacuum state does not possess the full symmetry of the field equations (the dynamics). The "order" *is* indeed such a "lack of symmetry."[83] When symmetry is broken, "the invariance of the field equations implies the existence of quanta, the so-called Nambu Goldstone (NG) quanta."[84] These NG quanta propagate through the system and are the carriers of the ordering information, "they are long range correlation modes;"[85] in crystals, for example, the ordering information is that which specifies the lattice arrangement. The NG quanta for crystals are the phonons. Thus, not only are these NG quanta involved in informational gain, they are also involved in the dynamic ordering of the system. for instance, with magnets, the symmetry broken is that of the magnetic dipole of the electrons, thus the magnetization comprises the correlation amongst all the electrons so that they all choose, among all available directions, one particular direction of the magnetization vector (the NG quanta for magents are magnoni). The NG quanta are masseless scalar bosons. Thus, they

---

[80] Ibid. When symmetry is broken, a quanta, a masseless scalar with no spin, appears, this masseless scalar according to Vitiello, is the carrier of the ordering information and therefore the quantum mediating the long range correlation among the atoms. This scalar is a boson, which means that many of them can be found in the same state with similar quantum properties (charge, energy, numbers etc). Symmetry can be restored via condensation of the bosons, one that is controlled by the Bose-Einstein distribution function (referred to as the Bose-Einstein Condensate). According to Vitiello, At conveniently high temperature, above a certain critical temperature T_c the condensed bosons may "evaporate": condensation is destroyed and symmetry is restored. Symmetry is restored and broken by means of an occurrence known as phase transitions.

[81] G. Vitiello, *My Double Unveiled*. John Benjamins Publishing Co., Amsterdam and Philadelphia, 2001, 30.

[82] Ibid, 30-31. According to Vitiello, «the word "spontaneous" means that the symmetry of the dynamics can be rearranged in any one of the possible ordering patterns observable at the physical level (in other words any of the physical phases can be dynamically realized).» (G. Vitiello, *My Double Unveiled*, 31)

[83] G. Vitiello, *The Dissipative Brain*, in Brain and Being - at the boundary between science, philosophy, language and arts, Globus G.G., Pribram, K.H. and Vitiello, G., (eds), John Benjamins Pub. Co. Amsterdam, 2004, 317-331.

[84] G. Vitiello, *The Dissipative Brain*, in Brain and Being.

[85] Ibid.

are to be differentiated from the other type of boson involved in the different energy fields known as the gauge bosons (the photons of the EMF, the gluons of the strong field, the $W^\pm$ and Z bosons of the electroweak fields). The gauge bosons are mediators of the energy exchanges among the interacting elements they correlate, because they are effectively quanta of the energy field they mediate (that is the $W^\pm$ and Z bosons are the quantum of the weak field). The NG bosons (NGB) are not mediators of the interactions among the elements of the system. They determine only the modes of interaction among them. Due to the masselessness of the NGB, their condensation does not necessitate a change of energy state of the system. This is because in their "lowest momentum state NG quanta do not carry energy."[86] This is needed to enable the NG quanta cut across the full system volume, sending long distance informational correlation in the system, "thus setting up an ordered pattern."[87] In living biological systems, the human body, the NG quanta are the Dipole Wave Quanta (DWQ), since they arise from "the breakdown of the electrical dipole rotational symmetry."[88]

How does symmetry breaking happen in the QBD? According to Vitiello, this happens by interaction, for the "brain is a system in interaction with the external world from which it receives stimuli carrying information. These stimuli put the brain into states."[89] The brain-body is not a closed system, but an open system that stands in physical entanglement with the environment. According to Streltsov et al., entanglement can arise from incoherent operations, provided one of the communicating systems is coherent. This can be illustrated thus:

S (incoherent)	*A (incoherent)*	*S (Coherent)*	*A (Incoherent)*
	Incoherent Op.	*Incoherent Op.*	
	S is separable from A	*S is entangled with A.*[90]	

Thus, the personal unit brain-body-environment has its physical foundation in the quantum entanglement brain-body-environment. The entanglement "represents the impossibility of cutting the links between the brain and the external world;"[91] the quantum model of the brain is based on the fact that the brain "is an open system in interaction with the external world."[92]

---

[86] Ibid.

[87] Ibid.

[88] Ibid. According to G. Vitiello, «In QFT the dynamics (i.e. the Lagrangian or the Hamiltonian, or simply the field equations) is in general invariant under some group, say G, of continuous transformations. Spontaneous breakdown of symmetry occurs when the minimum energy state (the ground state or vacuum) of the system is not invariant under the full group G, but under one of its subgroups.» (G. Vitiello, *My Double Unveiled*. John Benjamins Publishing Co., Amsterdam and Philadelphia, 2001, 93).

[89] G. Vitiello, *My Double Unveiled*, 73.

[90] A. Streltsov et al, *Measuring Quantum Coherence with Entanglement*, in Physics Review Letters, Number 115, June 2015, pp1-8..

[91] G. Vitiello, *The Dissipative Brain*, in Brain and Being - at the boundary between science, philosophy, language and arts, Globus G.G., Pribram, K.H. and Vitiello, G., (eds), John Benjamins Pub. Co. Amsterdam, 2004, 317-331.

[92] G. Vitiello, *My Double Unveiled*, 104.

For information printing on the brain "is achieved under the action of external stimuli, which produce the breakdown of the symmetry associated with the electric dipole vibrational field."[93] Thus, emphasis is laid on the brain being entangled or "coupled to the environment."[94][95]

The centrality of the brain, as constantly noticed in the foregoing lines, should not lead to a hasty consideration of the body as inconsequential in the entire dynamics that defines the human person, for the three components, of body-brain-environment, stand as integral to a valid comprehension of the human person. According to Capolupo, Freeman and Vitiello,

> Brains are thermodynamics systems that use chemical energy to construct knowledge from information. The oxidative metabolism of glucose provides the energy, as measured by oxygen depletion and carbon dioxide production. The sensory receptors in the body and on the body surface provide the information by absorbing energy of various types impinging from the internal and external environments. The role of each sensory receptor is to selectively convert a microscopic quantity of energy first to ionic currents (receptor potentials), then to a train of pulses (action potentials, units, spikes) on its axon.[96]

Once the external stimuli are intercepted by the body, a necessary SBS occurs, a definite ground state, from the many infinite ground states or vacua, is chosen. Masseless NGB are observed, which carry long-range correlation waves observed in the brain dynamics. As a consequence of this, the time-reversal symmetry is also broken, because the choice of a ground state entails that the information has been recorded.[97]After information has been recorded, the brain state is fixated and the brain cannot be brought to the state configuration in which

[93] Ibid.

[94] Ibid.

[95] Each personal conscious state of a human being corresponds to a complex phase-coherence among the oscillating electromagnetic force fields of some material parts (molecules) of the three components involved. That is - for instance in the personal state of me as seeing now the computer screen in front of me - some (effectively many trillions) of molecules of the neurons of a part of the visual cortex involved, many and many trillions of the molecules constituting the parts of the ocular system involved (ocular nerve, ocular muscles, cones and rods of my retina, of the crystalline membrane in front of my retina etc), many and many trillions of molecules constituting the gases forming the air between me and the computer screen, and finally the many and many trillions of the molecules of the part of the screen I am seeing and emitting the electromagnetic radiation putting in phase the molecules of screen, of airs, of my oculomotor system, of my visual cortex, on its turn influencing the oscillation in phase of my emotional system: limbic system, amygdala etc. This is a personal state unified at the material level by the electromagnetic fields, ordered and then unified informationally by the Nambu-Goldstone bosons characterizing univocally this so complex phase coherence domain of electromagnetic, oscillating force field.

[96] A. Capolupo et al, *Dissipation of Dark Energy by Cortex in Knowledge Retrieval* in Physics Life Review, Volume 10, Issue, 1, March 2013, pp85–94.

[97] G. Vitiello, *My Double Unveiled. The dissipative Quantum Model of the Brain*, 107.

it was before the information printing occurred, for before the information recording process, the brain can in principle be in anyone of the infinitely many (unitarily inequivalent) vacua.[98]

THE BRAIN AS AN OPEN/DISSIPATIVE SYSTEM

The brain is an open, dissipative system; the brain closed on the world is a dead brain, physiology tells us. Isolation of the brain (closure to the world) produces serious pathologies. Thus, the extension of the quantum model of brain to the dissipative dynamics appears to be a necessity.[99] The dissipation of the brain, and its inherent openness, is a mark of the interaction that exists between the brain and the environment, for the brain (/body) is not a closed system, but an open system that stands in physical entanglement with the environment. We ought to note that the entirety of the human person, as a biological system, stands in relation to other biological systems (other human persons and the environment). As a biological system, the human person is a dynamic comprising the brain and the body. The human person is an open-dissipative biological system in relation to the environment (that was why it was earlier asserted that the human person stands in relation, a relation of brain-body-environment). The human body (brain-body) operates dynamically in a phase coherent order. This macroscopic level of a high degree of coherence is referred to as order parameter. The order parameter is the macroscopic variable that characterizes the new emerging level of matter organization and is related to the matter density distribution. The emergent properties are neither the properties of the elementary constituents nor their summation. Rather, they are new properties, depending on the modes in which they are organized, that is to say, on the dynamics controlling their interaction. A point to recall is that "the ordered pattern which is actually realized is the output of the system's internal dynamics."[100] This pattern is realized through a process known as spontaneous symmetry breaking.[101]

Then, the mathematical formalism for quantum dissipation *requires* the doubling of the brain degrees of freedom.[102] The doubled degrees of freedom, say A˜ (the tilde quanta; the non–tilde

---

[98] Ibid.

[99] G. Vitiello, *The Dissipative Brain*, in Brain and Being.

[100] G. Vitiello, *The Dissipative Brain*, in Brain and Being.

[101] Symmetry breaking can also be explicit, referred to as Explicit Symmetry Breaking. In this case, the dynamical operations are modified by adding one or more terms that are not consistent with the symmetric terms.

[102] The conventional approach in introducing the QFT algebraic structure consists in assigning the canonical commutator or anticommutator relations for the boson or fermion case, respectively. However, one needs also to specify which one is the prescription for adding primitive observables such as energy, angular momentum, etc. It could seem that such a prescription does not belong to the algebraic structure of the theory. Effectively, this is not the case. In fact, in order to specify, e.g., the total energy E of two identical particles, one writes $E = E1 + E2$. The meaning of the labels in such a formula is that $E1$ refers to the first particle and $E2$ to the second particle. However, it is easy to realize that $E1 = E \times 1$ where the index 1 thus refers to the first position. Similarly, $E2 = 1 \times E$. Thus, $E = E1 + E2 = E \times 1 + 1 \times E$, and similarly $J = J1 + J2 = J \times 1 + 1 \times J$, for the angular momentum, which are nothing but the commutative coproducts of a coalgebra.

quanta A, denoting the brain degrees of freedom), are meant to represent the environment to which the brain is coupled. The physical meaning of the doubling is the one of ensuring the balance of the energy flux between the system and the environment. The environment thus represented by the doubled degrees of freedom appears described as the "time–reversed copy" (the *Double*) of the brain.[103] The environment is "modelled" on the brain. Time–reversed since the energy flux outgoing from the brain is incoming into the environment, and vice versa.[104] The doubling of the degrees of freedom in the dissipative model thus arises as a consequence of the irreversible time evolution.

The superimposition of the dipole soliton and the water dipole moment in the brain lead to one defined degree of freedom known as corticon. This, according to G.G. Globus, "disregards the neuron's and neuroglia's boundary membrane"[105] that is the mark of classical physics. These corticons are created when an input from the environment comes into the vacuum. But let us understand the concept of vacuum in QBD.

Here, "commutative" refers to invariance of the coproduct under the permutation $1 \leftrightarrow 2$, as it needs to be on the premise that the particles are identical. We should be able therefore to go from the algebra A for the single particle to the algebra for two of them, namely, $A \to A \times A$. Of course, we need also to be able to go back to a single particle, namely, $A \times A \to A$. The conclusion is that the basic algebra to start with, in QFT is a bialgebra, that is the Hopf algebra. We thus see that the "doubling of the degrees of freedom" (DDF) implied in the Hopf mapping $A \to A \times A$ arises as a natural requirement in setting up the QFT algebraic structure. Most interesting is the case when the two systems need to be treated not on the same footing, as, for example, in thermal field theory, or when dealing with open systems in general, where the system under study and its thermal bath or environment are not exchangeable. In these cases the proper tool is provided by the q-deformed Hopf algebras with non-commutative coproducts, e.g., $\Delta aq = a \times q + q^{-1} \times a \equiv aq + q^{-1}\tilde{a}$, with $a \epsilon A$, and its hermitian conjugate, $\Delta a\dagger q = a\dagger \times q^* + (q^{-1})^* \times a\dagger$. Of course if q is real, $q^* = q$; if it is imaginary, then $q^* = q^{-1}$. The deformation parameter q may depend on temperature, decay constants, etc. The QFT formalism of the DDF has been introduced and used in many applications of the TFD formalism for many-body systems. The Hopf coalgebra thus describes the doubling of the degrees of freedom $a \to \{a, \tilde{a}\}$ and of the state space $F \to F \times \tilde{F}$, with the operators a and $\tilde{a}$ acting on F and $\tilde{F}$, respectively. We stress that the associated Hopf algebra is, as said, a non-commutative coalgebra. (G. Basti, G. Vitiello and A. Capolupo, *Quantum Field Theory and Coalgebraic Logic in Theoretical Computer Science*, in arXiv:1701.00527v1[quant-ph], 29th Dec, 2016, 1-20).

[103] G. Vitiello, *The Dissipative Brain*, in Brain and Being. When the system under consideration is dissipative, it accepts external energy without heating up, stores the order, and can later give it up to the surrounding heat bath environment. *Umezawa's innovation is to treat the heat bath environment as tilde.* The nontilde system exchanges energy with its ~environment, while the energy of the nontilde system + ~environment, that is, the energy of the closed system, remains constant in strict accordance with energy conservation laws. So when the nontilde system dissipates order to the ~system, its entropy increases and the entropy of the ~system in compensation decreases. The *total entropy* of nontilde and tilde systems, however, remains constant under any exchange. (G.G. Globus, G.G. Globus, *Quantum Closures and Disclosures. Thinking-Together Postphenomenology and Quantum Brain Dynamics* 36).

[104] The quantum dissipation formalism implies that the full operator describing the system time evolution includes the operator describing the coupling between the non–tilde and the tilde quanta. At the same time, such a coupling term acts as the mathematical tool to attach the label to the vacua (and thus to distinguish among different memories). This label is time–dependent: the system states are thus time–dependent states.

[105] G.G. Globus, *Quantum Closures and Disclosures. Thinking-Together Postphenomenology and Quantum Brain Dynamics,* John Benjamins Publishing Co., Amsterdam and Philadelphia, 2003, 22.

The concept of vaccum in QBD: Vacuum states are near-zero energy states, also called "ground states." In the case of ordered water, the momentum axes of the spinning water dipoles all point in the same direction in the θ-vacuum states upheld by the living brain.[106] As already stated, when input comes into this vacuum, corticons (dipole wave quanta) are created, they are quanta which undergo annihilation and creation dynamics. This input provokes corticon dynamics. In the corticon dynamics, the energy gained can be dissipated, with the system relaxing back into a *different* θ-vacuum state than before. (The θ-vacuum transformation is called the Bogoliubov transformation, which remarkably, in Russian literally means the love-of-God transformation. So we might say that we have memory, and so our humanity, through the love of God.) Input provokes corticon dynamics and a Bogoliubov transformation to a θ-vacuum state. (Memory – hence temporality – is derived through the Bogoliubov movement).[107]

Understanding Bogoliubov Transformation via the Hopf Coalgebra of QFT:

There is one more aspect of QFT and its intrinsic algebraic Hopf structure, which is relevant from the perspective of the coalgebraic logic and computer science: the tilde modes provide the intrinsic dynamic (coalgebraic) reference (semantics) for the non-tilde modes. The coalgebra structure of the doubling both the space, and the operators, turns into a strict correspondence between each operator and its tilde-copy (the doubled operator) so that one of the two provides the address of the other one. The result is the self-consistent dynamical inclusion of the "reference term" in the logical scheme. A sort of contextual self-embedding, or dynamical generation of meaning, a "local", not "absolute", but crucially meaningful truth, singled out of the infinitely many possibilities offered by the infinitely many representations of the CCRs. The simplest example is perhaps obtained by explicitly computing the expectation value of the number operator

$N_{Ak} = A^{\dagger}_k A_k$ in the ground state $|0(\theta)\}N$. By inverting the Bogoliubov transformations, we have $\forall k$

$$NA_k(\theta) \equiv N\{0(\theta)| A^{\dagger}_k A_k |0(\theta)\}N = N\{0(\theta)|A^{\sim}_k(\theta) A^{\sim\dagger}_k(\theta)|0(\theta)\}N = \sinh^2\theta_k, \quad (1)$$

which shows that for any k, the only non-vanishing contribution to the number of nontilde modes $NA_k(\theta)$ comes from the tilde operators. In this sense, these last ones constitute the dynamic address for the non-tilde modes. Through them, the total number $NA_k(\theta)$ of the A_k condensate is determined. Of course, the reverse is also true, namely the only non-zero contribution to $NA^{\sim}_k(\theta)$ comes from the non-tilde operators, and

---

[106] Ibid.
[107] Ibid.

$$NA_k(\theta) - NA\tilde{~}_k(\theta) = 0.$$

The whole condensate content of $|0(\theta)\}N$ is thus specified by the N-set $\equiv$ $\{NA_k(\theta), NA_k(\theta) = NA\tilde{~}_k(\theta), \forall k\}$.

Such a N-set is called the order parameter. It provides a characterizing parameter for the θ-vacuum $|0(\theta)\}N$ and explains the meaning of the N subscript. Its knowledge constitutes the "end point" of the computation, the searched result.[108]

The corticon fields in which corticon creation and annihilation dynamics take place are of the spontaneous symmetry-breaking type. At the ground, there is sameness before difference, vacuum states without preference – degenerate θ-vacua – and difference is achieved, intrinsic to the ground, in symmetry-breaking. In non-vacuum states, the unbroken symmetry of "a uniform rotation of the electric dipole moment vectors of the H_2O molecules does not change the fundamental dynamics of the water rotational field described by the Schrödinger equation." The field entity, with its various energy levels, makes no distinctions under uniform rotation in higher energy states. But in least energy vacuum states, the rotational symmetry can be broken: a change in the direction along which the electric dipole moment vectors lineup changes the vacuum. Symmetry-breaking in vacuum states thus permits distinction. Order becomes ontological through symmetry-breaking, without which there is only the degeneracy of uniformity.[109] So vacuum states support distinction, permit order. When input spontaneously breaks the rotational symmetry of the vacuum, the broken symmetry is specific to a particular input. However, fundamental energy conservation laws do not allow the loss of symmetry under these conditions. The "lost" invariance is in fact conserved in massless quanta known as Nambu-Goldstone (N-G) bosons.[110] The broken symmetry is preserved by the NGB. According to G.G. Globus, the NGB "in living brain tissue are none other than the "symmetrons" of the early Umezawa school, since they conserve the lost symmetry specific for input."[111]

How Does Consciousness Arise? The personal unit brain-body-environment has its physical foundation in the quantum entanglement brain-body-environment. The entanglement "represents the impossibility of cutting the links between the brain and the external world;"[112] the quantum model of the brain is based on the fact that the brain "is an open system in interaction with the external world."[113] For, information printing (this is also consciousness)

---

[108] G. Basti, G. Vitiello and A. Capolupo, *Quantum Field Theory and Coalgebraic Logic in Theoretical Computer Science*, in arXiv:1701.00527v1[quant-ph], 29th Dec, 2016, 1-20.

[109] G.G. Globus, *Quantum Closures and Disclosures. Thinking-Together Postphenomenology and Quantum Brain Dynamics*, 23.

[110] Ibid.

[111] Ibid. G.G. Globus refers to these symmetrons as Goldstone symmetrons, to remind all that they are massless quanta which conserve the symmetry specifically broken by input order.

[112] G. Vitiello, *The Dissipative Brain*, in Brain and Being.

[113] G. Vitiello, *My Double Unveiled*, 104.

on the brain "is achieved under the action of external stimuli, which produce the breakdown of the symmetry associated with the electric dipole vibrational field."[114] Thus, emphasis is laid on the brain being entangled or "coupled to the environment."[115][116] The centrality of the brain, as constantly noticed in the foregoing lines, should not lead to a hasty consideration of the body as inconsequential in the entire dynamics that defines the human person, for the three components, of body-brain-environment, stand as integral to a valid comprehension of the human person. According to Capolupo, Freeman and Vitiello,

> Brains are thermodynamics systems that use chemical energy to construct knowledge from information. The oxidative metabolism of glucose provides the energy, as measured by oxygen depletion and carbon dioxide production. The sensory receptors in the body and on the body surface provide the information by absorbing energy of various types impinging from the internal and external environments. The role of each sensory receptor is to selectively convert a microscopic quantity of energy first to ionic currents (receptor potentials), then to a train of pulses (action potentials, units, spikes) on its axon.[117]

Once the external stimuli are intercepted by the body, a necessary SBS occurs, a definite ground state, from the many infinite ground states or vacua, is chosen. Masseless NGB are observed, which carry long-range correlation waves observed in the brain dynamics. As a consequence of this, the time-reversal symmetry is also broken, because the choice of a ground state entails that the information has been recorded.[118] After information has been recorded, the brain state is fixated and the brain cannot be brought to the state configuration in which it was before the information printing occurred; for before the information recording process, the brain can in principle be in anyone of the infinitely many (unitarily inequivalent) vacua.[119]

---

[114] Ibid.

[115] Ibid.

[116] Each personal conscious state of a human being corresponds to a complex phase-coherence among the oscillating electromagnetic force fields of some material parts (molecules) of the three components involved. That is - for instance in the personal state of me as seeing now the computer screen in front of me - some (effectively many trillions) of molecules of the neurons of a part of the visual cortex involved, many and many trillions of the molecules constituting the parts of the ocular system involved (ocular nerve, ocular muscles, cones and rods of my retina, of the crystalline membrane in front of my retina etc), many and many trillions of molecules constituting the gases forming the air between me and the computer screen, and finally the many and many trillions of the molecules of the part of the screen I am seeing and emitting the electromagnetic radiation putting in phase the molecules of screen, of airs, of my oculomotor system, of my visual cortex, on its turn influencing the oscillation in phase of my emotional system: limbic system, amygdala etc. This is a personal state unified at the material level by the electromagnetic fields, ordered and then unified informationally by the Nambu-Goldstone bosons characterizing univocally this so complex phase coherence domain of electromagnetic, oscillating force field.

[117] A. Capolupo et al, *Dissipation of Dark Energy by Cortex in Knowledge Retrieval* in Physics Life Review, Volume 10, Issue, 1, March 2013, 85–94.

[118] G. Vitiello, *My Double Unveiled*, 107.

[119] Ibid.

There is the presence of time-reversal symmetry which means that the human person assumes a present state of affairs, one that can be distinguished from the past and the future, what Vitiello calls, "NOW you know it!"[120]

According to Vitiello, "Consciousness appears to be intimately related to dissipation."[121] He adds further that "Consciousness seems thus to emerge as a manifestation of the dissipative dynamics of the brain."[122] This dissipative dynamics has to do with the coupling of A (the nontilde subject) with Ã (the tilde object), which describes nonlinear dynamical features of the dissipative model. The nonlinearity of the dynamics describes a self-interaction process for the A system. Ã thus also plays a role in such self-coupling or *self-recognition* processes. The Ã system is the *mirror in time* image, or the *time-reversed copy* of the A system.[123] It actually duplicates the A system. It is the A system's *Double*, and since it can never be eliminated, the A system can never be separated from its Double. The role of the Ã modes in the self-interaction processes leads me to conjecture that the tilde-system is actually involved in consciousness mechanisms.[124] Dissipation manifests itself as a *second person*, the Double or *Sosia*, to dialogue with. In this way, consciousness appears to be not solely characterized by a subjective dynamics; its roots, on the contrary, seem to be grounded in the permanent *trade* of the brain (the subject) with the external world, on the dynamical relation between the system A and its Sosia[125] or Double Ã, permanently joined to it.[126]

Consciousness is reached *through* the opening to the external world. The crucial role of dissipation is that self-mirroring is not anymore a *self-trap* (as for Narcissus), the conscious subject *cannot* be a monad. Consciousness is only possible if dissipation, openness onto the

---

[120] Ibid.

[121] Ibid, 123.

[122] G. Vitiello, *Quantum Dissipation and Information. A route to consciousness modeling*, in NeuroQuantology 2003; 2: 266-279.

[123] According to G.G. Globus, that the tilde object is a mirror image of the nontilde object, this representation is only in the mathematical sense, for There is no world running forward in the nontilde system and running backward in the ~environment, and so a metaphor of time and time-reversal as a movie run forward and backward respectively would be an inappropriate metaphor. (G.G. Globus, *Quantum Closures and Disclosures. Thinking-Together Postphenomenology and Quantum Brain Dynamics*, 36-37).

[124] Ibid. The mathematical and physical meaning of the tilde-system is to describe the environment to which the brain is permanently coupled (linked). Since the brain is intrinsically an open system, the tilde-system can *never* be neglected. The tilde-modes thus might play a role as well in the unconscious brain activity. This may provide an answer to the question "as whether symmetron modes would be required to account for unconscious brain activity. As already observed, the tilde modes might tell us something about that fuzzy region between fragile consciousness and the obscure unconscious core of the dream activity.

[125] The "doubling" of the self is actually a very old literary metaphor. Plautus invention of the "doubling" of Sosia in his comedy Amphitruo (Plautus, 189 B.C.), or even the falling in love of Narcissus with himself mediated by his "reflection" in the water, are famous examples of such a metaphoric use of the "doubling ". On the other hand, in the ancient Vedic tradition (Kak 1996), consciousness also flows between two poles: an identity of self and an identity with the processes of the Universe. G. Vitiello, *My Double Unveiled*, 141.

[126] Ibid.

outside world, is allowed. Without the *objective* external world, there would be no possibility for the brain to be an open system, and no Ā system would at all exist. The very same existence of the external world is the *prerequisite* for the brain to build up its own *subjective simulation*, its *own representation* of the world. The informational inputs from the external world are the *images* of the world. Once they are recorded by A, they become the *image* of A; Ā is the *address* of A, it is identified with (is a copy of) A.[127] In Vitiello's formulation, the brain is an open system exchanging energy with the external world. There is a "permanent 'trade' of the brain (the subject) with the external world." This trade is reiterated in the relation between the brain (subject) and its ~Double.

> ...the unavoidable coupling with the external world is 'internalized' in the dialectic, permanent relation with the Double.[128]

So now there is a subject/object dialectic where subject is nontilde and object is tilde, and a subject/Double dialectic where again subject is nontilde and Double is tilde. Consciousness arises for Vitiello where tilde and nontilde come together, where nontilde subject meets a world that is "in some sense" tilde, a meeting of time-reversed mirror images, self meeting Double. Consciousness, in Vitiello's account, is the case of subject self-recognition in a ~conjugate mirror. In his metaphor, consciousness is not on either side – neither nontilde/subject nor tilde/object, but at the tail of a mirror in which the mirror image comes up in an alter universe.[129] In Vitiello's thermofield QBD formulation, consciousness lies in the vacuum states where an interaction match takes place. Dasein's dissipative quantum brain, which supports controlled interactions in its ground states, does it all. So Vitiello's formula resolves to:

nontilde subject self-recognizing world representation → consciousness.

Vitiello gives no justification for thinking of nontilde as subject. It has the very same symmetry as the ~object, only time runs oppositely in the latter. Tilde and nontilde modes here are perfectly symmetrical, so they cannot support the categorical distinction between subject and object, indeed their only distinction is the time reversal.[130] In the very mathematical formulation, the self recognition or match is *assumed*. Vitiello "requires" that the condensate contain an equal number of A and A~ modes, which insures "that the flow of the energy exchanged between the system and the environment is balanced."[131] The equation of subject and object here is imposed by fiat; their equality is simply postulated, in the dominating fashion typical of still metaphysical modernity.[132]

---

[127] Ibid.

[128] G. Vitiello, *My Double Unveiled*, 141.

[129] G.G. Globus, *Quantum Closures and Disclosures. Thinking-Together Postphenomenology and Quantum Brain Dynamics*, 31.

[130] Ibid, 32

[131] G. Vitiello, *My Double Unveiled*, 111.

[132] G.G. Globus, *Quantum Closures and Disclosures. Thinking-Together Postphenomenology and Quantum Brain Dynamics*, 32.

CONCLUSION

Consciousness, as a nonphysical entity that is pertinent to the rationality of the human person, is an issue that has for long defied any explanation. Yet, with the findings of the QBD, based on QFT, it is now seen that the age-long truth of "no man is an island" comes to bear in what has been elaborated upon thus far. Consciousness arises in the brain-body-environment interaction or, to put it in quantum terms, entanglement. The environment referred to here is all that is outside the subject, the "I", including the "other", that is the "You". That is to say that the environment is not limited to the inanimate, or the brute, or the vegetative life that resides outside the subject. It also encapsulates other subjects, who in reference to the subject under study, is the object. The mode in which consciousness arises also makes reference to the view that opposes solipsism, but speaks for interaction, community, solidarity and togetherness. These latter qualities have been championed in philosophical debates under titles such as existentialism, personalism, Interpersonalism, especially in *Igwebuike* philosophy[133]. What

---

[133] Kanu, Ikechukwu Anthony. *Igwebuike and the Logic (Nka) of African Philosophy*, 14. Kanu, I. A. (2018). *Igwe Bu Ike* as an Igbo-African hermeneutics of national development. *Igbo Studies Review. No. 6.* pp. 59-83. Kanu, I. A. (2018). *Igwebuike* as an African integrative and progressive anthropology. *NAJOP: Nasara Journal of Philosophy.* Vol. 2. No. 1. pp. 151-161. Kanu, I. A. (2018). New Africanism: *Igwebuike* as a philosophical Attribute of Africa in portraying the Image of Life. In Mahmoud Misaeli, Sanni Yaya and Rico Sneller (Eds.). *African Perspectives on Global on Global Development* (pp. 92-103). United Kingdom: Cambridge Scholars Publishing. Kanu, I. A. (2019). Collaboration within the ecology of mission: An African cultural perspective. *The Catholic Voyage: African Journal of Consecrated Life.* Vol. 15. pp. 125-149. Kanu, I. A. (2019). *Igwebuike* research methodology: A new trend for scientific and wholistic investigation. *IGWEBUIKE: An African Journal of Arts and Humanities* (IAAJAH). 5. 4. pp. 95-105. Kanu, I. A. (2019). *Igwebuikeconomics*: The Igbo apprenticeship for wealth creation. *IGWEBUIKE: An African Journal of Arts and Humanities* (IAAJAH). 5. 4. pp. 56-70. Kanu, I. A. (2019). *Igwebuikecracy*: The Igbo-African participatory cocio-political system of governance. *TOLLE LEGE: An Augustinian Journal of the Philosophy and Theology.* 1. 1. pp. 34-45. Kanu, I. A. (2019). On the origin and principles of *Igwebuike* philosophy. *International Journal of Religion and Human Relations.* Vol. 11. No. 1. pp. 159-176. Kanu, I. A. (2019b). An *Igwebuike* approach to the study of African traditional naming ceremony and baptism. *International Journal of Religion and Human Relations.* Vol. 11. No. 1. pp. 25-50. Kanu, I. A. (2017). *Igwebuike* as an Igbo-African philosophy for Christian-Muslim relations in Northern Nigeria. In Mahmoud Misaeli (Ed.). *Spirituality and Global Ethics* (pp. 300-310). United Kingdom: Cambridge Scholars. Kanu, I. A. (2017). *Igwebuike* as an Igbo-African philosophy for the protection of the environment. *Nightingale International Journal of Humanities and Social Sciences.* Vol. 3. No. 4. pp. 28-38. Kanu, I. A. (2017). *Igwebuike* as the hermeneutic of individuality and communality in African ontology. *NAJOP: Nasara Journal of Philosophy.* Vol. 2. No. 1. pp. 162-179. Kanu, I. A. (2017a). *Igwebuike* and question of superiority in the scientific community of knowledge. *Igwebuike: An African Journal of Arts and Humanities.* Vol.3 No1. pp. 131-138. Kanu, I. A. (2017a). *Igwebuike as a philosophical attribute of Africa in portraying the image of life*. A paper presented at the 2017 Oracle of Wisdom International Conference by the Department of Philosophy, Tansian University, Umunya, Anambra State, 27-29 April. Kanu, I. A. (2017b). *Igwebuike* as a complementary approach to the issue of girl-child education. *Nightingale International Journal of Contemporary Education and Research.* Vol. 3. No. 6. pp. 11-17. Kanu, I. A. (2017b). *Igwebuike* as a wholistic response to the problem of evil and human suffering. *Igwebuike: An African Journal of Arts and Humanities.* Vol. 3 No 2, March. Kanu, I. A. (2017e). *Igwebuike* as an Igbo-African modality of peace and conflict resolution. *Journal of African Traditional Religion and Philosophy Scholars.* Vol. 1. No. 1. pp. 31-40. Kanu, I. A. (2017g). *Igwebuike* and the logic (Nka) of African philosophy. *Igwebuike: An African Journal of*

this goes to certify is that the human person is not a closed system, but is an open system who is in continuous interaction and rapport with others (rational, animate and inanimate alike). The human person becomes a closed system when he dies; as QFT records it, this is when he attains to the state of maximum entropy. The exchange between him and the environment is cushioned under the second law of thermodynamics, such that there is a balance, even in this exchange of energy (for what is exchanged is energy). The human person is one with other, and not one with himself, his rational consciousness attests to this. That the human person is linked to the other is what makes consciousness arise, one which is rational and cognitive. What is to be said is that our solidarity and complementarity, our interpersonal interaction, our "Igwebuikeness" as human persons, is neural, it is cognitive and it is quantum.

BIBLIOGRAPHY

A. Capolupo et al, *Dissipation of Dark Energy by Cortex in Knowledge Retrieval* in Physics Life Review, Volume 10, Issue, 1, March 2013.

A.S. Davydov, *Solitons in molecular systems*, in Physica Scripta, *20*, 1979.

A. Streltsov et al, *Measuring Quantum Coherence with Entanglement,* in Physics Review Letters, Number 115, June 2015,

B. Skinner, *A Children's Picture-Book Introduction to Quantum Field Theory*, in Ribbonfarm Online Journal, 20th August, 2015, https://www.ribbonfarm.com/2015/08/20/qft/ retrieved 12th May, 2020.

C.I.J.M. Stuart., Y. Takahashi, H. Umezawa, *On the stability and non-local properties of memory*, in Journal of Theoretical Biology, 71, 1978.

C.I.J.M. Stuart., Y. Takahashi, H. Umezawa, *Mixed-system brain dynamics. Neural memory as a macroscopic ordered state*, in Foundation of Physics, 9, 1979.

D.M. Rosenthal, *Concepts and Definitions of Consciousness*, in The Encyclopedia of Consciousness, W.P. Banks ed, Academic Press, Elsevier Inc, Oxford, 2009.

G. Basti, G. Vitiello and A. Capolupo, *Quantum Field Theory and Coalgebraic Logic in Theoretical Computer Science*, in arXiv:1701.00527v1[quant-ph], 29th Dec, 2016.

Arts and Humanities. 3. 1. pp. 1-13. Kanu, I. A. (2017h). *Igwebuike* philosophy and human rights violation in Africa. *IGWEBUIKE: An African Journal of Arts and Humanities.* Vol. 3. No. 7. pp. 117-136. Kanu, I. A. (2017i). *Igwebuike* as a hermeneutic of personal autonomy in African ontology. *Journal of African Traditional Religion and Philosophy Scholars. Vol. 2. No. 1. pp. 14-22.*

G.G. Globus, *Quantum Closures and Disclosures. Thinking-Together Postphenomenology and Quantum Brain Dynamics,* John Benjamins Publishing Co., Amsterdam and Philadelphia, 2003,

G. Vitiello, *My Double Unveiled.* John Benjamins Publishing Co., Amsterdam and Philadelphia, 2001.

G. Vitiello, *The Dissipative Brain*, in Brain and Being - at the boundary between science, philosophy, language and arts, Globus G.G., Pribram, K.H. and Vitiello, G., (eds), John Benjamins Pub. Co. Amsterdam, 2004.

G. Vitiello, *Quantum Dissipation and Information. A route to consciousness modeling*, in NeuroQuantology 2003; 2.

I. A. Kanu. Igwebuike as an Igbo-African Hermeneutic of Globalization. *Igwebuike: An African Journal of Arts and Humanities*, Vol. 2 no. 1 2016:1-6.

I. A. Kanu. *Igwe Bu Ike* as an Igbo-African hermeneutics of national development. *Igbo Studies Review. No. 6.* pp. 59-83. 2018

I. A. Kanu. *Igwebuike* as an African integrative and progressive anthropology. *NAJOP: Nasara Journal of Philosophy.* Vol. 2. No. 1. pp. 151-161. 2018

I. A. Kanu. New Africanism: *Igwebuike* as a philosophical Attribute of Africa in portraying the Image of Life. In Mahmoud Misaeli, Sanni Yaya and Rico Sneller (Eds.). *African Perspectives on Global on Global Development* (pp. 92-103). United Kingdom: Cambridge Scholars Publishing. 2018

I. A. Kanu. Collaboration within the ecology of mission: An African cultural perspective. *The Catholic Voyage: African Journal of Consecrated Life.* Vol. 15. pp. 125-149. 2019

I. A. Kanu. *Igwebuike* research methodology: A new trend for scientific and wholistic investigation. *IGWEBUIKE: An African Journal of Arts and Humanities* (IAAJAH). *5. 4.* pp. *95-105.* 2019

I. A. Kanu. *Igwebuikeconomics*: The Igbo apprenticeship for wealth creation. *IGWEBUIKE: An African Journal of Arts and Humanities* (IAAJAH). *5. 4.* pp. *56-70.* 2019

I. A. Kanu. *Igwebuikecracy*: The Igbo-African participatory cocio-political system of governance. *TOLLE LEGE: An Augustinian Journal of the Philosophy and Theology. 1. 1.* pp. 34-45. 2018

Kanu, I. A. On the origin and principles of *Igwebuike* philosophy. *International Journal of Religion and Human Relations*. Vol. 11. No. 1. pp. 159-176. 2019

I. A. Kanu. (2019b). An *Igwebuike* approach to the study of African traditional naming ceremony and baptism. *International Journal of Religion and Human Relations*. Vol. 11. No. 1. pp. 25-50.

I. A. Kanu. *Igwebuike* as an Igbo-African philosophy for Christian-Muslim relations in Northern Nigeria. In Mahmoud Misaeli (Ed.). *Spirituality and Global Ethics* (pp. 300-310). United Kingdom: Cambridge Scholars. 2017

I. A. Kanu. *Igwebuike* as an Igbo-African philosophy for the protection of the environment. *Nightingale International Journal of Humanities and Social Sciences*. Vol. 3. No. 4. pp. 28-38. 2017

I. A. Kanu. *Igwebuike* as the hermeneutic of individuality and communality in African ontology. *NAJOP: Nasara Journal of Philosophy*. Vol. 2. No. 1. pp. 162-179. 2017

I. A. Kanu. *Igwebuike* and question of superiority in the scientific community of knowledge. *Igwebuike: An African Journal of Arts and Humanities*.Vol.3 No1. pp. 131-138. 2017

I. A. Kanu. *Igwebuike as a philosophical attribute of Africa in portraying the image of life*. A paper presented at the 2017 Oracle of Wisdom International Conference by the Department of Philosophy, Tansian University, Umunya, Anambra State, 27-29 April. 2017

I. A. Kanu. *Igwebuike* as a complementary approach to the issue of girl-child education. *Nightingale International Journal of Contemporary Education and Research*. Vol. 3. No. 6. pp. 11-17. 2017

I. A. Kanu. *Igwebuike* as a wholistic response to the problem of evil and human suffering. *Igwebuike: An African Journal of Arts and Humanities*. Vol. 3 No 2, March. 2017

I. A. Kanu. *Igwebuike* as an Igbo-African modality of peace and conflict resolution. *Journal of African Traditional Religion and Philosophy Scholars. Vol. 1. No. 1. pp. 31-40.* 2017

I. A. Kanu. *Igwebuike* and the logic (Nka) of African philosophy. *Igwebuike: An African Journal of Arts and Humanities. 3. 1. pp. 1-13.* 2017

I. A. Kanu. *Igwebuike* philosophy and human rights violation in Africa. *IGWEBUIKE: An African Journal of Arts and Humanities.* Vol. 3. No. 7. pp. 117-136. 2017

IKECHUKWU ANTHONY KANU

I. A. Kanu. *Igwebuike as a hermeneutic of personal autonomy in African ontology. Journal of African Traditional Religion and Philosophy Scholars. Vol. 2. No. 1. pp. 14-22.* 2017

J.R. Searle, *Consciousness,* Originally published October 8, 1999 as an academic paper at the University of California at Berkeley, Posted on KurzweilAI.net August 13, 2001.

K. Cherry, *Consiousness is the Psychology of Awareness,* in VeryWellMind online journal, February 24th, 2020, https://www.verywellmind.com/what-is-consciousness-2795922, Received 12th May, 2020.

M. Asorey, *A Concise Introduction to Quantum Field Theory,* in International Journal of Geometric Methods in Modern Physics, October 2018,.

M. Jibu-K. Yasue, *Quantum Brain Dynamics and Quantum Field Theory,* in Brain and Being: At the Boundary Between Science, Philosophy, Language and Arts, G.G. Globus, K.H. Pribram and G. Vitiello eds., John Benjamins Publishing Company, Amsterdam/ Philadelphia, 2004.

M. Jibu-K. Yasue, *Magic without Magic. Meaning of Quantum Brain Dynamics* in the Journal of Mind and Behaviour, Vol 18, No2/3.

M. Kuhlmann, Quantum Field Theory, in the Stanford Encyclopedia of Philosophy, Sept 27th, 2012, https://plato.stanford.edu/entries/quantum-field-theory/ retrieved 12th May, 2020.

M. Saleem, *Quantum Mechanics,* IOP Publishing Ltd, 2015.

M. Velmans, *How to Define Consciousness and How not to Define Consciousness,* in Journal of Consciousness Studies, 16(5), 2009.

T.W.B. Kibble, *Spontaneous Breaking of Symmetry In Gauge Theories,* in Phil. Trans. R. Soc. A 373: 2015 http://dx.doi.org/10.1098/rsta.2014.0033.

W.J. Freeman-G. Vitiello, *Dissipation and spontaneous symmetry breaking in brain dynamics,* in Escholarship.org, 2008, https://escholarship.org/uc/item/5c43n596.

'IGWEBUIKE' PHILOSOPHY AND HUMAN RESOURCE MANAGEMENT

OMOJOLA Immaculata Olu, (SSMA), PhD
Department of Business Administration and Management
Villanova Polytechnic, Imesi Ile, Osun State
omojolassma@yahoo.co.uk

EXECUTIVE SUMMARY

This paper discussed the relationship between 'Igwebuike' philosophy and human resource management. This philosophy emphasizes togetherness, collegiality and collaboration. HRM is concerned with administrators overseeing people within a particular organization using the rules and policies. Six parts of HRM processes were discussed - human resource planning, recruitment, selection, professional development, performance appraisal and compensation. In arriving at a connection between these two concepts, the work disclosed that they both deal with people and their affairs; working together and depending on others for achievements were identified as related. The links in the process of HRM were also acknowledged to be common to the two thoughts, which are important factors toward individual and general development. It was then recommended that HRM departments and administrators can use 'Igwebuike' philosophy to form policies for organizational goals. Phenomenological method of research was used for the purpose of this study.

Keywords: *Igwebuike* philosophy, Human Resource Management, Recruitment, Selection, Kanu Ikechukwu Anthony, Professional Development, Performance Appraisal, Compensation and Policies.

INTRODUCTION

This paper has its aim in discussing the link between *Igwebuike* philosophy and human resource management. Human resource management and personnel management are two terms that have always been used interchangeably until human resource management became more popular. Armstrong (2006) gives a clue to the transformation of the term, personnel management, to human resource management. Personnel management began around the end of the 19th century, when welfare officers (sometimes called 'welfare secretaries') came into being. They were women who were concerned only with the protection of women and girls. The creation of this welfare secretaries was a reaction to the harshness of industrial conditions, coupled with pressures arising from the extension of the franchise, the influence of trade unions and the labour movement, and the campaigning of enlightened employers, often Quakers, for what was called 'industrial betterment.' When men became part of this process, personnel management, as a term, began to fade, and human resource management came to play.

Supporting this assertion, Lundy (2008) opines that the First World War accelerated change in the development of personnel management, with women being recruited in large numbers to fill the gaps left by men going to fight, which in turn meant reaching agreement with trade unions (often after bitter disputes) about 'dilution'– accepting unskilled women into craftsmen's jobs. During the 1920s, jobs with the titles of 'labour manager' or 'employment manager' came into being in the engineering industry and other industries where there were large factories, to handle absence, recruitment, dismissal and queries over bonuses, and so on. Employers' federations, particularly in engineering and shipbuilding, negotiated national pay rates with the unions, but there were local and district variations and there was plenty of scope for disputes.

According to Mello (2001), during the 1930s, with the economy beginning to pick up, big corporations in these newer sectors saw value in improving employee benefits as a way of recruiting, retaining and motivating employees. The Second World War brought about welfare and personnel work on a full-time basis at all establishments producing war materials, because an expanded Ministry of Labour and National Service insisted on it. The government saw specialist personnel management as part of the drive for greater efficiency and the number of people in the personnel function grew substantially; there were around 5,300 in 1943. This development, as in the view of Armstrong, brought human resource management into popularity because the term left the level of being use for women and girls to include management of people (men inclusive) and their affairs.

In the opinion of Cole (2002), while stating why HRM is preferred to personnel management states that, "use of HRM language also helps to bypass 'politically incorrect' terms used in the past, such as manpower planning"p8. Although Cole's distinction between the two terms has been shared by numerous authors, like Lunnernburg and Ornstern (2008), some scholars, like Ajayi and Ayodele (2002), are still of the opinion that personnel management and human resource management can be used to mean the same thing. Kamoche (2001) gives a simple closure to this discussion. To him, whether human resource management is called "personnel management, personnel administration or strategic human resource management is immaterial" (p.1). By implication, the four terms are the same, since they are all about managing people and their affairs to achieve the objectives of organization; even Drucker (1986) calls HRM personnel administration and human relations.

Human resource management is a deliberate style of managing people or workforces in an organization for the accomplishment of company's goals. In an attempt to develop an adequate definition for human resource management, scholars came up with series of descriptions. To understand the exact meaning of the term 'human resource management' and its scope, the following definitions formulated by eminent scholars on management science, as put together by Miller and Miller (1973) will be very useful. They are as follows: human resource management is concerned with obtaining and maintaining a satisfactory and a satisfied work force. Human resource management is an extension of general management that promotes and stimulates every employee to make fullest contribution to the purpose of the business. Human resource management is that aspect of management having as its goal the effective utilization of the labour resources of an organization.

Manpower management is the function of activity aiding and directing working men and women in maximizing their contributions and satisfaction in employment. It helps workers, including all those who work, from unskilled common labourer to corporation president to public administrator,combine their efforts with those of others in providing the services and products we all want. The personnel function is concerned with procurement, development, compensation, integration and maintenance of the workers in an organization for the purpose of contributing towards the accomplishment of that organization's major goals or objectives. Therefore, the researcher feels that personnel management is the planning, organizing, directing and controlling of the performance of those operative functions.

According to Brech (2010), human resource management is that part which is primarily concerned with human resource of organization. It includes the function of employment, development and compensation. These functions are performed primarily by the human resource manager in consultation with other departments. Human resource management is an extension to general management. It is concerned with promoting and stimulating competent work force to make their fullest contribution to the concern. Personnel management exists to advice and assists the line managers in personnel matters.

Therefore, HRM department is a staff department of an organization. Personnel management lays emphasis on action, rather than making lengthy schedules, plans and work methods. The problems and grievances of people at work can be solved more effectively through rationale personnel policies. It is based on human orientation. It also motivates the employees through its effective incentive plans so that the employees provide fullest co-operation. HRM deals with human resources and all that has to do with them. In context to human resources, it manages both the individual as well as the organization.

Willie (2010) gives a picture of human resource management as the management of employees' knowledge, aptitudes, abilities, talents, creative abilities and skills/competencies. It is a continuous, on-going development function aimed at improving human processes. Human resource management follows the systems thinking approach. It is not considered in isolation from the larger organization and takes into account the linkages and interfaces. It is considered a strategic management function.

Ajayi and Ayodele (2002) define human resource management as "the careful selection of and placement of new employees and the development and effective utilization of existing ones with a view to attain the potential of individual employees and organizational goals and objectives" (p.152). In the definition of Stoner, Freeman and Gilbert (2002), human resource management is a process "that tries to keep the organization supplied with the right people in the right positions, when they are needed" (p.376). To Akindutire (2004), however, personnel administration "is the process of getting qualified personnel to provide instructional services for the goal achievement of the school system" (p26).

The common factors in these definitions are the fact that the above authors focus on obtaining, using and maintaining a satisfied workforce. It is a significant part of management concerned with employees at work and with their relationship within the organization. Human resource management is the planning, organizing, compensation, integration and maintenance of people for the purpose of contributing to organizational, individual and societal goals. Simply put, it is about managing people, about working together for organizational targets, development of people and the company, and finally, HRM processes are connected, which means they are not separated as visibly shown in the model.

In describing the roles the Human Resource Management Department performs for an organization, Arum and Roksa (2010) agree with the following: conducting job analyses, planning personnel needs and recruitment, selecting the right people for the job, orienting and training, determining and managing wages and salaries, providing benefits and incentives, appraising performance, resolving disputes and communicating with all employees at all levels. These are what it takes to be a human resource manager. In line with this, Kamoche (2001) says that human resource management "is concerned with the management of people, the employer-employee relationship or labour regulation" (p.1). And Akindutire feels that the functional aspects of personnel administration are: placement of personnel, training and development and service activities related to welfare of personnel. The functions presented by Kamoche and Akindutire have recently been broken into ten responsibilities by Meich (2019) as planning for the future, recruiting top talent, succession (career) planning, evaluating job functions, incentives and rewards, employee engagement and internal marketing, employee wellness, general administration, employee off-boarding, safety and health standards. All these descriptions of the HRM department can be compressed to be getting proper staff to meet objectives, organize, motivate and communicate appropriately, evaluate and develop workforce,, all of which, to the researcher, will reflect in the HRM process.

HUMAN RESOURCE MANAGEMENT PROCESS

Human resource management is a planning unit in any organization that has a manager and other staff that carry out the process of making the affairs of all personnel in the organization realizable. Therefore, Stoner et al have analyzed human resource process to be in seven parts as follows: human resource planning, recruitment, selection, training and development, socialization, performance appraisal and promotions/transfers/demotions and separations. In the same vein, Lunnernburg and Ornstern (2008) break the process into six parts in this way: human resource planning, recruitment, selection, professional development, performance appraisal and compensation. For the purpose of this work, however, Lunnernburg and Ornstern's pattern will be adopted, taking for granted that socialization that is added to the first one is embedded in professional development or training and development of the processes, while, promotions/transfers/demotions and separations are entrenched in performance appraisal and compensation, because compensation is about reward, and if no reward, there will be demotions or lay-off. Below is human resource management model.

HUMAN RESOURCE MANAGEMENT PROCESS MODEL

The human resource model is a reflection of what the human resource department does in the organization to make the affairs of personnel achievable. The model reflects connections or networks between all the phases, step by step. It must begin with **Human Resource Planning**- this is logical planning and forecasting to see that there are no dearth of personnel in an organization. It will pay attention to job analysis that is divided into two parts - job specification which is the outlining of the required qualifications of any interested person to take up a job. Job description, therefore, is the stating clearly of the job title, the superior of the staff to be employed, statement of job goals and duties /responsibilities. This exercise gives the organization reasons to be proactive and exist without fear that there can be disappointment in relation to manpower shortage.

Recruitment: This is referred to as "the process of generating a pool of competent applicants needed to fill the available positions in an organization" (Lunenburg and Ornstein, 2008p.492). The HRM department has the responsibility of attracting, shortlisting, selecting and appointing candidates for permanent or temporary jobs in an organization. It can be done through internal or external sourcing, since there can be some qualified staff among the existing ones to fill in the gaps. If there are, it is a matter of deploying them to the given positions for new ones to occupy their places. It is a good way of motivation and a reliable method of improving the organization. Therefore, HRM department will get personnel to replace them. This stage is always preceded by an interactive session with the team approved by the organization to do it. This must be done by Human Resource Management department before selection.

Selection: This is a way of picking the best candidates out of the recruited ones. Mahek (2019) proposes the following as steps in the selection process in any organization - preliminary interview, screening of applicants, employment tests, selection interview, checking of references, medical examination, and final selection/hiring. This process, in the mind of the researcher, is combining the entire HRM process, not taking a step at a time. The first four processes should be left for the recruitment stage, while the selection phase should be concerned with checking reference, medical examination and final selection and hiring. Although Mahek insists that "the selection process varies from industry to industry, company to company and even amongst departments of the same company" (p.2). After recruitment and selection, the next step is professional development.

Professional Development: This is a way of teaching administrators and professionals the skills needed for both present and future positions. It has dual benefits: confidence to perform better on a given assignment and ability to improve the standard of the organization, now and in the future. Nevertheless, Trammel (2019) suggests ten ways of professional developments for those who long to be few steps ahead of others as follows; hone a learning mindset, examine your decisions, read regularly, write regularly, attend training programs, teach what you know, build self-awareness, gather feedback, find mentors and cultivate peer relationships.

These proposals have merits because they include assessment, training and evaluation which have been the regular ways of developing workers in organizations. And to this, Drucker (1986) warns that apart from the fact that individuals should make regular efforts to develop their careers, the work environment must maintain this fact when he stresses that "the work therefore must encourage the growth of the individual and must direct it-otherwise it fails to take full advantage of the specific properties of the human resources" (p.266). There should be regular assessment of workers in HRM to see if they are responding to the needs of the organization. This can only be achieved through consistent performance appraisal.

Performance Appraisal: Performance appraisal is a method that HRM adopts to assess employee response and contributions to an organization. It is done for the following reasons: 1. to check the effectiveness of personnel selection procedure. 2. The outcome of it is used by administrators to make decisions for compensation, promotions, transfer, demotions and lay-off. 3. Also, it reveals areas in an organization where improvements and developments are needed. This exercise is often called annual review, performance review or employee appraisal, since it also focuses on how an organization is progressing through the workforce.

Compensation: Compensation is a vital part in HRM process. Employees develop serious anxiety if they are not adequately compensated. Apart from this, they talk ill about their organization and administrators. They can become less effective and committed, which will have adverse effect on the organization in question. Compensation includes fringe benefits or bonuses, profit sharing, overtime pay, even promotions, responsibilities and recognition rewards are parts of compensation. These processes in HRM are to be followed step by step and properly planned. As it reflects in the model, the processes are connected with each other and none is less important as in the spirit of *Igwebuike* philosophy.

IGWEBUIKE PHILOSOPHY

According to Alalama (2018), while citing Kanu, "*Igwebuike* philosophy is based on the Igbo-African worldview of complementarity, that is, the manner of being in African Ontology. It is a worldview in which individuating differences must work towards a corporate existence where the "I" does not stand as the "I" but as a 'We', where life and living makes meaning. In a scenario of this kind, difference does not divide neither does it constitute a threat, but rather unites and gives hope that future existence would have meaning" (p.20).

Kanu (2017) had earlier explained this philosophy in this assertion. It (Igwebuike philosophy) "is anchored on the African worldview, which is characterized by a common origin, common world-view, common language, shared culture, shared race, colour and habits, common historical experience and a common destiny. Life is a life of sharedness" (p.17).

Igwebuike philosophy has its worth in paying attention to people and, by extension, the environment in which people live or work. It also emphasizes togetherness and sharing which can easily prompt the development of the individual and the entire group. Above all, it highlights being connected with a given group that can simply foster support and encouragements for improvement.

IGWEBUIKE PHILOSOPHY AND HUMAN RESOURCE MANAGEMENT

The link between *Igwebuike* philosophy and human resource management is paramount to this work. The following important characteristics, which also explain the nature of human resource management, can be deduced from the various definitions and explanations given above. It concerns employees: it is primarily concerned with the efficient utilization and conservation of these human resources; it considers employees as individuals and also as members of a group; it is concerned with personnel policies in formulating policies with regard to recruitment, selection, training, promotion, transfer, job evaluation, merit rating and working conditions. *Igwebuike* philosophy is also concerned with people being together for growth and development, and connected with other members in a group.

As human resource management is the strategic approach to the effective management of people in a company or organization such that they help their business gain improvement, so also is *Igwebuike* philosophy giving attention to people, and it emphasizes togetherness and sharing, with much importance on what you have in common. As Kanu explained, it is "characterized by a common origin, common world-view, common language, shared culture, shared race, colour and habits, common historical experience and a common destiny. Life is a life of sharedness" (p.17). Also, it has a connection or link with the HRM process as in the model where all the processes stand as one and none could be omitted at any point, if truly the HRM department must function as it should be, which is closely associated with the thought of Alalama "'I' does not stand as the "I" but as a 'We'" (p.20), in defining *igwebuike* philosophy.

Another common factor is development. Since development of staff is a must in HRM and indeed the system must be able to naturally develop personnel, so also will the association with a group in *Igwebuike* philosophy certainly develop every member of the group.

RECOMMENDATIONS

Based on the discussions above, the following recommendations are offered.

That since human resource management is about people and their welfare, human resource managers are, therefore, encouraged to make the office to be more people-oriented and to be more preoccupied with their dealings as in the *Igwebuike* philosophy which stresses 'we' not 'I'.

On the part of workers, however, there should be cooperation with the administrator or HRM manager to achieve all the laid-down rules. Attention should not be given to individual interest but to the group for the benefit of all. It is important to keep in mind that HRM processes are connected, so also is *Igwebuike* philosophy about life of sharing, as Kanu states "Life is a life of sharedness" (p.17).

Working together harmoniously must equally be underlined. Where ever you find people, there must be understanding for development. Therefore, managers are encouraged to lead their members in a manner that will enhance their growth, as in the mind of Maxwell while citing Firestone that "It is only as we develop others that we permanently succeed" (p.112).

CONCLUSION

This work has been able to show the link between HRM and *Igwebuike* philosophy. Human resource management is an integral but distinctive part of management, concerned with people at work and their relationship within the enterprise, seeking to bring together inter-effective organization men and women who staff the enterprise, enabling each to make his/her own best contribution to its success, both as an individual and as a member of a working group. It seeks to provide relationships within the firm that are conducive both to effective work and human satisfaction. *Igwebuike* philosophy is about paying attention to one another and not being individualistic in a group. It advocates the idea that all members should always seek the growth and progress of the group, for the group. Like the saying goes, if you want to walk fast, walk alone and if you want to walk far, walk together. Walking together is always the focus of any organization. This brings about back-up and assistance for success, which is the view point of *Igwebuike* philosophy that HRM can also adopt.

REFERENCES

Ajayi I. A and Ayodele J. B (2002). *Fundamentals of Educational Management.* Nigeria. Greeline Publication.

Akindutire I. O. (2004). *Administration of Higher Education.* Lagos. Sunray Press. Alalama V.E (2018). *Igwebuike* as an African Philosophy for Peace and Conflict Resolution in Obeama-Nguru of Aboh-Mbaise L.G.A. Imo State. Retrieved (5/5/2020) from https://www.academia.edu/37608513/.

Armstrong, M. (2006). *A handbook of human resource management practice. International student edition.* (10th ed). Kogan page, London and Philadelphia.

Arum, R., & Roksa, J. (2010). *Personnel management.* Retrieved (5/4/2020) from http://www.businessdictionary.com/definition/personnel-management.html

Brech, C. (2010). *Academically adrift: Limited learning on college campuses.* Chicago: University of Chicago Press.

Cole, G. A. (2002). *Personnel and human resource management.* TJ International Ltd. Padstow, Cornwall.

Drucker P. F. (1986). *The Practice of Management.* New York. Harper.

Kamoche, N. (2001). *Understanding Human Resource Management.* Buckingham. Open University Press.

Kanu, I. A. *Igwebuike* as an Igbo-African hermeneutics of globalisation. *IGWEBUIKE: An African Journal of Arts and Humanities*, Vol. 2 No.1. pp. 61-66. 2016

Kanu, I. A. *Igwebuike* as the consummate foundation of African Bioethical principles. *An African journal of Arts and Humanities* Vol.2 No1 June, pp.23-40. 2016

Kanu, I. A. *Igwebuike* as an expressive modality of being in African ontology. *Journal of Environmental and Construction Management. 6. 3.* pp.12-21. 2016

Kanu, I. A. African traditional folktales as an integrated classroom. *Sub-Saharan African Journal of Contemporary Education Research.* Vol.3 No. 6. pp. 107-118. 2016

Kanu, I. A. *Igwebuike* as an Igbo-African philosophy for Christian-Muslim relations in Northern Nigeria. In Mahmoud Misaeli (Ed.). *Spirituality and Global Ethics* (pp. 300-310). United Kingdom: Cambridge Scholars. 2017

Kanu, I. A. *Igwebuike* as an Igbo-African philosophy for the protection of the environment. *Nightingale International Journal of Humanities and Social Sciences.* Vol. 3. No. 4. pp. 28-38. 2017

Kanu, I. A. *Igwebuike* as the hermeneutic of individuality and communality in African ontology. *NAJOP: Nasara Journal of Philosophy.* Vol. 2. No. 1. pp. 162-179. 2017

Kanu, I. A. *Igwebuike* and question of superiority in the scientific community of knowledge. *Igwebuike: An African Journal of Arts and Humanities.*Vol.3 No1. pp. 131-138. 2017

Kanu, I. A. *Igwebuike as a philosophical attribute of Africa in portraying the image of life.* A paper presented at the 2017 Oracle of Wisdom International Conference by the Department of Philosophy, Tansian University, Umunya, Anambra State, 27-29 April. 2017

Kanu, I. A. *Igwebuike* as a complementary approach to the issue of girl-child education. *Nightingale International Journal of Contemporary Education and Research.* Vol. 3. No. 6. pp. 11-17. 2017

Kanu, I. A. *Igwebuike* as a wholistic response to the problem of evil and human suffering. *Igwebuike: An African Journal of Arts and Humanities.* Vol. 3 No 2, March. 2017

Kanu, I. A. *Igwebuike* as an Igbo-African modality of peace and conflict resolution. *Journal of African Traditional Religion and Philosophy Scholars.* Vol. 1. No. 1. pp. 31-40. 2017

Kanu, I. A. *Igwebuike* and the logic (Nka) of African philosophy. *Igwebuike: An African Journal of Arts and Humanities.* 3. 1. pp. 1-13. 2017

Kanu, I. A. *Igwebuike* philosophy and human rights violation in Africa. *IGWEBUIKE: An African Journal of Arts and Humanities.* Vol. 3. No. 7. pp. 117-136. 2017

Kanu, I. A. *Igwebuike* as a hermeneutic of personal autonomy in African ontology. *Journal of African Traditional Religion and Philosophy Scholars.* Vol. 2. No. 1. pp. 14-22. 2017

Kanu, I. A. African philosophy, globalization and the priority of 'otherness'. *Journal of African Studies and Sustainable Development.* Vol. 1. No. 1. pp. 40-57. 2018

Kanu, I. A. *African traditional philosophy of education: Essays in Igwebuike philosophy.* Germany: Lambert Publications. 2018

Kanu, I. A. Igbo-African Gods and Goddesses. *Nnadiebube Journal of Philosophy.* Vol. 2. No. 2. pp. 118-146. 2018

Kanu, I. A. *Igwe Bu Ike* as an Igbo-African hermeneutics of national development. *Igbo Studies Review. No. 6.* pp. 59-83. 2018

Kanu, I. A. *Igwebuike* as an African integrative and progressive anthropology. *NAJOP: Nasara Journal of Philosophy.* Vol. 2. No. 1. pp. 151-161. 2018

Kanu, I. A (2017). *Igwebuike* Philosophy and the Issue of National Development. IGWEBUIKE: An African Journal of Arts and Humanities Vol. 3 No 6.

Lundy O. (2008). From Personnel Management to Strategic Human Resource Management. *International Journal of Human Resource Management. 5 (3): 687-720.*

Lunnernburg F. C. and Ornstern A. C. (2008). *Educational Administration: Concept and Practices.* USA. Wadsworth: Cengage Learning.

Mahek S. (2019). Selection Process in HRM. Retrieved (5/5/2020) from http://www.economicsdiscussion.net/human-resource-management/selection-process-in-hrm/31871.

Maxwell J.C. (2001). *The Power of Leadership.* Nigeria: Joint Heir Publications Ltd.

Meich C (2019). 10 Core Functions of Human Resource Management. Retrieved (5/5/2020) from https://tracktime24.com/Blog/10-core-functions-of- human-resource-management

Mello J. A (2001). *Strategic Human Resource Management.* South Western, Cincinnati.

Miller J. B. & Miller M. G. (1973). *Personnel and industrial relations: A managerial approach.* New York: Macmillan Company.

Stoner J. A. F., Freeman R. E. and Gilbert D. R. (2002). Management. Sixth Ed. New Delhi: Asoke K. Ghosh.

Trammel J. (2019). 10 Ways to Maximize Your Professional Development. Retrieved (5/5/2020) from https://www.inc.com/joel-trammell/10-ways-to-maximize-your-professional-development.html

COVERT MILITARY OPERATIONS, BIOENGINEERING AND THE WEAPONIZATION OF VIRUSES: AN IGWUEBUIKE DISCOURSE

Hilary Ugwu, MSW
University of Oklahoma
School of Social Work
Norman, USA,
hiugwu@yahoo.com

EXECUTIVE SUMMARY

In the Art of War, Sun Tzu (544 B.C – 496 B.C), the ancient Chinese military tactician, outlined combat subterfuges to dismantle the enemy. His strategies not only involve physical combat. It also includes using swift psychological dexterities to paralyze the opposition. Military generals around the world have studied Sun Tsu, mastered his tactics and made exponential improvements. Thus, the portrait of modern warfare is that of a theater of apocalyptic death. Think of the horrors of mass-killer viral attacks, thermonuclear pulverization, sonic sound-frequency weapons, lethal gaseous nerve agents, the manipulation of electromagnetic spectra for destructive purposes, etc. The threat of nuclear annihilation hunted humanity during the time of the Cold War. The Cold War indeed ushered in an era of rapid anti-human scientific and technological intensification. Two super heavyweight economic ideologies, viz the Anglo-American capitalism, and Soviet Communism, were masturbating and exhibiting their erectile military narcissism. It was a time of looming fear— unbridled arms race, socio-economic sabotage and psychopathic war-mongering. It was also be beginning of race to conquer the space, hence the installation of space-based complex planetary reconnaissance spy satellite systems. The Cold War era spiked-up mass brainwashing and unmitigated propagandas. We were told that the battle line was drawn between 'demon-' driven Marxist-Leninist authoritarian eastern communism and 'angelic' Anglo-American exploitative imperial capitalism. However, these two world powers pushed the rest of mankind into taking sides. The Cold War gave mischief makers insatiable Dracula-kind of bloody appetite for developing and stockpiling mass destroyer-weapons, including bioweapons (BW) which herein is my main focus.

Keywords: Igwebuike, Kanu Ikechukwu Anthony, Military Operations, Bioengineering, Weaponization, Viruses

INTRODUCTION:

Ancient myths abound which portray man as acting wickedly against his own kind. The Latinized aphorism, '*homo homini lupus*'—man is wolf to man, captures tersely mankind's deep-rooted belief that man is a predator as well, just like the wild wolf. The statement reveals man's psycho-traumatic paranoid fear relative to him being preyed on by his own kind. The human experiences of trauma and victimization find their ways into the linguistic lexicons. Man would not have created words such as homicide, infanticide, genocide, holocaust, pogrom, etc., if he had not traumatically experienced them. These words elicit dark creepy feelings. They also re-trigger repressed collective anxieties. Humanity's primal psycho-trauma exists in all of our collective minds. The Swiss analytical psychologist, Carl Jung, calls this realm of collective minds, the "objective psych." This is the realm of our congenital unconscious mind. The darkest and deepest part of our collective fears has manifested throughout history in storytelling and mythologies.

In ancient Kemet (what Greek erroneously called Egypt), there was a mythology that tells of the drama of the death of one man in the hand of another by a deliberate act of killing. This is the myth of Seth and Osiris. Seth/Set (original name, Setesh) premeditatedly killed his brother, Osiris (original name, Asar) in the vilest and sadistic manner. The myth paints a picture of gory precision medical assassination. Seth dismembered Osiris' body into fourteen pieces and scattered the remains all over the River Nile. The name, Seth, has continued to migrate into the human conscious history. Seth invokes certain nomenclatural diabolism: Shaitan, in Arabic, and Satan, in Christian theology, both of which derive from the Kemetian Seth/Set. Whether you call him Seth, Set, Sheth, Setesh, Sutekh, Setan, Satan, Shaitan, I am referring to the same primordial character in African mythology. The drama of Seth/Set is deeply encoded within the human collective psychology. Modern Anglo-linguistic formation identifies Seth with darkness, since the word Sun-Seth (sunset). Seth is the Prince of Darkness, and his coming foreshadows night/darkness and evil in the ancient African mind. This primordial human trickster (Seth) became the god of evil as well as the god of the barren WILDERNESS. He causes death and chaos. Seth was referred to as the Apep or Apophis, that is, the Great Dragon/Monster/Serpent/Beast (Remler, 2010). Jesus was in the Seth's (Satan's) wilderness and was tempted by him.

While this article is not a recapitulation of ancient African theological construct, I must not fail to point out that the atrocious deed of this prehistoric man (Seth) has become the objective embodiment of evil as a monstrous entity within the collective human psyche. My point is that man is capable of inverted evolution (devolution) into Sethian-likeness (Satan-like) through his deliberate act of wickedness against his own kind and nature.

Similarly, the myth of Cain and Abel, specific to the Hebrew scripture, continues to warn us about the murderous instinct encoded in the human freewill. The Hebraic myth introduces mankind to the dramatic prelude of man's premeditated killing of his own kind. This biblical story is the primeval blueprint to murder consciousness. Cain's method was simplistic, anachronistic and crude. When the deity, Elohim, asked him the whereabouts of his brother, he gave a classical response "Am I my brother's keeper?" This Cainite response would set the future stage for humanity's careless, irresponsible and unaccountable predisposition toward their own bio-kinds. The point is that those we trust to protect us have continued to exhibit Cainite psychopathic nature, narcissism and antisocial proclivities.

The above prehistoric Sethian/Cainite murder mythos serve as reminders that man, in fact, does exterminate his bio-kind for diabolical intentions. It is not completely irrational to make apriori assumptions that man's darker nature easily succumbs to the lures of cruel, nefarious and murderous instructs embedded in his free choice. Today, modern man has perfected his inherited Sethian/Cainite killing skills, using advanced scientific and technological methods. Modern man is obsessed with anti-human sciences and seems to reach a state of orgasmic euphoria when he is able to unleash death and destruction on the planet. Man can now, through molecular engineering, create and spread deadly bio-synthetic terminator pathogens that can wipe out any crowded cities.

VIRUSES: THE INVISIBLE DEMON

The English natural philosopher, Robert Hooke (1635—1703), changed the world after he discovered that organisms have cells. This finding was possible through the use of light microscope. Antonie Leeuwenhoek (1632—1723) made another significant discovery, the bacteria. Following similar trend, a Russia scientist, Dmitry Ivanovky (1864—1920), was able to discover a much smaller micro agent, the virus. These discoveries opened some doors into the microscopic universe of microorganism. Ivanosky found that viruses are filterable micro agents. His experiments indicated that viruses were able to pass through Poreclain Chemberland Filter which bacteria could not pass through. Thus, scientists, for the first time, learned that there are micro agents that are much smaller than bacteria.

The word "virus" derives from Latin and implies poison. Viruses and bacteria are completely different. Viruses have no cellular structure as bacteria. Another distinguishing feature of viruses is their extremely small size. A bacterium is a giant in comparison to a virus (Zimmer, 2011). Scientists, in their taxonomic classifications, exclude viruses from living organisms. In other words, viruses are non-living biological agents. So, if viruses are non-living organisms, what are they? They are infectious virions which are capable of entering a cell and initiating a replication cycle (Payne, 2017). A virus carries a single nucleic acid encased within its protein coats. They parasitize off of all other forms of life on earth. They have replication cycle which means that they have the capacity to change their genome rapidly. This is why viral mutations are very common. They have fluidity of adaptation on new hosts. The mysterious artificial-like nature of virus makes it difficult to fight. Bacteriological attack is more manageable than virus attack. Some viruses can mutate so quickly it is nearly impossible to create an effective single medical solution to eliminate their mutation variants. Bacteriophages is a scientific terminology which points to the fact that viruses can infect and destroy bacteria (This sounds like top gangster.). Due to their small sizes, they are described as "filterable diseases." They can pass through filters that bacteria cannot filter through. Viruses lack ribosomes and must steal ribosomes from its host for translation of their mRNA. Scientists report that viruses are known for their geometric sophistication which are not observed in natural microbial organisms (Tennant et all, 2018). They sort of behave like invisible demons.

BIOLOGICAL WEAPON (BW): A HISTORICAL MORPHOGENESIS

Bioweapon (BW) skeptics who are uncomfortable with the idea that man uses viral attacks on his own kind often recite litanies of epidemics throughout history as a 'proof' that intentional viral attack is made-belief. Their argument is that if man, in the context of historical ecosystems, has always experienced death by germs, it is, therefore, 'unreasonable' to think that germs are intentionally created and deployed to attack humans. The most cited example is the bubonic black plague that ravaged Europe in the Middle Ages (I will provide a new viewpoint on this as you read on.). No reasonable person denies the fact that disease-causing agents have always existed in man's natural environment. The real question which skeptics of BW miss is this: Has man used germ as a BW? The answer is yes. Let's outline the historical progression of BW from four fundamental point of views, viz: (a) pre-microbiology era (pre-germ discovery era), (b) the era of applied microbiology, (c) the era of aerobiology and industrial microbiology and, (d) the era of molecular biology and biotechnology. I will provide a brief theoretical description of these for eras of BW expansion histories.

Pre-Germ Era: The use of germs as BW has always been practised by man throughout ancient time, even before the discovery of microbial agents via microscope. Soldiers are familiar with diseases due to high level of exposures to unsanitary battlefields conditions. Thus, military tacticians of ancient time learned to harness pathogenic agents for bio-attacks on their enemies. Valerius Maximus, a Roman author— more than two thousand years ago - provided a historical testimony that diseases were used for purposes of war (Guilemin, 2005). In ancient times, the army deployed carcasses of diseased animals or corpses of highly infected people to contaminate water supplies in populated areas to cause mass death on the side of the enemies. They sent infected and highly contagious people to enemy cities and towns as a way of spreading the diseases. Ancient Greece Army used extremely poisonous extracts from plants to contaminate water sources on the enemy side. The eye-opening written account of Gabriele de' Mussi, concerning the battle siege of Caffa in 1346, indicates that the Black Death in Middle Age Europe was a distinctive case of BW. Mussi reported that the Black Death (which killed an estimate of 50 million people) was as a result of soldiers' flinging rotten diseased corpses into the besieged walled City of Caffa to cause infection and contamination. He indicated that contaminated fleeing Italians brought the plague to Europe. Evidence indicates that rats helped to spread this plagues, but according to Mussi, the initial cause was traced to military BW.

Advent of Microbiology: The next shift in man's BW capacity was brought in by the science of microbiology. Man is able to, through advancement in science, identify in a test tube specific microbial agents as the cause of illnesses. Man learned to isolate, modify and deploy pathogenic agents. Thus, military strategists saw a ripe opportunity for weaponization of viruses. This was the beginning of the scientific development of BW which changed the concept of warfare forever. On a positive side, man's capacity to understand, prevent and fight germs improved exponentially with the science of microbiology. Microbiology leads to the knowledge that simple preventive measures like sanitization was able to prevent diseases.

Progress in Industrial Aerobiology and Microbiology: Aerobiology deals with the study of the spread and effect of biological agents for public health purposes. Following World War II, industrial societies entered a new era of industrial microbiology. This era ushered in industrial-scale pharmaceutical production and customization of microbial organisms for various purposes. Breweries, baking industries, allopathic pharmaceutical companies, etc., utilized bacteria massively for product manufacturing. Some bacteria are beneficial and necessary for the survival of the human organism. With this era also came a problem, the mass production of death-causing viruses for BW purposes.

The Era of Molecular Biology and Biotechnology: In the early 1950s, Francis Crick and James Watson discovered the double helix structure of DNA. A new scientific revolution was born (Koblentz, 2009). Thus began the new era of genetic engineering. This propelled microbiologists into a new form of BW heights. The ability to manipulate gene code made bioweaponeers demigods. Viral strands cannot only be studied from their genetic composition, but the humane genetic strands are also carefully studied. With this mixture, it became easy to create virus that can target specific people based on genetic history. Gene editing has positives but lots of negatives as well.

The Military Weaponization Viruses

"In this age of technological inhumanity
Scientific atrocity
Atomic mis-philosophy
Nuclear mis-energy
It's a world that forces lifelong insecurity"
Bob Marley—Survival (song)

The lyrics above is from Bob Marley's SURVIRAL album. Marley offers a prophetic glimpse into the inordinate and gloomy empirical materialism of modern civilization. He paints a portrait of the age of draconian scientism, epistemological imperialism as well as scientific atheism. It is the era of dictatorship that passes for science. The consequence of man's exaggerated fanatical faith in material science is leading man into an apocalyptic horror. This is the age where man has to face the demon of invisible micro-bug created in laboratory. Some of the world's most powerful governments and their elite military intelligences, in collaboration with some civilian 'mad scientist', have engaged in secret BW research and development.

Certain research institutes have been exposed as having engaged in Bioweaponry, for instance, The Pasteur Institute in France, Porton Down Research Center in England, Ivanofsky Institute of Virology in Russia, Fort Detrick Military Research Institute in the United States, The Tokyo Institute, Japan etc. These institutions are linked to underground anti-human-anti-God-anti-nature BW research activities (Horowitz, 1998). Countries such as Isreal, Lybia, Egypt, China, Iran, North Korea, Pakistan, Taiwan, Syria, to name but a few, are reported to have engaged in the use of bioweapon (Koblenz, 2009).

The notion of BW involved microorganism used intentionally to cause illnesses and death. What makes microbial BW agents lethal is their capacity to mutate, reproduce and spread. A bio agent released within a given environment could linger for years, just waiting for activation inside a host. Chemical weapon is easily detected and felt. But BW could take days and months before victims become symptomatic. BWs are relatively cheaper to make compared to other forms of mass weapons (Cole, 1990). This could explain its appeal to mischief makers. According to expert advice to the United Nations, large-scale attack against a civilian population costs $2000 per square kilometer, using conventional weapon, $800 with nuclear weapons, $600 with nerve–gas weapons, and only $1 with BW. To think that the military could ignore such low-cost budget in international arms' race would be to play the ostrich. In 1980, the U.S. annual budget, involving BW development, is $1 billion. There is no question that viruses are being made in test tubes. Experts indicate that certain viruses can be cultured in test tubes "by mixing purified genomes and protein." The said genomes may have been synthesized (Payne, 2017).

The modern rise in BW research and development came from warmongering mindset of industrialized nations. As way back as 1920s, France was working on the use of microbial agents as weapons. Japan may have started working on BW in the early 1930s. The United Kingdom, Soviet Russia as well the United States have engaged in BW research and development as means of winning wars and dominating their enemies. The military proponents of BW development believe that mass death of civilians will bring a battle-resistance nation on her knees (Guillemin, 1999). There are sufficient historical reasons to conclude that some deadly man-made bio agents which at one time or another have ravaged human society might have come from clandestine military laboratory bases and may have been either released accidentally or by deliberate intent. Looking back at the mid-19th century, one could notice that the threats of global catastrophe and the end of life on earth by thermonuclear pulverization was widespread in newspaper headlines, books, televisions and radio talk shows. Even then, the media paid less attention to the possibilities of human-induced virological outbreak of similar apocalyptic proportion. I would assume that the reason threats from BW mass death are given less attention is because viruses are microbes and are imperceptible to the naked eyes, unless with special equipment. So if people didn't see it, they think it posed less threat. Viral attacks usually sneak into a population and cause mass death undetected. So they are not as dramatic as thermonuclear destructive explosions.

The period between 1945 and 1991 has been classified by military historians as The Cold War era. World War II was crucial in understanding man's weaponization of microbes. Molecular sciences, like microbiology and other nano-based sciences, provide man with the tool for detailed study of structures, systems and behaviours of microscopic organisms. Man's scientific ability to understand the structures of Deoxyribonucleic Acid as well as Ribonucleic Acid offers him the endless mastery of post-transcriptional modification, that is, the ability to control gene's expression. The ability to splice genes means that man has acquired the science of the gods. He too can create or destroy at his whims and caprices. Those who weaponize microbial agents for dark evil agendas will not hesitate to use such knowledge to instigate mass pandemic, bioterrorism, disorientation of population, Pavlovian-style mass behaviour modifications/social control, economic collapse, political control, social systems collapse and mass death. There are people who believe in and want to implement Malthusianism and Nazi-style eugenics.

SOVIET RUSSIA AND MICROBIAL WARFARE

During the Cold War, Russia's Ostrov Vozrozhdeniya (translated as Rebirth/Renaissance Island) was used as one of the BW research, development and test locations. Multiple reliable sources, including declassified documents, implicate elite Soviet military intelligence for the existence of so many weaponized strands of killer viruses. Some prominent Russian BW facilities were, at least according to official report, dissolved in the early 1990s, following the collapse of communist Russia. However, it would be unwise to trust official reports and believe that Russia's BW capacity has been disarmed.

BWs were developed and used during World War II. In 1942, as both the Russian and the German fronts were preparing for the battle of Stalingrad, a virus outbreak occurred. This virus was named Tularemia, and it was a BW. It was uncertain if this came from the German side from the Russian side. What is clear, however, was that Russia had a well-established BW capacity. Russia's Biopreparat Agency was dedicated to research and development of unnatural pathogens as BW. The Agency was created through a clandestine decree and has top military officials who were themselves dedicated scientists. The reason most of BW activities around the world are strictly under military secrecy is because bacteriological warfare is prohibited by the Geneva Protocols of 1925. This deceptive prohibition is nothing but a toothless dog. Virological weapon continues to be developed by the world's most sophisticated militaries and nothing happens. These deadly germs are deployed for all kinds of agenda. Other Soviet military facility used for BW development include, the Center for Military Technical Problems of Anti-Bacteriological Defense, Sverdlovsk; Scientific Research Institute of Microbiology, Kirov; the Center of Virology, Zagorsk; Leninggrad's Scientific Research Institute of Military Medicine, to name a few.

Russia's Biopreparat Agency was overseen by Russia's Fifteenth Directorate. This covert agency came under different army chiefs at different times, including, General Yury Tikhonovick, as well as General Vsenolod Ogarkov. Russia boasted possession of SS-18 killer missile capable of conveying active bio agents to target destinations. The Communist Red Army strategists were obsessed with this mission of 'conquering the world' through epidemiological attacks and mass death if need be. Russia's viral capacity was enormous. Cities were marked around the world for viral attacks. Many will not want to imagine that genetically modified infectious microorganism have been used on the masses around the world in the past and have continued to be used in the present time for nefarious reasons. There are enough information to make intelligent assertion that as far back as 1920s, Soviet Communist Russia has enlisted the best and brightest of their scientists in the development of killer viruses to be used as BW. Russian military strategists were using low-flying airplanes loaded with deadly microbes, spraying them around (Alibek, 1999).

IMPERIAL JAPAN AND WEAPONIZATION OF VIRUS

Japan has been involved in the development and use of BW for anti-human purposes. During World War II, Japan invaded the Chinese region of Manchuria. What made this invasion additionally horrific was that the Japanese military deployed death-causing bio agents on the population of the region. Japanese history of atrocities in China was immense. Their war atrocities continue to define the Chinese bitter enmity against Japan today. Chinese school teach their children the horrific Japanese terror in their land during World War II. These children are growing up to detest Japan as evil. The imperial Japanese military facility responsible for the dark mission in China was known as Water Purification Unit 731. Unit 731 was under the command of Lieutenant General Shiro Ishii. This facility was in full operation for a very long time. Japan was working with viral strands, such as anthrax, plague, cholera, dysentery and many other deadly agents. The Japanese military was dropping canisters infested with deadly bio agents, like plagues. We have to understand that before they deployed such agents, they must have engendered it to be even deadlier when in contact with human organism. When the Soviet Red Army invaded the regions occupied by Japan in China, they gained access to documents and materials implicating Japan for BW atrocities. When the Soviet Communist Leader, Stalin, was briefed as to Japan's use of BW in China, he ordered that Russia increase its germ weaponization exponentially. Japan was also implicated for flying low-airplane in the town of Chuhsien in Chekiang Province, South of Shanghai in China. They were spreading clouds of deadly viruses on the population. Sometimes in 1941, Japanese airplane flew over the city of Changteh in Hunan Province in China and sprayed what is now understood to be bubonic plagues on the population. There were reports of people having their lymph nodes swollen and they died from the contamination.

Japan was determined to weaponize every germ they could obtain. Japanese Army Medical Collage, Tokyo was running covert BW research in the later 1930s. The U.S. officials were concerned that the Japanese intelligence unit was sending secret agents to obtain yellow fever strand from Rockefeller Institute of Medical Research in New York (Croddy et al, 2002). In the 1990s, a renegade cult-like subversive group in Japan known as Aum Shinrikyo was in possession of BW which they were planning to use on the masses. This group was responsible for chemical attack on vulnerable innocent people inside a mass transport train in 1995. Possession of BW means, capacity as well as the intention to use especially in the hands of local or international terrorists groups should concern everyone.

THE UNITED STATES' BIOWEAPON PROGRAMS

In 1969, the U.S. president, Richard Nixon, made a speech in which he vaguely promised the world that the United States was abandoning its BW program. The U.S. demonstrated her commitment to Nixon's promise by reportedly destroying some of their BW stockpiles. However, people did not believe Nixon and the whole official narrative. Many around the world thought he was making false declaration and surreptitiously moving the offensive BW program even deeper underground. The Russian military bioweaponeer, Alibek (1999), expressed Russia's attitude regarding Nixon's statement. He stated that the Russian government did not believe Nixon in any shape or form. Russia believed that U.S. was being deceptive.

Evidence of the United States history of BW activities can be discerned from the U.S Senate Subcommittee on Health and Human Scientific Research of the Committee on Human Recourses hearing in 1977. It proved that the United States was not just researching and developing bioweapons but was carrying out germ testing on civilian population. The hearing also revealed that disease-causing microorganisms have been tested on densely populated civilian locations between 1949 and 1969. The named Senate hearing also linked mysterious outbreak of illnesses on civilian population in those areas of test. It has been reported that the United States Army was spraying Serratia Marcescens on the population in San Fransisco during the 1950s for tests. The United States' Project Jefferson and Project Clear during the 1990s were alleged to be involved in that which violated international BW convention. Whistleblower and independent researcher confirm that Fort Dietrick located in the state of Florida is one of the facilities that have engaged in secret BW activities. AIDS was said to have developed in this highly secretive military facility (Henderson, 2019). Henderson further reported that AIDS was developed as a means to depopulate the world of undesirable masses.

The U.S. Army Medical Research Institute on Infectious Diseases was alleged have history of BW programs that contravened international BW convention. Vigo Facility, Indiana, Pine

Bluff Arsenal, Arkansas, Dugway Proving Ground, Utah, all in the United States, have been identified as having engaged in germ activities for BW at one time or the other. The U.S has a Biological Defense Research Program. This program exists for a reason—preparedness for possible mass viral attacks. Mass attack by the enemy might not necessary be in time of war. Foreign enemy might use mass viral attacks to destabilize a population, slow down economy and create damaging stress on nation's resources.

The Regan administration in 1986 had a budget of 1 billion dollars for biological and chemical weapons research and development. Regan presidency was during the Cold War era. So it was easy for the U.S. government to earmark such a huge sum of money for viral and chemical bioweapon research by constantly feeding taxpayers official and media propaganda about Russia.

AIDS VIRUS AS A BW

According to a whistleblower, Cooper (1991), who served as a United States Naval intelligence officer, AIDS is a biological weapon. Cooper was shot and killed in an altercation with a law enforcement officer. Many believe he was assassinated because he exposed too much of the dark secrets of the U.S government as an insider military intelligence officer. There are no cases of AIDS virus prior to 1975. Research has linked the World Health Organization to an agent of infecting African population with AIDS. In 1977, the WHO started smallpox vaccination program in Africa. Copper linked the smallpox vaccination project of 1977 by WHO to the origin of AIDS in Africa. He stated that Africans were first injected with AIDS virus during this time. It has been estimated that 100 million Africans were injected with AIDS virus camouflaged as smallpox vaccine in 1977. According to Cooper, some population in the United States (gays) was also intentionally targeted and injected with the virus one year later in 1978 through government deceptive hepatitis B. vaccine program. The hepatitis B. vaccination in New York and with the gay population were how AIDS virus was introduced in the United States. This "vaccination' program by National Center for Disease Control was meant to remove the undesirable from the planet, in this case, 'useless Africans and homosexuals.' Cooper reechoed a few times that "whatever caused AIDS was in the vaccine" (Cooper, p168, 1998). This might explain why some distrust all vaccine agenda and programs, especially the so-called free mass vaccinations coming from the WHO. This organization is diabolical when one looks underneath the presumed global humanistic public face. The global Malthusian eugenicist usually uses this organization for evil intents. Currently, President Trump is proposing that the United States will not fund this organization further. Trump has gained deep insight into the WHO.

There are several other renowned scientists who reported that AIDS epidemic was man-made. Dr. Horowitz (1998) reported that AIDS virus was cultured as a BW and intentionally released on the masses. He also re-affirmed Cooper's report that among the initial victims of

AIDS virus during the late 1970s were black Africans and homosexuals. Certain population controllers see both the black masses and homosexuals as undesirables who ought to be reduced or eliminated. And yes, AIDS reduced African population drastically. There are too much convergence of propositions to ignore all these glaring pink elephants in the room. Eugenic genocidal maniacs are bent on depopulating the world based on Malthusian devilish principles and other fanatical ecological reasons. Certain elitist agenda, such as "green revolution," mask fanatical eugenics principles which include geo-engendering via genetic modification of every biological taxonomy on this planet. When government and world leaders talk about 'Depopulation Policy' as the dangerous Zionist and Malthusian eugenicist, Henry Kissinger—the former U.S Secretary of States - was fond of doing, all critical thinkers must understand the concept in its true nature, i.e., eugenic mass depopulation.

Molecular biologists as well as virologists who have studied the behaviour of AIDS virus believe that there is a strong behavioural similarity between AIDS and Bovine Lymphotrophic Virus (BLV). The 'official' reports around the world, including deceiver scientists from the WHO, claim that AIDS came from African green monkeys. However, independent scientists have long debunked this bogus claim and have continued to report that AIDS virus was laboratory-cultured. Dr. Robert Strecker, a U.S. distinguished, practitioner of internal medicine and gastroenterologist, pathologist and pharmacologist, was another whistleblower who reported that AIDS was an artificial and unnaturally engineered pathogen. He concluded through his medical research that AIDS was intentionally released on the population for nefarious reasons. In 1969, the United States Defense Department provided funding in the sum of $10 million for researchers to create a deadly strand of virus. The strand of virus was meant to target mostly black African population. Dr. Strecker expressed that there was research going on in T-Cell-destroyer virus in the early days. According to him, the success of this research led to the creation of a virus which destroys completely the immune system of a human organism. Dr.Strecker indicated that this was possible by the crossing of the viral strand such as Bovine leukemia virus and Visna viruses. He reported that Bovine predominantly attack cows. Visna is known to attack sheep. He stated that these two strands were then cultured in the herpes to get what undeniably turned out to be AIDS. Bovine leukemia virus does not naturally attack the human organism. That is why it has to be carefully cultured in a test tube before being released to infect people. In other words, it was weaponized. Dr. Strecker then debunked the claim that AIDS came from simian monkey. He alleged that it was the International Agency for Research on Cancer that was responsible for introducing AIDS to African population. IARC is an extension of World Health Organization and it came into existence in 1965. Dr. Leonard Horowitz was another person who reported that cancer causing AIDS-like viruses found in livestock was engineered to infect humans. In his book, *Emerging Viruses: AIDS and Ebola-Nature, Accident or Intentional*, he discussed some procedures scientists used to manufacture AIDS from combining strands of naturally occurring viruses in livestock.

IKECHUKWU ANTHONY KANU

RED ALERT: VIRAL ATTACKS AND BW SUSPICIONS

Anthrax: Anthrax is a single-celled bacterium originally known as Bacillus anthracis. This strain is found in livestock such as sheep and cattle. It forms spores which grow in lymph and blood. Anthrax has been called the 20th century BW. Many people have forgotten that in October 2001, in the wake of the attack on the World Trade Center in the United States, there was mass panic about anthrax used on American population as BW. It was reported that this virus was deployed through contaminated envelopes sent out to people, prominent media personalities. Following this attack on the population, President George W. Bush established the National Biodefense Analysis and Countermeasures Center which is overseen by the Department of Homeland Security.

According to ex-Soviet bioweaponeer, Ken Alibek (Alibek et al, 1999), a hundred kilograms of anthrax spores would, (intentionally released) in optimal atmospheric condition kill up to three million people in any of the densely populated metropolitan areas of the United States." He reported that a single SS-18 (laced with viral weapon) could wipe out the population of a city as large as New York. Anthrax as a bio-agent is considered an effective bioweaponary by world military elites. The deadly outbreak of Anthrax in the city of Sverdlovsk, Russia, in April and May 1978, was due to a release from massive stockpile of anthrax by the military (Cole, 1990). Anthrax virulent strain is difficult to obtain. If this is the case, it would take an extreme scientific knowledge to understand how to work with it and use it on the population. Scientists report that anthrax attack mimic cold flue. Victims exhibit slight nasal congestion, joint pain, lethargy, lingering cough and more. Due to the mild nature of initial symptomatology, it is often not taken serious. Thus, the virus would continue to metastasize in the lymph, node thereby ravaging the body's general immune system. The toxicity generated by the virus then overwhelms the internal human biomechanics completely with invasive acidic fluids and block the body's oxygenation mechanism. Anthrax virus induces difficulties in bronchial systems, breathing issues persists. The blockage of oxygenation system leads to victim's bluish/pale unnatural pigmentation, death is imminent.

Smallpox: Russian scientists worked on modification of smallpox to serve as biological agent for weapon. By 1947, Russia had already established a large capacity smallpox BW production facility. The World Health Organization, during the 1970s, claimed that smallpox disease has been eradicated globally. For Communist Russia, this declaration created a new opportunity. Now, since the world no longer paid attention to fighting smallpox, it was a moment to genetically modify the strand for weaponization. It is estimated that the Russian stockpile of smallpox viral strands was about twenty tons as way back as the 70s. Smallpox is known to be highly contagious. Motility rate could be as high as 90 percent. One of the wicked ways they were spreading this virus was grinding it into power and dusting it over letters for BW delivery (Alibek, 1999).

Ebola: Ebola River in Zaire, modern-day Democratic Republic of Congo, continues to be associated with the name of a deadly virus. It has been claimed that Ebola (disease) originated in this region of Africa. Ebola is a hemorrhagic fever-causing agent. Some believe that Ebola is an offshoot of Marburg. Marburg virus surfaced in Germany so many years back. This begs the question, did scientists isolate Marburg in the laboratory and genetically modified it as the strand known as Ebola which was to be found in Zaire in years to come? Why Congo? Well, Congo is one of the world's most heavily blessed natural resources country on the planet. This country has been ravaged by internationally sponsored conflicts. Congo conflict is prolonged for the resource theft by international resource thieves. Even in the midst of conflict, local impoverished guerilla factions arms-funded by international cooperate criminals continue to supply resources to these foreign corporate overlords who fly helicopters and small airplanes into the Congo jungles to steal.

The outbreak of Ebola in Congo is very suspicious for one reason. Both Ebola virus and Marburg virus (found in Germany way back), when observed under electron microscope, share similar behavioural characteristics. They multiply by shooting out some monofilaments. According to Alibek (1999), Ebola and Marburg belong to the same family of viral agents named filoviruses. Filoviruses attack host cell by enveloping them with net-like strands. The appearance of Ebola in Africa is very suspicious. Could it be the military and international elite controllers tested Ebola on Africans? Could it be a way to continue to keep this resource-blessed people down forever? This needs to be investigated further.

BIOTERRORISM AND MEDIA MASS TRAUMATIZATION

Dr. Horowitz (2001) describes an aspect of bioterrorism as when the elite controllers frighten the masses into accepting every official recommendation which might include vaccine experimental trials, using people as test-tube guinea pig, etc. He further cites a case example where people have been sprayed with Malathion and Anvil as a "precautionary measures" against anthrax. He states that Malathion and Anvil, in themselves, are bad agents for humans. They are immune system suppressant, carcinogenic (cancer causing agent) and lethal for human organism to absorb. It was probably a test but people were deceived that they needed to take the vaccine for protection against anthrax. The masses are usually vulnerable and suggestible to the whims and caprices of the powers that be (PTB). Poisoning the masses using chemical and biological means for political, economic, military and medical reasons is not new. In ancient Rome, chemical agents (lead) were added into the public water systems. Lead is scientifically established to be a deadly neuro-suppressant and could lead to serious cognitive degeneration. If public water systems are contaminated with lead, it could lead to mass mental passivity, Alzheimer's disease, memory loss and so many other neuro-degenerative problems. Were ancient Roman elite trying to create a passive population so dumbed down through water-system 'vaccination' and who were unable to think for themselves and put up any resistance to the oppressive systems? In fact, many scholars believe that this was the case. Many think that the fall of Rome, among many other factors, is attributed to weakened neuronal systems as a result of mass lead poisoning. The elite were also affected. We see some of the most psychopathic Roman emperors emerging—pedophiles, incest, sadistic murders, including of family member, and any evil you can name. A neuro-psychological assessment of some of these Romans shows a serious mental health issues. Could it be lead poisoning causing these cognitive degenerative behaviours? Medical tests of archeological artifacts prove clue that Romans had mass lead poisoning. In modern society, it is a known fact that public water systems are treated with fluoride. Fluoride is a neuro-cognitive depressant as well. Toothpastes are also fluorinated. The argument of demented scientists is that fluorinated water helps with healthier teeth. But one should examine this argument, since there is clear evidence of cognitive degeneration through contamination with fluoride. That is, it could be a way of creating a mass of people with sedated neuronal and nervous systems. It is not completely irrational to think that mass public water is vaccinated with fluoride for cognitive mass repression. So, one does not even need to get a vaccine, since city water is already vaccinated secretly. Scholars are also linking GMO with their high level of pesticide, herbicide to future bio-genetic degeneration of humanity. This is a new form of homo-reengineering.

Many people seem excited with eating seedless fruits and not having to do the "hard work" of spitting out seeds. But seedless seeds bio-engineered mutant variant. They are called genetically modified organism (GMO) and are unnatural because the original divine genetic blueprint has been altered. Genetically modified food and meat appear to be a subliminal BW system to alter the original humans through gradual scientific molecular mutations? This is what the company called Monsanto does, modifying all living organism on the planet away from their divine origin. Monsanto now has patents on virtually all agricultural seeds on this earth and few people understood this. Bill Gates has millions of dollar worth of financial investment stake in Monsanto. Bill Gates is also part of the ownership of Alliance for a Green Revolution in Africa (AGRA). The term "green revolution" is a Malthusian fanatical eugenic global movement. The agenda have been pushed to Africa since the 80s and beyond. Gates is promoting terminator GMO seeds in Africa, seeds you can only plant once and when you have harvest them you can't plant them again because they were engineered to be sterile and impotent. You can harvest good yield, yes, but they are infertile to grow for your next planting season. So what do you do? You have to go back to these agro-based Malthusian corporatocrats to buy more seed every year. Famers around the world will be subjected to such global control. And world food supply will be in the hands of few wicked overloads. These elite-owned agro-bio-tech companies already have obtained patents on many seeds. So in the future it would be illegal for you to own their patented seed. The global agro beast called Monsanto and other emerging agro-biopharmaceutical companies are in the game of geo-engendering and tera-formation of all biosphere as we know it. This agenda of subliminal human genetic mutation is designed on a long term to change the original genetic code of man through food and other bio-synthetic toxicities.

The powers that be (PTB) can terrorize the population not just with actual BW but with virus-scare. Media manipulation through highly effective visual cinematographic mind control could induce mass panic. The public's visual and auditory apparatuses are constantly under media assault with hyped up apocalyptic-type viral invasion and induced food shortage. They heighten death statistics, parade few cases seriously night and day on the media. This is how you get the population to do whatever you prescribe. It is called Hegelian dialectics, action-reaction-solution. Various intelligences in the developed world are involved in media mind programming. The American CIA, the Russian KGB, the Israeli Mossad, the British M-16, etc., all have agents in popular media outlets. CIA's Operation Mockingbird is known for media psyop (psychological operation) program for mass mind control. The pretty face Anderson Cooper, while at school, interned for CIA's Operation Mockingbird. Many popular media casters are implanted there for mass behavioural social engineering. Many people do not do research. For these groups of people, nothing is true until it is reported in popular international media outlets, like CNN, AL Jazeera, etc. This sort of people stand to be manipulated, irrespective of their educational background. It does not matter if they have three PhDs.

GAME OF DEATH: HOW THE GLOBAL POWER SYSTEMS USE MASS DEATH TO ACHIEVE GOALS

Oppressive systems - social, political, economic, religious, familial, etc., - are like a self-sustaining parasitic organism in a closed system. For an oppressive system to evade its eventual cause of entropic decay, it must seek to expand its deceptions in order to continue to feed off on the people it oppresses. In so doing, the small privileged elite, in closed-system circuit, will continue their act of vampirism. Evil systems have perpetuated itself in power using every bio-chemical-military-neuro-linguistic-religoius-mind-controlling tools to keep itself in position of power and control. The Roman Emperor Nero (A.D. 37-68) would not have cared about setting Rome on fire for political agenda. He would not have cared about killing hundreds of his own people to stay in power if he needed to. Similarly, Emperor Gaius Caesar of Rome ruled from 37 A.D to 41 A.D. He is popularly known as Emperor Caligula. He used his debauchery, diabolism and perverted politicalcrafts to perpetuate himself in power. It would be irrational to think that if he had access to modern BW, he would hesitate to use it.

In our modern global politico-military and economic game of chess, the world elite have used any means possible, no matter how evil, to assert their dominance, not minding the consequence such as mass death. For example, the global financial elite have financed and used murderous instincts of the Islamic extremists for their geo-political control. One would be shocked to learn that both the ISIS terrorist organization as well as the Jabat Al-Nusra have been funded and utilized by certain Western power elite for geo-political control (Henderson, 2019). Russia's Center for Reconciliation in Syria and their intelligence gathered information implicating the Anglo-Western powers for secretly funding Jabat Al-Nusra terrorists in Syria.

Henderson (2019) reveals that clandestine Western elite provided Jabat Al-Nusra with chemical weapons in Syria's village of Serakab. This group provoked the chemical attacks which is now blamed on Syria's Bashar Al-Assad. The goal was to remove Syria Al-Assad from power. Once the masses hear (through CIA-controlled media agents) that Al-Assad used chemical weapon, everyone will turn against him and it becomes easy for PTB to get rid of him. What is reported on the news is not what is going on underground. And few people understood this global power games. In 2018, the only few countries whose central banks were not under the control of Anglo-American financial banking elite were Syria, Iran, Cuba and North Korea. Every central bank in the world is under the absolute control of Anglo-American Western power system. And anyone who wants to change this dynamic will be ready to die. Any country that wants to change it will be ready to be destroyed in few months. This is how things are and how things work. A critical look indicates that these named countries(Syria, Cuba, Iran, North Korea) are not in the good books of the Western PTB that are ready and willing to use their military puppets' knowledge of biological, chemical and conventional means to create new global paradigm shift and to subjugate all countries on the planet under their financial and military control. Gaddafi of Libya tried to create a different financial arrangement independent of the clandestine Anglo-American central bank control. They got rid of him immediately. In the process of killing Gaddafi, many people died and the country was destroyed. Do you think the covert global system of PTB care about humans dying? So, those who argue against the possibility of PTB using viruses to achieve certain agenda, locally, nationally and globally, need to reconsider their knowledge of the human power games. Perhaps, it is time for them to turn off too much watching of television which is another name for mind control.

BLACK MARKET AND VIRUSES

Military and civilian scientists go around the world secretly obtaining bacteria that are natural occurring in certain geographical areas. They then return to their clandestine laboratories and try to genetically engender them to specifically attack humans. The strand known as Machupio which causes Bolivian hemorrhage fever was smuggled by Russian agents from the United States for specific customization as weapon during the Cold War. Russia also may have obtained more strands of Marburg from Germany. Marburg virus is in the Ebola family. Inhaling as little as three microscopic particles of Marburg constitutes a terminal biohazard that leads to death (Alibek, 1999).

A U.S. congressional inquiry during the 80s found that batches of deadly BW agents were mysteriously missing from laboratories. One would make an intelligent guess; these batches probably were exchanged in black markets. They might have ended up in the hands of big corporate pharmacological establishments, other governments, or nefarious secret societies and elite researchers, including terrorists. The congressional inquiring body cited huge loopholes and safety concerns.

Recently, the U.S. Department of Justice arrested Dr. Charles Lieber. Dr. Lieber is the chair of the Chemistry and Chemical Biology Department at Harvard University. He was charged for lying to the U.S. government about details of his involvement with China. He was made a "Strategic Scientist" at Wuhan University of Technology (WUT), China. All businesses and institutions in China are rigidly under the Chinese communist state. Companies can be taken over at any time by the state at will if it serves states specific agenda. WUT (definitely under communist direction) was paying Dr. Lieber large sums of money for his nanoscience research. China is involved in global scientific and economic espionage. No doubt, they were utilizing Dr. Lieber to gain certain information of nanoscience, perhaps for bio engineering. The U.S government wanted to know all details. Also, two Chinese researchers, Yanqing Ye, 29 and Zaosong Zheng, 30, were also charged separately. Zaosong was accused of attempting to smuggle 21 vials of bio agents from the U.S to China. The bottom line is that China has so many highly disciplined communist agents around the world who are highly committed to their communist BW development agenda. They are everywhere in the world stealing bacteria for modification and weaponization. International underground germs market is a fact.

THE DARK CONNECTION OF SOME RESEARCH INSTITUTES AND PHARMACEUTICAL COMPANIES

The U.S. National Cancer Institute (NCI), University of Texas, University of Chicago, University of Virginia, the University of California, The University of New York, Yale University, to name but a few, have history of receiving funding from the government for the wily research project of BW. Research institutions are supposed to be independent and not controlled by the government. The government will always control, dictate and direct any research institution that is so eager to go for the money. The saying goes, he who pays the piper dictates the tune. Thus, institutions of learning and research centers so eager to get cash and be in the good books of the government usually become puppets of nefarious politicians and government secret agenda. Some of these agenda are dark and anti-human. One character whose name appears to be linked to the above-named government-backed clandestine university BW researches is Dr. Robert C. Gallo. Dr. Gallo's research at one time was funded by the National Institute of Cancer. While some of this research fundings appear innocent from a quick glance, usually government intelligence units use these individuals for evil agenda. Why Gallo is important in this article is because he has been linked by many independent sources to the creation of AIDS virus as a BW. Gallo is linked with the U.S. top military medical research facility at Fort Detrick, in Florida. This is the facility where AIDS was said to have originated from. Horowitz (1998) indicates that Gallo's research publication "detailed the steps involved in creating human-immune-system-destroying viruses…." Dr. Horowitz then concludes that Gallo spent decades of research creating and perfecting "AIDS-like" viruses.

The company, Litton Research Laboratories, which is a subsidiary of Litton Industries Inc., U.S.A, has a dark history with BW development, according to Horowitz. This company is a top American military contractor and has received millions of dollars from the government to engage in BW projects. Dr. Gallo, again, has an established history with this devious company which ought to be charged with genocidal actions against Africa via viruses.

The Former, U.S. Secretary of States, Henry Kissinger, as well as the U.S. Department of Health, Education and Welfare's Frank Carlucci and Joseph Califono, have also been implicated as culprits to introducing immune system destroyer in Africa as a form of BW. One of the political reasons for the introduction of AIDS in Africa was to subdue the alleged radical "communist" tendencies of the African Nationalists who "threaten" global democracy of the West. We should not forget that CIA was central in destroying Kwame Nkrumah's vision for Africa. Africa spent many decades and resources in the fight against AIDS epidemics which led to the total destruction and collapse of the spirit of Pan African nationalism that was in emergence in the 1960s and 1970s. (Umpenhour, 2005). The image of Africa around the world became associated with disease and poverty. Thus, a continent ravaged by disease does not have the strength to push the agenda of Pan Africanism and the spirit of national rebirth. This is a classic CIA long-term operation and it was effective. The spirit of African nationalism and liberation fizzled away. And colonization went underground. This time around, BW was one of the many tools.

The International Union Against Cancer (IUAC), under the WHO, in the 60s and 70s, became so obsessed with Africa in their research focus. This organization claimed to promote campaign against cancer. However, researching about this organization may prove that its name is an inversion of truth. This company has been reported as being the actual conduit through which AIDS was brought to Africa.

There seems to be a symbiotic relationship between certain big money pharmaceutical companies and some of the dark military BW programs. To understand the established power system in control, one must understand that the top secretive elite see themselves as family. They protect themselves in a network of financial, social, political and military brotherhood. In the United States, the Rockefellers own one third of the entire pharmaceutical industries which continue to push for mass vaccinations bringing billions of dollars to this economic empire (Henderson, 2019). The same people, through political lobbying, have been able to demonize homeostatic natural herbs. In some places, if you sell herbs, you go to jail. Pharmaceutical companies tell people that herbs are bad but allopathic synthetic chemicals are good. This is a typical inversion of reality by sheer use of legal force, and one of the ways people are being controlled.

The bio-pharmaceutical company known as Merck, Sharp & Dohme (popularly known as Merck) has suspicious BW history of research and development as well. The company's current website describes their vision statement thus: "To make a difference in the lives of people globally through our innovative medicines, vaccines, and animal health products. We are committed to being the premier, research-intensive biopharmaceutical company and are dedicated to providing leading innovations and solutions for today and the future."

A UK journalist, Miles Johnston, in an interview, has linked Bill Gates' funded Pirbright Institute, based in U.K, to current Covid-19 outbreak. Mr. Gates also has a foundation which he uses to promote mass vaccinations, especially for developing societies like Africa and India. Gates' vaccines program is accused of spreading sterilization for population control. The U.S government has official program for population control. Two outstanding evidence that cannot be ignored. The U.S. House Bill 5090 authorized the funding for Project MK-Naomi. There is no doubt that MK-NAOMI is a Malthusian depopulation project aimed at eliminating the undesirable poor people around the world. The U.S. also created The Office of Population Affairs. A deeper research into the activities of this office implicates global depopulation agenda. There is an elite political group in the U.S. which met in 1961 and created the famous Report from Iron Mountain. This report espoused ways to eliminate certain population, especially using wars - another case of Darwinian-fittest philosophy which was even implemented by Nazi Germany. Bill Gates is known for financing the Wuhan Institute of Virology which is also linked with the Covid-19 outbreak. Gates' seemingly global altruism might be covering up some darker Malthusian eugenic program. Malthusian population control fanatics like Paul Ehrlich, in his book, *The Population Bomb,* outlines global template for depopulation of the world.

New viruses will continue to emerge. In the past, the U.S. as well as Soviet Russian militaries tested viruses using low-flying airplanes for spraying. When viral outbreaks occur, government will likely start pushing and forcing vaccines on the masses. Governments have engaged in extreme draconian non-pharmaceutical biodefense measures such as martial-law-type response to these viral outbreaks. That is, restriction of freedoms, creation and enforcement of self-isolation, restriction of human contacts, travel bans, etc. Forced vaccination has always taken place around the world. A careful examination of molecular compositions of some of these vaccines by independent scientists reveals bigger concerns. A character named Dr. Maurice Hilleman has a history of research with Merck, Sharp & Dohme (cited above). He is credited for developing about 40 vaccines for this reticent company. He once confessed that vaccines injected to people were contaminated with cancer viruses as well as Leukemia viruses (Icke, 2013). We are all aware of how the rate of cancer is exploding exponentially around the world. There has also been connections made between vaccine and autism in children. However, mainstream scientists and academics, who are usually lackeys to mainstream power system, usually deny such reports. Research has also shown that some vaccines contain noxious agents such as mercury (deadly for humans), aluminum, Octoxinol 9 (sperm-killing agent), aborted fetal materials, insect and dog genes, Betapropiolactone (corrosive chemical found in disinfectant), Phenol (carbonic acid which could trigger dermatitis condition), Triton x-100 (detergent) ethylene glycol (antifreeze), etc., (Icke, 2005). Big Biotech companies are interested in big money. The masses become the experimental guinea pig and the sheep to fleece.

BACTERIOLOGICAL WARFARE PROHIBITIONS

Geneva Protocols of 1925. The protocol prohibits the use of BWs. The U.S. and Soviet Russia were signatories. But the U.S. did not ratify the Geneva Protocol until years later in 1975. I would make a rational assumption here. The U.S. congress utilized delay tactics in ratifying this prohibition. There is substantial evidence that the U.S was developing and stockpiling BW until the 70s, in view of The Cold War. By the time congress completed ratification, they had amassed as much BW as they needed. Geneva Protocol on a face value prohibits the use of bacteriological agents in warfare. However, the weakness and hypocrisy of this prohibition is clean; it did not prohibit possession. What a façade!

Biological Weapon's Convention of 1972. This convention prohibits the development, production and stockpiling of BW, except for prophylactic and military defense purposes. By 1996, close to 140 countries were signatories. One could already notice the hypocrisy and deception of this convention. Obviously, it is all talk-and-no-do. It was meant to pacify the masses who were starting to be worried about the apocalyptic nature of biochemical weapons. In fact, the convention clearly gave the military and as well as the pharmacological companies absolute freehand. Where there is profit, there is greed; where there is greed, evil is possible. Corporate conglomerates might decide to develop strands of viruses to experiment, in the name of research, on the people, since the Biological Weapon's Convention did not expressly forbid it. The military could claim defense purposes as well and continue to develop deadly viruses capable of depopulating any given society drastically.

THE MORAL AMBIVALENCE OF BIOWEAPON (BW) SKEPTICS

The great moral conundrum in germ research involves the "dual-use-dilemmas." The ethical ambivalence is between biodefense and bio-attack. Biodefense is the same as biosecurity. Biosecurity implies engaging in germ sciences as a means of protecting the population against disease outbreaks. Bio-defense also argues that it is ethical, especially for governments, to engage in germs research programs as "acts to defend a state's population against future biological attack" (Enemark, 2017). Proponents of this stand indicate that a clear scientific understanding of pathogenic organisms provides enormous protective benefits. That is, it saves lives. Critics, on the other hand, point out inherent risks and weaknesses of this argument. They contend that there is the possibility of using such knowledge for evil intention, such as the creation, proliferation and use of BW against a population, especially on an international scale. Both arguments are valid. However, my focus in this article is the fact that BW have been proliferated and used around the world at different times and continues to be used against vulnerable populations. Laboratory insiders in biosecurity programs have been reported as breaching all ethical codes, smuggling and marketing deadly strands in the black markets.

There are those who think that BW concerns or alarms are a product of "conspiracy theory." For instance, a high ranking U.S. Army Medical Corps, Major Leon A. Fox, during the early 1930s, published an article in the *Army Surgeon* journal in which he set out to debunk the possibility of BW use. His stand was that BW concerns came from conspiratorial "scare-heads" and "pseudo-scientists" who were seeking ephemeral mass media attentions. He unequivocally stated that deploying, successfully, death-causing bio agents was a practical impossibility. His argument was that noxious bacteriological organism could not linger on open surface for long due to exposure to heat and other harsh factors. Thus, they could not be successful as a mass weapon. Obviously, this argument defies common sense. It undermines the ability of genetic engineering in virological sciences to modify strands and make them mutable for evolutionary adaptations. One wonders if this sort of official denial was a covert psychological operation for mass distraction. Despite official lies, it soon became crystal clear that BWs were not only possible as a means of mass attack but were, actually, being used especially during World War II. The Cold War efforts no doubt created lots of anti-human scientists in the industrialized high-tech "first world" societies. These military-controlled scientists have been implicated in the nefarious research and development in virological sciences. The purpose of the development is for mass death, population control as well as behaviour modifications. This is not hard to conclude for those who do research BW.

Some people do not want to imagine or accept that viruses can be cultured in laboratories to be used as BW. This sort of lackadaisical attitude vindicates the famous existentialist observation of Albert Camus that man is a creature who spends his whole life trying to convince himself that his existence is not full of absurdities. As far-fetched as this idea of BW research and deployment may sound, there are some evidences to substantiate such claims. During the 19th century, there were indications of underground proliferation of BW research laboratories and projects aiming assiduously to develop strands of viruses that could destroy the human immune system and terminate the entire human organism. Governments funded some of these evil researches. While these clandestine BW research activities were being carried out, there were whistleblowers who continued, like foresighted prophets, to sound warning alarms to humanity about accidental and intentional releases of these lethal viruses on the masses. When such alarms were raised, "official" medical reports from government representatives continued, as they still do, to hide these atrocities with their skillful scientific sophistry aimed at neutralizing and subverting all clues to malevolent scientific programs. Mainstream elite medical authorities, as well as so called academia, often serve as lackeys to the powers that be (PTD). In cases of viral onslaught on the masses, these officials usually invent shambolic cock-and-bull 'scientific' explanations as to the origin of some deadly viruses that have ravaged humanity at different times. For instance, African monkeys have been accused of so many responsibilities for viruses. This is laughable, especially knowing that the despicable World Health Organization and their mind-controlled scientists often peddle these lies that are even found in textbooks.

If man is capable of evil at all, it would be naïve and irresponsible to exempt him from the capacity to develop and deploy bioweapon (BW). Man's scientific advancement in biotechnology offers him a rapid paradigmatic thrust into a new era of BW possibilities. Guillemin (1999) lamented thus: "should the deliberate infliction of disease and other hostile application of biotechnology come into widespread use, the nature of war and the future course of civilization itself could be disastrously altered." Guillemin was speaking hypothetically. Although he was making a valid point, he appeared to be ignoring the real world in his probability statement. The fact is that military elite are, in fact, engaged in clandestine operations of research, development and testing of BW on the people. Declassified documents provide some evidence that between 1949 and 1970, virological warfare program was in constant progress by the U.S. government. Not only that these germ weaponization was going on, they were being tested on the people. Leonard (1988) explained that the U.S. military has a history of testing new BW on the U.S. population. My point is this: If they can test it on their own citizen, what makes one believe they cannot test it on other populations around the world with weak government and defense systems? Leonard further cited some evidence of the U.S. Navy spraying the people with microbial agents as "testing." This kind of dark bio-experimentation is not new as far as the United States government is concerned. The U.S. has a long dark history of medical experimentation on vulnerable population. There was the Tuskegee Syphilis Experiment where the United States government researchers carried out atrocious Nazi-style controlled experimentation on black people from 1932 until about 1972. Government's Public Health Services intentionally left these "Negros" untreated for syphilis, while deceptively providing them with placebo medical cares. At that time, ordinary penicillin could have cured those blacks inflicted with syphilis. But the government wanted to study the behaviour of syphilis on infected people and in this case vulnerable and poor black sharecroppers. It is also a well-documented history that between 1837 and 1838, the imperial European expansionists and colonialists in the Americas were intentionally giving the native people they met in the land blankets laced with chickenpox as a form of BW to exterminate the people.

Today, we live in a time of bio-nano-genetic sciences. These highly advanced sciences have made possible the engineering of molecular/atomic destructive machines, both biological and synthetic. Sometime ago, I read Michael Crichto's book **Prey**. Even though written in a sci-fi style, he depicted a vision of the future that is already possible, the futuristic technology which many whistleblower reports military elite already possess, that is, man-made nano particles (nano dusts) that are self-aware and self-preserving. These sentient molecular agents got released from secret military laboratory and ended up posing the greatest death threat man has ever known. The point is that molecular engineering is now possible and viral agents are being engineered every day in underground laboratories around the world. Unfortunately, part of these futuristic sciences deals with development of invisible bio-synthetic soldiers that could attack and kill people.

In their book, *The Soviet Biological Weapons Program: A History*, Milton Leitenberg and his colleagues observe that the reason the concept of BW awakens such dismissive cynicism in those who seek to "debunk" the fact is because "... the idea that someone can and is willing to apply science and medicine in order to manipulate and grow microorganism for the purpose of deliberately brining about illness and death contravenes so much of our societies ethnics that is beyond the pale of civilized behavior" (Leitenberg et al, 2012). Echoing the same line of thinking, Leonard (1988) wrote that one of the reasons BW is seen as abhorrent is because they infringe on the essential moral values among civilized people and "contradicts human sensibility." This might be why those who deny the possibility of BW deployment and use tend to dangle between ethical ambivalences. One the one hand, they count on the good nature of man, and on the other hand, they understood man's possibility to initiate endless plethora of evil on his own kind. In a perfect world, man is supposed to be good and do the right thing of fighting bad germs and saving lives, and not use germs to cause death. Unfortunately, this is an imperfect world and man is in a "fallen state." Cognitively, the relationship between 'ought to' and what actually obtains is like the metaphysical relationship between appearance and reality. Those who take reality as given and feed on what they are being told by the government and their official media outlets will fall into abysmal epistemological error.

The threat of biological warfare is to be taken serious. I would conjecture, at least, that any coherent mind would do so. This planetary biosphere is in danger if we ignore the truth about man's virological weapons capacities. The degenerate instincts of man to deploy such cannot be undermined. Critics who deny the possibility of modern man weaponzing viruses for mass death often cite plethora of epidemics throughout history. Deniers seem to reassure themselves of their stance through constant re-echoing of the noisy notion that disease has always been here with us and had always plagued mankind. However, the difference between our time and primitive times is molecular atomic sciences and genetic engineering. These sciences have enabled man to understand the invisible universe around of germs and viruses. Do we actually believe that if 'mad scientists' could build nuclear weapons that could end life on earth that they cannot develop and use viral strands to kill? This is a monologue that calls for reflection.

CONCLUSION

My intention in this article has been to point out that anti-human scientific proclivities abound and man has, in fact, intentionally engineered viruses in laboratory as BW. The military industrial complexes around the world have been implicated multiple times in BW research and development projects. Whistleblowers who sound alarms on these covert scientific atrocities often face hard times in the hands of the almighty draconian government officials as well as from mainstream established intellectuals. Mass media psychological operations are often a good tool used to centralize information by the powers that be (PTB). Once information system is centralized and forced into the psyche of the general population, independent researchers and counter-voices are seen and categorized as crazy conspiracy theorists. The nefarious projects of viral engineering have only one goal - creation of mass death-agents. Mad scientists splice, mutate, modify and strengthen various harmful bio-synthetic microbial strands found in nature to be used as invisible super soldiers, BWs. Any reasonable person ought to ask, 'how come people, corporations and governments owe patents to viruses?' Doesn't this imply that people created or modified these pathogenic plagues; hence, they can lay claim to ownership? I have no doubt that there are people whose sole intentions are to subjugate all categories of taxonomy under their control as a means of power and wealth. The history of military techno-scientific offensive/defensive research and development power is incomplete without a reflection on viral BW. Corporate pharmaco-epidemiological profit drives have also been implicated for many strands of viruses that attack humans.

Nazi-style anti-human research and development is in progress in our world today and we must not sleep to that fact! If we do, our entire planetary biosphere will be subjugated under taxonomic apocalypse as well as consent viral terrorizations. There are 'mad scientist', surrogated by powerful military elite and governments who are immoral. There are large pharmaco-conglomerates backed by big money as well as arcane political force who would not hesitate to use BW on the population to achieve their agenda.

Scientific and military Machiavellianism is a reality. Machiavelli's Prince is a conscienceless immoral entity. The mad scientist like Machavelli's Prince has perfected a system of scientific authoritarianism. The mad scientist idolizes himself as "homo deus," the god man. This nomenclatural title is an inversion of his true nature. His anti-human-anti-nature consciousness best fits with the title 'homo diablos,' the human devil. The 'mad scientist' has corrupted true science. He coerces humanity to bow to his religion of scientism. He is an empirical fanatic. For him, empiricism is the only conduit wherein reality is studied, understood and improved. His acclaimed empirical objectivity hides a narrow materialistic relativism. He presents his scientism as a base for a new universal paradigm. Since his scientism is seen through the relativistic lens of empirical materialism, he is an atheist. His appetite for terror, death and destruction is insatiable.

REFERENCES

Christine Enemark, *Biosecurity Dilemmas: Dreaded Diseases, Ethical Responses, and the Health of Nations*, Georgetown University Press, Washington Dc, 2017.

Cole, Leonard, *Clouds of Secrecy: The Army's Germ Warfare Tests over Populated Areas*, Rawman & Littlefield Publishes Inc., 1988.

David Icke, *The Perception Deception*, David Icke Book Ltd, Isle of Wight, UK, 2005.

Dean Henderson, *Nephilim Crown, 5G Apocalypse,* USA, 2019.

Ed Regis, *The Biology of Doom: America's Secret Germ Warfare Project,* Henry Holt & Company, LLC, 1999.

Eric Croddy, Clarisa Perez-Armendariz, John Hart, *Chemical and Biological Warfare: A Comprehensive Survey for the Concerned Citizen*, Springe Science and Business Media, LLC, NY, 2002.

Gregory Koblentz: *Living Weapons: Biological Warfare and International Security*, Cornell University, NY, USA, 2009.

Jeanne Guillemin, *Anthrax: The Investigation of a Deadly Outbreak*, University of California Press Ltd, 1999.

Jeanne Guillemin: *Biological Weapons: From the Invention of State-Sponsored Programs to Contemporary Bioterrorism*, Colombia University Press, 2005.

Kanu, I. A. *Igwebuike* as an Igbo-African philosophy for the protection of the environment. *Nightingale International Journal of Humanities and Social Sciences*. Vol. 3. No. 4. pp. 28-38. 2017

Kanu, I. A. *Igwebuike* as the consummate foundation of African Bioethical principles. *An African journal of Arts and Humanities* Vol.2 No1 June, pp.23-40. 2016

Kanu, I. A. *Igwebuike* as the hermeneutic of individuality and communality in African ontology. *NAJOP: Nasara Journal of Philosophy*. Vol. 2. No. 1. pp. 162-179. 2017

Kanu, I. A. *Igwebuike* philosophy and human rights violation in Africa. *IGWEBUIKE: An African Journal of Arts and Humanities*. Vol. 3. No. 7. pp. 117-136. 2017

Kanu, I. A. Igbo-African Gods and Goddesses. *Nnadiebube Journal of Philosophy*. Vol. 2. No. 2. pp. 118-146. 2018

Kanu, I. A. *Igwe Bu Ike* as an Igbo-African hermeneutics of national development. *Igbo Studies Review*. No. 6. pp. 59-83. 2018

Kanu, I. A. *Igwebuike* and question of superiority in the scientific community of knowledge. *Igwebuike: An African Journal of Arts and Humanities*.Vol.3 No1. pp. 131-138. 2017

Kanu, I. A. *Igwebuike* and the logic (Nka) of African philosophy. *Igwebuike: An African Journal of Arts and Humanities*. 3. 1. pp. 1-13. 2017

Kanu, I. A. *Igwebuike* as a complementary approach to the issue of girl-child education. *Nightingale International Journal of Contemporary Education and Research*. Vol. 3. No. 6. pp. 11-17. 2017

Kanu, I. A. *Igwebuike* as a hermeneutic of personal autonomy in African ontology. *Journal of African Traditional Religion and Philosophy Scholars. Vol. 2. No. 1. pp. 14-22.* 2017

Kanu, I. A. African philosophy, globalization and the priority of 'otherness'. *Journal of African Studies and Sustainable Development.* Vol. 1. No. 1. pp. 40-57. 2018

Kanu, I. A. African traditional folktales as an integrated classroom. *Sub-Saharan African Journal of Contemporary Education Research.* Vol.3 No. 6. pp. 107-118. 2016

Kanu, I. A. *African traditional philosophy of education: Essays in Igwebuike philosophy.* Germany: Lambert Publications. 2018

Kanu, I. A. *Igwebuike as a philosophical attribute of Africa in portraying the image of life.* A paper presented at the 2017 Oracle of Wisdom International Conference by the Department of Philosophy, Tansian University, Umunya, Anambra State, 27-29 April. 2017

Kanu, I. A. *Igwebuike* as a wholistic response to the problem of evil and human suffering. *Igwebuike: An African Journal of Arts and Humanities.* Vol. 3 No 2, March. 2017

Kanu, I. A. *Igwebuike* as an African integrative and progressive anthropology. *NAJOP: Nasara Journal of Philosophy.* Vol. 2. No. 1. pp. 151-161. 2018

Kanu, I. A. *Igwebuike* as an expressive modality of being in African ontology. *Journal of Environmental and Construction Management.* 6. 3. pp.12-21. 2016

Kanu, I. A. *Igwebuike* as an Igbo-African hermeneutics of globalisation. *IGWEBUIKE: An African Journal of Arts and Humanities,* Vol. 2 No.1. pp. 61-66. 2016

Kanu, I. A. *Igwebuike* as an Igbo-African modality of peace and conflict resolution. *Journal of African Traditional Religion and Philosophy Scholars.* Vol. 1. No. 1. pp. 31-40. 2017

Kanu, I. A. *Igwebuike* as an Igbo-African philosophy for Christian-Muslim relations in Northern Nigeria. In Mahmoud Misaeli (Ed.). *Spirituality and Global Ethics* (pp. 300-310). United Kingdom: Cambridge Scholars. 2017

Ken Alibek with Stephen Handelman, *Biohazard:* The Chilling True Story of the Largest Covert Biological Weapon in the World—Told from Inside by the Man who Ran it, Random House, Ny,2002

Milton Taylor, *Viruses and Man: A History of Interactions,* Springer International Publishing, Switzerland, 2014

Paula Tennant, Gustavo Fermn, Jerome Foster, *Viruses: Molecular Biology. Host Interactions and Application of Biotechnology*, Elsevier Inc., 2018.

Remler Pat, *Egyptian Mythology A to Z*, Chelsea House Publishing, New York, 2010.

Stephanie Dalley, *Myths from Mesopotamia: Creation, the Flood, Gilgamesh, and Others*, New York: Oxford University Press, 1989.

Susan Payne, Viruses: *From Understanding to Investigation,* Elsevier Inc., London, UK, 2017.

William Cooper, *Behold A Pale White,* Light House Publishing, Flagstaff, AR, 1991

IN SEARCH FOR NATIVE COMMUNICATION: IGWEBUIKE AND SHIKROT PHILOSOPHICAL RENDERINGS

Justine John Dyikuk
University of Jos, Plateau State
justinejohndyikuk@gmail.com

EXECUTIVE SUMMARY

The ancients developed their modes of communication which helped them to relate with one another and communicate with the divine. These forms of communication also distinguished them from others while providing meaning about life and the eternal destiny of man. Unfortunately, the arrival of the colonialists and the advent of the Internet with its razzmatazz of new media expressions showed an exit door to native media. This qualitative study, "In Search for Native Communication: Igwebuike and Shikrot Philosophical Renderings" investigated the matter with the help of Native Theory of Communication theoretical framework. While dissemination of information, public relations and entertainment were found as native forms of communication in Igbo philosophy, it was discovered that being persuasive, active listening and saying the truth are elements of communication in Ngas culture. The paper recommended revamping African traditional education, embracing public relations and encouraging divine encounter as veritable ways of inculcating traditional values of community among people of the two cultures. It concluded that notwithstanding the use of the new media, if various forms of communication are married to newer expressions, Africans are capable of finding solutions to contemporary challenges in an African way.

Keywords: Communication, Kanu Ikechukwu Anthony, Native, *Igwebuike, Shikrot.*

INTRODUCTION

Before the arrival of White imperialists to Africa, the people of the continent used oral tradition as a vital vehicle for information gathering, sharing and worship. While living their normal lives, they cultivated, built, ate, sang, danced, healed their sick, created and communicated through various modes such as incantation (Duru, 2016). Most importantly, language which has also been a veritable tool for communication, alongside other linguistic

183

forms of communication among *Homo Sapiens,* was employed through sound and the acoustic effects they produced (Ahamefula & Odii, 2014). This meant that the people crafted their modes of communication and attached meaning to them. These traditional forms of communication were part and parcel of the people's philosophy. For example, the Igbos of the South East and Ngas people of North Central Nigeria enjoyed rich communication values which helped the people to distinguish themselves and fulfill their destiny.

However, the advent of the digital age with all its attractions seems to have pushed these erstwhile local media to the background. Worse still, for Africans, traditional or native forms of communication which made a lot of sense to people are gradually being replaced by digital formats. The coming of the Internet plus Smartphone technology is also truncating the traditional forms of human interaction. In societies where having a meal together, sharing banters with friends, telling children stories under the moon light and other indigenous types of communication are gradually being faced out, the implication is that interpersonal, intrapersonal, group and extra-communication are now considered as older ways of communication. What is now trending is surfing the Internet and communicating through various social media platforms, like Facebook, WhatsApp, Twitter, Instagram, Emails, to mention a few.

The ease with which information is now being transmitted creates an instantaneous sensation of satisfaction. Because social media is characterized by speed, media convergence and interactivity, it creates a feeling that these media can perfectly replace older forms of human communication. In a bid to embrace this new technology, Africans now stand the risk of missing out on sharing common meals, going out to enjoy traditional dance in the village square, bonding as an extended family or members of the same kindred or paying regular visits to friends and family. This is because new media could provide an avenue to contact them. Inspired by this anomaly, this qualitative research aims at:

1. Presenting a resume' of the Igbos of the South East in juxtaposition with the Ngas people of North Central Nigeria;
2. Investigating native communication in *Igwebuike* philosophy;
3. Exploring traditional communication in *Shikrot* philosophical outlook;
4. Searching for common grounds regarding native communication in *Igwebuike* and *Shikrot* philosophical thoughts, and;
5. Stimulating academics (media scholars and philosophers) to encourage the young not to lose their *Africanness* in a digital age which seems to supply all things Western.

CONCEPTUAL ANALYSIS

Native Communication

Also known as traditional or trado-rural communication, native communication is communication from an African perspective. It is a kind of communication which starts from a person's birth to his death, as it affects every aspect of life. Africans communicate with themselves, their neighbours, the deities, ancestors, and God. It consists of both verbal and non-verbal cues. In the context of *Igwebuike* (Igbo) and Shikrot (Ngas) philosophies, this means the transmission of essential values which catapults the worldviews of these people towards appreciation by others (Dyikuk, 2019) and finding local solutions to African problems.

Igwebuike Philosophy

Igwebuike, which simply means "number is strength" or "number is power," is at the heart of African philosophy. It is the idea that when human beings form a united front, their solidarity and complementarity becomes an unbreakable union, such that nothing can defeat their collective resolve (Kanu, 2016a & b). As the lungs or vital organ of Igbo tradition, *Igwebuike* is a driver of communication as it engenders complementarity, harmony and communality. It is the philosophy of the Igbo people which helps them in transmitting values, mores and customs.

As the mechanism for ensuring complementarity, harmony and communalism in the community, *Igwebuike* brings about unity and synergy between the Igbos at home and those in diaspora. It is the core or underlying principle of African philosophy and a manner of being in African ontology, which translates as complementarity, harmony and communality. The worldview persuades everyone in the community to work towards corporate existence by creating a situation where "we" becomes lauder than "I" (2015 & 2016c&d).

Although the community means much to the individual, it does not suppress him/her, as the individual's talents do not constitute any threat to the society. *Igwebuike* unites all and gives hope that the future is full of meaning. It argues that it is the community that gives meaning to a person's existence based on his/her identity (Kanu, 2017 & 2018a). Here, the family and community which the individual belongs to are indisputable and inevitable. The community-oriented philosophy posits that life and living makes meaning because of the community (Kanu, 2016 & 2018b). This philosophy takes cognizance of divine and human realities, methods of traditional education and native communication as invaluable ways of transmitting Igbo culture.

Shikrot Philosophy

Literally translated as "talk of love," *Shikrot* philosophy encapsulates the religious, political and socio-cultural life of the Ngas people of Plateau State. It includes the philosophy, ethics and behavioural patterns as well as the cultural-ideology of the people. As the worldview which helps them to raise the stakes, *Shikrot* philosophy provides that Ngas sons and daughters should be knitted in love and also live out values such as truthfulness, straightforwardness, honesty, heroism, accountability and ingenuity. Notwithstanding the barrier between the *nkarang* (bona fide citizens) and *nlap* (foreigners), this philosophy invites all to love unconditionally (Dyikuk, 2008 & Dyikuk, 2019).

Based on the communitarian dimension of *Shikrot*, the people exuded the spirit of charity and solidarity, sharing their farmlands with members of the kindred and close allies. "Built on love, communalism and a high sense of fellow-feeling, Shikrot philosophy reveals the various forms of communication in the society. It also showcases the revered culture of the people such as their mores, customs and traditions. Because the community emphasizes a communitarian way of life, it frowned at those who had rebellious tendencies" (Dyikuk, 2019,p.5). The same author opines that from manhood training which was based on circumcision (*Vwang*) to naming and wedding ceremonies and funerals, native communication was used as a vehicle of communicating values and customs. Comedians (clowns), town criers, messengers, dancers and musicians had a crucial role to play in the community as they served as conveyors of information, masters of ceremony, consolers and producers of comic relief.

THEORETICAL FRAMEWORK

This study adopts Native Theory of Communication as theoretical framework. This indigenous theory engenders collaborative decision-making processes about socioeconomic and environmental sustainability as well as diverse stakeholder interests in various communities and organizations (Deetz, 2020). The theory makes case for a culture-bound development that is all-round, which meets the needs of the people and attempts answers to the puzzles of life. Native Theory of Communication is a 21st century assumption which argues that an African model of communication should be developed by Africans for Africans, which takes into the cognizance the culture, norms, mores, values, traditions as well as wishes and aspirations of the people towards finding home-grown solutions to problems.

As a theory which engenders integral development, it insists that for "Africans to freely communicate with themselves and find lasting solutions to the issues that affect them, both capitalist post-colonialism and neo-colonialism with their ingredients of hierarchical and linear approaches to governance must be kept at the back door. An erstwhile linear model of communication must necessarily give way to a grassroots, people - oriented or participatory model of communication which indicates that power belongs to the people; something akin to strict principles of democratic governance" (Dyikuk, 2018,p.15). This theory is in tandem with the study because native communication is key to revitalizing the African philosophical worldview in the light of *Igwebuike* and *Shikrot* renderings.

LITERATURE REVIEW AND DISCUSSION

Igbos of South Eastern Nigeria: A Synopsis

The Igbos have a very rich history - Igboid languages are said to have originated from Volta–Niger family. As one of the biggest and most inflectional ethnic groups in Nigeria with about 40 million people throughout Nigeria, they have an ancient and well-organised culture. The well-urbanized ethnic group lives in Igbo land, which consists of such cities like Onitsha, Owerri, Nnewi, Okigwe, Aba and Orlu. They have a variety of dialects and were predominantly farmers, traders and craftsmen. Their style of pottery is traced back to 2500 BCE. Genetic research finds them close to Niger-Congo-speaking peoples (Agu, 2020 & Adeboyejo, 2018).

According to one school of thought, the Igbos originated from the Nri Kingdom where Eri, a king-figure, held sway. Although the Nri Kingdom was theocratic in nature, the people practiced a quasi-democratic governance without centralized states. Scholars put the five groups of Igbo people as Northern Igbos, Western Igbos, Igbos of North-Eastern Nigeria, Igbos of South-Eastern Nigeria and Igbos of Eastern Nigeria. Another school of thought traces Igbo roots to ancient Hebrews. It is believed that they migrated from the Middle East to their present ancestral home. A third version simply suggests that the tribe originated from ancient Orlu or Awka towns (Agu, 2020 & Adeboyejo, 2018).

Unlike other cultures, the Igbos did not have a centralized system of government. They had title holders who were respected for their achievements, but were not revered as kings. They had a traditional republican system of government that is consultative in nature, which guarantees equality to citizens. They cultivate roots and tubers like yam and cassava, which explains why most of their cuisines are pounded yam and garri eaten with vegetables soup of different variety (*oha, nsala, akwu, okazi* and *ofe owerri*), alongside fruits and seeds. Little wonder during the new yam festivals (Iri Ji), the harvest of yams is celebrated (Adeboyejo, 2018).

Regarding marriage in Igbo culture, there are four stages: The first stage is "knocking the door," known as *Iku aka. The second stage is the* visit of the groom with his family members to the woman's family where her extended family members are supposed to give their consent. The third visit involves paying of bride price and collection of list for wedding items from the prospective in-laws. The fourth and final stage, called *Igba nkwu* or "wine carrying," is the wedding itself; here, the groom will hide in the crowd and the bride will look for him and offer him a cup of palm wine to show everyone that he is the man. After this, the couple is blessed by family, friends and all present as celebration continues (Adeboyejo, 2018).

Built on *Igwebuike*, Igbo culture encapsulates various customs, practices and traditions of the people. It comprises ancient practices and modern concepts which have evolved due to external influences. Some of these customs and traditions are visual art, religious beliefs, birth, marriage and death rituals, use of language, music and dance forms, cultural attire, food and language or dialect. The Igbos express their culture through customs, beliefs, war, burial, social norms, religion, racial and social or material traits. They often seize every opportunity to educate the world about their rich culture and traditions through festivals of arts and culture (Obindigbo, 2020). For the Igbos, traditional education or philosophy includes moral and religious instruction that is meaningful to all (Osuagwu, 2006).

NGAS PEOPLE OF NORTH CENTRAL NIGERIA: A HISTORICAL OVERVIEW

Ngas or Angas is an Afro-asiatic language spoken by certain dwellers in North Central Plateau, Nigeria. They are said to have migrated from Bornu from where they passed through villages before settling in their present homes on the highlands of Plateau and splintered into sub-groups in Pankshin, Ampang, Amper and Kabwir. The major city of the Ngas people is Pankshin (Tolu, 2020). They have many festivals, such as *Pus Dung* which brings all Ngas sons and daughters from diaspora to celebrate cultural diversity and rendition. This is celebrated annually at Nefur Arena. Other such festivals are *Tsati Tar or Mos Tar,* the "Shooting the Moon," which is celebrated during harvest to mark the end of the farming season and the beginning of a new season. The *Moslum* festival, which occurs around March or April, features the preparation of local brew *Mus* which the people use in a ritual to ask for blessings from the gods for a bumper harvest. The masquerade, *Wong,* comes out during this event (Tolu, 2020).

As regards marriage rites, the people practice match-making. "The child then gets to know about this when they are fully grown. Paying for a wife involves farming for the eventual in-laws and this lasts for as long as the courtship lasts. Cakes of tobacco and salt are also offered to the girl's father and mother respectively. There is no specific bride price here. Goats are also offered as part of the marital rites" (Tolu, 2020). Since it is difficult to separate a people's religious life from their social life, the historical and social life of the Ngas man reveals that they are deeply religious people. Ngas people are divided into Hill Ngas (Pankshin LGA) and the Plain Ngas (Kanke LGA) (Gyang, 2020).

They, however, have similar beliefs and practices with few variations in one village or the other. Shikrot is the worldview of the Ngas people. Most inhabitants of Pankshin and Kanke Local Government Areas in North-Central geopolitical zone are Ngas by tribe. While Christianity is currently the major religion there, there are few Muslims and pockets of those who still practice African Traditional Religion (ATR). The rural population still practices extended family system and common farming activities as well as animal husbandry. The *Ngolong* Ngas is the paramount traditional ruler in the two LGAs who superintends over the traditional affairs of the Ngas populace (Gyang, 2020). *Shikrot* sums up the ontology or philosophy of the Ngas people.

NATIVE COMMUNICATION IN IGBO CULTURE: VIEWPOINTS FROM *IGWEBUIKE* PHILOSOPHY

1. **Dissemination of Information:** Announcements concerning public or community works, duties or responsibilities of the collective citizenry are carried. Defaulters in the community often faced automatic sanctions. The traditional authority could send certain groups of people or individuals to make announcements or disseminate information about upcoming events. The news takes the form of passing information about new or impending events which are of importance to the community (Akakuru, Nwokedi & Edi, 2015).

2. **Advertisement, Public Relations and Entertainment:** Advertisement was carried out through displaying products on a table, tree stump or flay pole, peripatetic hawkers and vendors. The merchants often sang, accompanied by drumming while naming the product for sale. In *Igwebuike* philosophical thought of communication, Public Relations (PR) was achieved through person-to-person or on a person-to-organisation basis, where the individual tries to promote the image of his organization through singing. Entertainment was done through music, dance and drama, which were carried out either free of charge or paid for in some circumstances. It could also take the form of performances and announcements that were made to enhance communication in the community to a greater level (Akakuru, Nwokedi & Edi, 2015).

3. **Education:** In Igbo culture, educating the people is at the heart of all cultural expressions. As such, education is derived through informal means from parents to their children or through a more formal means where membership into certain societies through membership of other socio- cultural groups in the community could afford one the chance to learn (Akakuru, Nwokedi & Edi, 2015).

4. **Signs and Symbols:** In Igbo land, various forms of traditional communication include: idiophones, membranophones, aerophones, symbology. As instruments which produce sound without using an intermediary medium, idiophones produce sound when shaken, scratched, struck, pricked (pulled) or pressed with the feet. Examples are: gong, woodblock, wooden drum, bell and rattle. Membranophones are skin or leather drums which produce sounds through the vibration of membranes when beaten specially with carved sticks. As media which comprise flute family, whistle reed pipes, hones and trumpets, aerophones produce sound as a result of the vibration of a column of air. In *Igwebuike* tradition, symbology are a descriptive representational device for conveying meaning. They are known as "uri" in Igbo, which stands for writings or painting on a wall or human body (Akakuru, Nwokedi & Edi, 2015).

5. **Sound and Acoustics:** In a paper which investigated the various non-verbal forms of cultural communication among Igbo people, Ahamefula and Odii found "that sound patterns and acoustic effects (extra linguistic) other than the sounds from the vocal tract system of man play a significant role in human communication, especially in cultural communication" (2014.p.35). The authors noted that aside from the 'oja' (flute), there are many other Igbo traditional instruments such ikoro (giant gong), igba (membrane drum), ekwe gong), ogene (metal gong) that are employed in cultural communication.

6. **Ikpe Ekpere (Prayers):** As a central part of the life of Igbo people, **Ikpe Ekpere, as prayer is called,** serves as a direct link to *ala mmu*o (the spirit land). In traditional Igbo beliefs and practices, morning prayer was carried out every day by the head of each household. As he does that, he offers *oji* (kola nut) to the different divinities (Ogbukagu cited in Duru, 2016). It is essential to communicate with the divine before one communicates with his/her fellow human beings. This is what *Igwebuike* philosophy stimulates.

7. **Incantation**s: Incantation is a collection of special words that are either uttered or sung to have magic effect on someone. It also involves an activity through employing special spiritual passwords. In line with *Igwebuike* philosophy of communication, in Igbo thought, incantation belongs to an extra-mundane form of communication which takes place between the living and the dead, supernatural and Supreme Being. This mode of communication includes: rituals as 'Igo-ofo' (traditional worship), *Iwa oji* (breaking of kolanut) and *itu oza mmii* (pouring of libation). These are secret ways of giving or practicing traditional medicine for the purpose of love or imprisoning mosquitoes to stop them from biting the person making the incantation in some localities, like Umunoha in Mbaitoli Local Government Area of Imo State (Duru, 2016).

NATIVE COMMUNICATION IN NGAS CULTURE: SHIKROT PHILOSOPHICAL PERSPECTIVE

1. **Being Persuasive:** In Ngas culture, persuasiveness, referred to as *man le shitok den'en gurum* or *man shitok*, means talking to make an influence or impact on your audience. Usually, children would sit behind elders in order to listen so as to learn from them (Govwang, cited in Dyikuk, 2008). Ngas people believe that the ability to speak persuasively is a gift from God, although some people who admire orators can learn. Those with this gift are often asked to represent the people, especially in modern times. *Man shitok* connotes making a good speech. In olden times, those who were talented in public speech were sent on errands to deliver messages to the people. Due to lack of formal education, children imitated orators and mimicked them while playing (Jurshak, cited in Dyikuk, 2008). This was an essential element of socialization.

2. **Active Listening:** Ngas people hold good listening ability as a most cherished type of native communication. *Ten kom,* as it is referred to, means listening attentively with mind and heart alert. Children are not expected to speak when elders are discussing. They just listen and only reply when they have better knowledge of what their elders are talking about. In this custom, children are taught the basics of active listening, especially when they are before their seniors or visitors (Govwang, cited in Dyikuk, 2008). Also known as *Fot Shitok,* active listening is fundamental to the people's communication. When a child refuses to listen or pay attention to what is being said, we say, *gem de po fot kom ka,* which translates as – "this child does not pay attention and is stubborn" (Jurshak, cited in Dyikuk, 2008).

3. **Saying the Truth:** *Le zin* is speaking the truth in Ngas language. One is expected to speak the truth at all times. As one grows, one is taught to speak the truth all the time; as such, dishonesty is abhorred (Govwang, cited in Dyikuk, 2008). Truth-telling is symbolized by the one-one facial tribal mark on each side of the chick. Because of this, the Hausa's nicknamed the Ngas as *"Aska daya, magana daya"* – One mark (on each side), one word. Children learn how to tell the truth from their parents. Sanctions such as flogging are consequences for lies. To buttress this point, a typical Ngas man would say: *"Shikok gak do mun la shi nyi"* – which literally translates as "we will only follow one thing (message) that is said (Jurshak, cited in Dyikuk, 2008). Saying one thing underscores truth in the culture. Usually, children would sit in *kantang* and are taught about the dangers of stealing or fighting over other people's property as these contradict truth.

4. **Showing Respect:** Respect in Ngas is, *pen warang, pen kun or nang kun.* Showing respect, especially to elders, is fundamental to many cultures in Africa. This is because doing so is also associated with the divine. Ngas people believe that "One who respects a human being, respects God." When a child shows lack of respect, it is concluded that such a child is not from a disciplined home. To this end, children are trained to respect their elders. As a sign of respect, children are expected to help someone who is older to carry load. At home, they are taught to wake up very early in the morning, greet their elders and run errands. As a mark of respect, a younger person is expected to be the last person at meals – he/she cannot leave the plate for his/her seniors, even if he/she is satisfied. Any member of the community who is elderly, not necessarily his/her parents or guardians, can discipline an erring child (Yeldung, cited in Dyikuk, 2008). Also, food is distributed to children according to their age. Disrespectful children are beaten squarely to serve as a deterrent to others. As such, showing respect is a non-negotiable native form of communication.

5. **Sense of Followership:** Because the leader comes across as a vanguard, gadfly and shining star, the led are expected to follow the leader. This underlines the importance of followership among the Ngas people as a form of native communication. "The idea of an individual standing alone on his or her on does not really make sense in Ngas thought" (Govwang, cited in Dyikuk, 2008). That is why members of the community

hold communality, submissiveness and followership in high esteem. Since togetherness enhances progress, followership is an invaluable traditional asset. In solidarity, respect, humility and search for the common good, the people follow the leader. This is closely connected to respect. In the light of respect for constituted authorities, the people are groomed to be loyal to superiors and all those in authority. As such, a leader must be followed and respected as a sign of loyalty, submission and good followership (Yeldung, cited in Dyikuk, 2008).

6. **Traditional Entertainment:** Another critical form of native communication is amusement or *nang shuar*. Since humour creates comic relief, excitement and eases tension, amusement or traditional entertainment helps people in the community to feel relaxed and enjoy a good life. In a typical Ngas community, there are comedians who entertain people at various occasions, such as traditional festivals, weddings and funerals. Although these comedians (clowns) are not trained, they, nonetheless, act in an impromptu manner to make people laugh to the admiration of women and children (Yeldung, cited in Dyikuk, 2008). *Nang shuar* by the amuser (*go tok barak*) is cherished by the people as a gift or talent. Usually, he demonstrates these abilities during funerals to make people forget the pain of their loss (Yeldung, cited in Dyikuk, 2008).

7. **Sense of Community:** Like other cultures in Africa, the Ngas have a high sense of communality expressed through the extended family system. For them, the individual realizes himself/herself in and through the community. That is why they live together, farm together (*nwok*) and eat as a family in groups of men, women and children. An individual's problem becomes a problem of the community. Women use common utensils and go to the farm as well as the stream in groups to fetch water and bathe their babies. This is usually accompanied by a melodious traditional song which inspires team spirit and keeps the body alive. For the Ngas people, "...co-operative community effort [is] considered necessary for the development of good character" (Fafunwa, 1975,p.24).

RECOMMENDATIONS: COMMON GROUNDS FOR NATIVE COMMUNICATION IN *IGWEBUIKE* AND SHIKROT PHILOSOPHICAL THOUGHT

Although Moemeka (1998) suggested that African communalism is anchored on supremacy of community, sanctity of authority, respect for old age, usefulness of the individual and religion as a way of life, we shall consider common features in both the *Igwebuike* and *Shikrot* philosophies of native communication in the light of education, public relations, divine encounter and interpersonal relations:

1. **African Traditional Education:** In *Igwebuike* philosophical rendering, the system of education created multiple personalities in the society. Traditional education included moral and religious instruction that was meaningful to all. It encapsulated the world view of the people which takes into cognizance language, culture, morals, proverbs,

signs and symbols, even as it provided answers to the people's questions about life and afterlife (Osuagwu, 2006). Children were taught by their parents in the kindred or extended family system. The use of proverbs, songs and dance was part of preparing children for a holistic appreciation of Igbo culture. Like the philosophy of Ohazurume (Umeogu, 2007), *Igwebuike* is the sum total of the people's realities, places, thoughts, language and actions.

In *Shikrok* philosophy of communication, children receive their earliest education from parents, guardians, elders or seniors within the kindred. For a holistic socialization, children are trained to respect their elders (Dyikuk, 2008). They are also taught about religious and moral values, especially during *Vwang* rite of initiation into adulthood. Although informal, this education was a gateway to who the child would grow to be in the future. Everything was done in love so as to groom the young into a descent and invaluable member of the community as well as a mature citizen. Therefore, it is evident that both *Igwebuike* and *Shikrot* worldviews hold African traditional education of the young as a form of native communication dearly. This is aimed at preparing a person for the future. It is crucial for traditional rulers, religious leaders and stakeholders in the education sector to encourage parents/guardians as well as other custodians of culture to incorporate teaching African traditional education into contemporary curricular so as equip children with the love of language and culture and how to communicate same.

2. **Public Relations:** We saw earlier that another vital form of native education in *Igwebuike* philosophy is public relations, with its twin variables of advertisement and entertainment. The Igbos value performances and announcements because they are carried out to enhance communication in the community (Akakuru, Nwokedi & Edi, 2015). Through the use of signs and symbols, such as idiophones, membranophones, aerophones, symbolography, local entertainers, performers and dancers communicate important messages and provide useful entertainment for the people. For example, sound and acoustics from local instruments, like Igba Membrane drum), Ekwe gong), Ogene (metal gong) (Akakuru, Nwokedi & Edi, 2015), are useful recipes for the social life of the people. "Traditional communication in Igbo land is a continuous process of information dissemination" (Akakuru, Nwokedi & Edi, 2015,p.17).

In like manner, the Ngas consider amusement or *nang shuar* as a useful vehicle for transmission of values. For this ethic group, the comedian who performs at funerals is one endowed with the gifts of persuasion and humour so as to provide comic relief for people in moments of tension. As a traditional form of communication, public relations makes room for amusement or local entertainment which helps people in the community to feel relaxed and enjoy a good life (Dyikuk, 2008). Since public relations is a common denominator in the two cultures, in the face of decaying cultural values, African academics from these extractions should drum support for revamping this important element of native communication in both localized and urbanized settlements. This will go a long way in connecting young people who may have lost their roots to be reconnected to the rich traditions of the past.

3. **Divine Encounter:** In view of *ikpe ekpere*, Igbos believe that prayer is a direct link to *ala mmu*o (the spirit land) which is why morning prayer is offered by the custodian of the family, accompanied by *oji* (kola nut) and other divinations (Ogbukagu cited in Duru, 2016). *Igwebuike* philosophy is built around the idea of *Igwe*, God as the Supreme Being who holds all things in being and to whom other smaller gods like *amadioha,* the god of thunder, are subject to. Everything about the life of this people, from birth to death, is associated with divine realities.

In the same vein, the Ngas cannot understand life outside of religion. This is why, for instance, children are taught that God must not be excluded from education; the Plateau people hold that *Nen* is the supreme God, while other lesser ancestors and spirits are within the environment to whom libation is made in form of food and drink (*Mus or Pito*) (Gyang, 2020). From when a child is born and prayers are offered, to the time of death, the idea of God is central to all affairs. Another meeting point in the two cultures is the supremacy of God and dependence of man on him. What is more, it behooves sages and scholars to canvas for an acculturation of the good aspects of this overt reliance on God as a resource for a native form of communication that is inculturated, especially in the light of Christian faith.

4. **Interpersonal Relations:** One of the finest expressions of *Igwebuike* philosophy is the concept of universal brotherhood and love. This form of native communication among the Igbos comes from the concept of the love of God who in turn inspires human beings to love one another. This is why the extended family or kindred, *umunna,* practice communalism and fellow-feeling. This is also why events like the new yam festival (*iri ji*) and marriage ceremonies bring people together for common celebrations (Adeboyejo, 2018). All these point to interpersonal relations as ways of expressing native communication in Igbo society.

The sense of followership, traditional entertainment by comedians and dissemination of information by the town crier reveals various levels of traditional communication among Ngas people. Because interpersonal relations is paramount to this ethnic group, the people engage in certain common practices such as eating together in groups of men, women and children, using common utensils for fetching water, drinking from the well and engaging in commercial farming (Dyikuk, 2008). At every point, the people must interact. This common feature in Igbo and Ngas cultures underscores the place of traditional communication in Africa and the need to restore same in formal settings. The right place to start is the home, followed by local communities where community or traditional leaders are custodians of the traditions of the people.

5. **Respect for Authority:** Igbo philosophy is built around *Igwebuike* which connotes that the people ought to help one another to succeed. As the Igbo saying goes, "A child who washes his hands well eats with the elders." When someone is of age or the person is married, he/she is respected by both the young and old alike. The person can even take part in discussions with his kinsmen and participate in meetings with elders. Respect is deeply rooted in truth, honesty and transparency. Interestingly, persons who have excelled in their fields, brought about development, or those who possess exceptional abilities, qualities and achievements are given titles (Nairaland, 2017).

The youths who are initiated into the "Ngas cult" are taught how to respect their elders, keep secrets, show love and make sacrifice for the good of the society. "In Ngas tradition like other cultures in Africa, elders are repertoires of knowledge who communicate or transmit those values to their children. In line with traditional African education, parents teach their kids how to eat, greet, dress and treat others with respect" (Dyikuk, 2019,p.11). In a society where traditional values of communication, like respect for authority are challenged due to advances in technology and loss of touch with cultural roots, it is expedient that a new model of African traditional education is developed to remind the young on the need to respect constituted authorities.

CONCLUSION

The study was able to demonstrate that dissemination of information, advertisement, public relations and entertainment, education, signs and symbol, sound and acoustics, *i*kpe ekpere **(prayers)** and i**ncantations** are veritable forms of *Igwebuike* philosophy of communication in Igbo thought. In like manner, the article provided evidence that being persuasive, active listening, saying the truth, showing respect, sense of followership, traditional entertainment and a high sense of community are elements of native communication in Ngas culture. Since the study set out in search for native communication in *Igwebuike* and *Shikrot* worldviews, a common ground was found. This was why revamping African traditional education, public relations, divine encounter, interpersonal relations and respect for authority in the communities under study, through educational policies, were recommended as useful ways of restoring native communication in the two cultures. This can be achieved if the requisite communication values are infused into primary and secondary curricula for education.

It is worth reiterating that traditional communication affects every aspect of an African's life. These common grounds are not exclusive to the Igbos or Ngas people of Nigeria, as they are also found in other parts of the global south. Be that as it may, in a society where homegrown solutions seem to be taking the centre stage in almost every part of the world, educationists of African extraction need to think out of the box to find lasting remedies to challenges in the African way. Indeed, native communication, like native intelligence which entails taking a helicopter view of contemporary issues, should propel various academics, especially media scholars and philosophers, to encourage the young not to lose their *Africanness* in a digital age which supplies all things Western.

REFERENCES

Adeboyejo, A (2018). An introduction to Nigeria's Igbo people. https://theculturetrip.com/africa/nigeria/articles/an-introduction-to-nigerias-igbo-people/.Accessed 4/28/2020.

Agu, Z (2020). Origin of Igbo tribe in Nigeria www.legit.ng/1151109-origin-igbo-tribe-nigeria.html. Accessed 4/27/2020.

Ahamefula, N.A & Odii, B (2014). Preliminary study on the use of sound and acoustics in Igbo cultural communication. Innovare Journal of Social Sciences. 2(2), [35-39].

Akakuru, O.C; Nwokedi, C.I & Edi, T.O (2015). Means and forms of traditional communication in Igbo Land in contemporary socio-cultural interactions. Journal of Humanities and Social Science (IOSR-JHSS). Volume 20, Issue 6, Ver. IV, [17-20]. DOI: 10.9790/0837-20641720.

Deetz, S (2020). Native Theory. www.cu.edu/ptsp/native-theoryAccessed 4/27/2020.

Duru, W. (2016). The communicativeness of incantations in the traditional Igbo society. Journal of Media and Communication Studies, 8(7), 63-70.

Dyikuk, J.J (2008). Ngas values of social communication as vital tools for effective homiletics: A case study of Bwarak. Bachelor's Degree in Theology (BTH) Thesis. University of Jos, Nigeria.

Dyikuk, J.J (2018). Communicating the Marshall plan to Africa: Challenges and responses. Sumerianz Journal of Social Science. Vol. x, No. x, [11-18].

Dyikuk, J.J (2019).Communication and culture in Igwebuike and Shikrot philosophies: A critical evaluation. Igwebuike: An African Journal of Arts and Humanities. Vol. 5 No 8 [1-16].

Fafunwa, A.B (1975). History of education in Nigeria. London: George Allen and Unwin Ltd.

Gyang, L.J (2020).The effect of Western Education on Africa traditional values. www.academia.edu/37705415/THE_EFFECT_OF_WESTERN_EDUCATION_ON_AFRICA_TRADITIONAL_VALUES. Accessed 4/27/2020.

Kanu I. A. (2018a). Sources of Igwebuike Philosophy. Towards A Socio-Cultural Foundation. *International Journal of Religion and Human Relations* Vol. 9 No 1 June.

Kanu, I. A. (2016a). Igwebuike as a trend in African philosophy. *Igwebuike: An African Journal of Arts and Humanities.* Vol.2. No. 1.[97-101].

Kanu, I. A. (2016b). Igwebuike as an Igbo-African hermeneutic of globalization. *Igwebuike: An African Journal of Arts and Humanities.* Vol.2. No.1. [1-7].

Kanu, I. A. (2018b). Igwebuike and Being in Igbo ontology. *Igwebuike: An African Journal of Arts and Humanities.* Vol. 4 No 5. [12-21].

Kanu, I. A. (2015b). *Igwebuike as an ontological precondition for African ethics.* International Conference of the Society for Research and Academic Excellence. University of Nigeria, Nsukka. 14th -16th September.

Kanu, I. A. (2015c). *Igwebuike as an Igbo-African Philosophy of Education.* A paper presented at the International Conference on Law, Education and Humanities. 25th -26th November 2015 University of Paris, France.

Kanu, I. A. (2014). *Igwebuikology* as an Igbo-African philosophy for Catholic-Pentecostal relations. *Jos Studies.* 22. pp.87-98.

Kanu, A. I. (2017c). *Igwebuike* as an Igbo-African philosophy of inclusive leadership. *Igwebuike: An African Journal of Arts and Humanities.* Vol. 3 No 7. pp. 165-183.

Kanu, A. I. (2017d). *Igwebuike* philosophy and the issue of national development. *Igwebuike: An African Journal of Arts and Humanities.* Vol. 3 No 6. pp. 16-50.

Kanu, A. I. (2017f). *Igwebuike* as an Igbo-African Ethic of Reciprocity. *IGWEBUIKE: An African Journal of Arts and Humanities.* 3. 2. pp. 153-160.

Kanu, I. A. *Igwebuike* as the hermeneutic of individuality and communality in African ontology. *NAJOP: Nasara Journal of Philosophy.* Vol. 2. No. 1. pp. 162-179. 2017

Kanu, I. A. *Igwebuike* philosophy and human rights violation in Africa. *IGWEBUIKE: An African Journal of Arts and Humanities.* Vol. 3. No. 7. pp. 117-136. 2017

IKECHUKWU ANTHONY KANU

Kanu, I. A. *Igwe Bu Ike* as an Igbo-African hermeneutics of national development. *Igbo Studies Review. No. 6.* pp. 59-83. 2018

Kanu, I. A. *Igwebuike* and question of superiority in the scientific community of knowledge. *Igwebuike: An African Journal of Arts and Humanities.*Vol.3 No1. pp. 131-138. 2017

Kanu, I. A. *Igwebuike* and the logic (Nka) of African philosophy. *Igwebuike: An African Journal of Arts and Humanities. 3. 1.* pp. 1-13. 2017

Kanu, I. A. *Igwebuike* as a complementary approach to the issue of girl-child education. *Nightingale International Journal of Contemporary Education and Research.* Vol. 3. No. 6. pp. 11-17. 2017

Kanu, I. A. *Igwebuike* as a hermeneutic of personal autonomy in African ontology. *Journal of African Traditional Religion and Philosophy Scholars. Vol. 2. No. 1. pp. 14-22.* 2017

Kanu, I. A. (2018). New Africanism: *Igwebuike* as a philosophical Attribute of Africa in portraying the Image of Life. In Mahmoud Misaeli, Sanni Yaya and Rico Sneller (Eds.). *African Perspectives on Global on Global Development* (pp. 92-103). United Kingdom: Cambridge Scholars Publishing.

Kanu, I. A. (2019). *Igwebuike* Research Methodology: A New Trend for Scientific and Wholistic Investigation. *IGWEBUIKE: An African Journal of Arts and Humanities* (IAAJAH). *5. 4.* pp. *95-105.*

Kanu, I. A. (2019). Igwebuikeconomics: The Igbo Apprenticeship for Wealth Creation. *IGWEBUIKE: An African Journal of Arts and Humanities* (IAAJAH). *5. 4.* pp. *56-70.*

Kanu, I. A. (2019). Igwebuikecracy: The Igbo-African Participatory Socio-Political System of Governance. *TOLLE LEGE: An Augustinian Journal of the Philosophy and Theology. 1. 1.* pp. 34-45.

Moemeka, A. (1998). Communalism as a fundamental dimension of culture. Journal of Communication, 48(4) [118–41].

Nairaland.com (2017). Respect in Igbo land and it general misconception in Nigeria(debunking the lies). www.nairaland.com/3676537/respect-igbo-land-it-generalAccessed 4/28/2020.

Obindigbo.com (2020). Igbo Culture. http://obindigbo.com.ng/category/igbo-culture/. Accessed 4/27/2020.

Osuagwu, P.C (2006). The education of the whole person: The Igbo moral perspective. *ETD Collection for Fordham University*. AAI3222144. https://fordham.bepress.com/dissertations/AAI3222144.

Tolu, (2020). Facts about the angas tribe of Nigeria. https://everyevery.ng/facts-about-the-angas-tribe-of-nigeria/. Accessed 4/27/2020.

Umeogu, B. (2007). Ohazurume: A Philosophical Definition of Communalism as the Typology of Igbo Being. In I. Odimegwu (Ed.), Perspective on African Communalism. Pp. 107 - 112. Canada: Trafford.

THE ROLE OF UMUNNA IN CONFLICT RESOLUTION AS AN EXPRESSION OF IGWEBUIKE PHILOSOPHY

Francis N. C. IWUH
Modibbo Adama University of Technology
Yola, Adamawa State
nduemerem16@yahoo.com

EXECUTIVE SUMMARY

Knowledge of the traditional ways of resolving conflict is highly needed at a time and period when people are losing and abandoning their history and tradition. We approached this article from the expository point of view, to study the role traditional institution (umunna) has played in restoring warring members of the society. The presence of modern conflict management has posed a great challenge to the existing traditional method. In this study, the term "umunna" was descriptively explained through the way in which they resolve conflicts in Igbo land, which has become an expression of Igwebuike philosophy of peace and conflict resolution. The elders, acting as arbiter, resolves conflict in umunna kindred. In this regard, they act as peacemakers and have kept the community running smoothly. The conclusion of this paper is that umunna instituion has contributed a lot to the resolution of conflict in Igbo land and their role in conflict resolution has been very interesting and effective. The knowledge acquired through this study will help appreciate and empower the umunna traditional conflict resolution mechanism in Igbo land.

Keywords: Igwebuike Philosophy, Kanu Ikechukwu Anthony, Conflict Resolution, *Umunna*, Tradition

INTRODUCTION

Disputes are an integral part of human nature which dates back to the origin of man. This is so because human beings live in families, hamlets, villages and in large communities. As they interact amongst themselves, disputes are likely to occur. Since we are created differently and can hardly share the same view, there is bound to be divergent opinions as when friends or members of a family disagree, or as what countries or states hold tenaciously, views that are diametrically opposed. In traditional African society, conflicts are common phenomena among communities, families and individuals. Africa as a continent has diversity of cultural and religious practices. This diversity affects the approaches to dispute and conflict management in the traditional setting. Apparently, the approach tends to differ from the Western dispute management in several respects. Even then, in Africa itself, the approach may also differ from one culture to another. Igbo traditional African society has a well-organized and systematic conflict resolution strategy. It is a healing process in which all stakeholders contribute positive energy. These stakeholders range from family heads, the council of elders, or chiefs, religious leaders, leaders of age-grades, *umuada* and to *umunna*. Igbo people initially had neither chiefs nor kings who would manage their conflict, and would not wait for conflict to start before they control it; they rather had institutions for managing the suppression of weaker persons from the stronger. One of those institutions that resolve conflict in traditional Igbo society to date is the "*umunna*."

This paper discusses "*umunna*" as an institution that resolves conflict in traditional Igbo society, drawing inspiration from *Igwebuike* African philosophy of peace and conflict resolution. *Igwebuike* is an indigenous Igbo philosophy, rooted within indigenous epistemologies, cultures and traditions based on the relationships and experiences of interrelationships and interconnections of the Igbo people. The study tends to commend and appreciate "*umunna*" for their great contribution in resolving conflict in traditional Igbo society.

CONFLICT AND CAUSES OF CONFLICT IN IGBO LAND

Conflict is part and parcel of every human society. Whenever two or more people are gathered in one interaction or another, conflict is bound to surface. Conflict is described in terms of what might have caused it, such as scarce resources, disagreement and competition. Conflicts will always occur due to ideological, political, social and economic differences which usually resulted in rivalry and competition. Conflict resolution aims at restoring social harmony, mending breached social ties, performance of rituals and offering apologies or compensation to ensure that the status quo before the dispute is restored. The pre-colonial Igbo society cannot be said to differ, as individuals and communities engaged in one form of interaction or the other - a situation which at times led to conflicts (Ezenwoko and Osagie, 2014, p. 135). Igbo peace scholars are unanimous on the causes of conflicts in Igbo land, which include issues arising from marriage, inheritance, chieftaincy tussle, land, territorial boundaries, among others. Matudi (2016) captures the sources of rift or conflict in African setting in different levels.

In the family level; conflict ensues through interpersonal relations, marital issues and property ownership. In economic level; conflict can take shape through land encroachment, territorial dislocation, terms of trade and failure to pay tribute. In the political level; conflict can arise through tussle for leadership, especially where rules guiding selection of traditional rulers are disobeyed. Conflict can also be manifested in non-compliance to religious obligations-violation or objection of shrine order and finally, non-allegiance to constituted authority such as elders and traditional rulers (p. 4).

Charles (2016) agrees with this when he said, "Conflict in Igbo land has always been either disputes over ownership of land, chieftaincy tussle, political authority and fears of domination and marginalization" (p.9). Thus, inter-tribal conflict over boundary and trade, marital conflict, conflict over inheritance and chieftaincy title tussle all exist in Igbo land.

The major cause of conflicts in Igbo traditional society has always been the struggle and ownership of land. Land is seen as valuable sources not only for food cultivation but also for exploitation of aquatic and other products. Land has much to do in human affairs, and whatever human beings do on the land affects the land positively or negatively, whether it is to grow food and cash crops, extract mineral resources or abode for its inhabitants. Land speculation is, therefore, an important source of communal conflicts today. According to Charles (2016), "This is because of the spirituality surrounding land in the Igbo culture as expressed in the prominence of the deity, 'ana' and the importance of the yam crop" (p.6). Land dispute is a serious issue among the Igbos, since it touches both the material and spiritual essence of Igbo ontology. The reason why land disputes are more complex in Igbo land is that all lands are usually owned; whether it is cultivated or not, it belongs to somebody or a community. Hence, claims and counter-claims over land ownership have become the order of the day in Igbo society till date.

Geographically, there is scarcity of land among the Igbos of southeastern part of Nigeria. Subsistence farming still accounts for a major part of their occupation. So dispute on the limited available land is rampant. In addition, most of the bitter territorial disputes have erupted among communities that have had strong ties that bounded them together for centuries. Charles gave example of a famous land boundary conflict between Aguleri and Umuleri. These two communities belong to the same ethnic stock, are neighbours, have the same ancestral origin (Eri), are in the same local government area (Anambra East), and the same state (Anambra). They have been living together, farming and intermarrying long before the coming of the white man. The major cause of the conflicts that have lasted for more than thirty (30) years is a piece of land called, 'Otuocha.' The two communities have been in court since 1920 and yet no lasting peace has been achieved until 2000 after the 1999 war that claimed many lives (2016, p. 6). Land conflict is one of the deadly conflicts in Igbo society. This is the reason why Nwolise (2004) posits that, "It was pressure on land resulting from a combination of expropriation, monetization of land by the colonial masters, rising population density, degradation and resurgence of pre-colonial communal competition has raised land into primal "casus belli" in rural." Thus, land is something that is worth fighting and dying for. There is too much pressure on the little cultivable land and this also causes conflicts among the people, especially during the farming seasons. Land is a non-renewable resource and, with concentration of population growth, will lead to conflict.

Another major source of conflict in family setting in Igbo land is sharing the inheritance or the properties of the dead among the living children and other family members. This source of conflict can be either among the living children of the deceased person or the brothers of the deceased with the wife/children. In Igbo society, the property of a man, on his death, was inherited by his sons, while that of a woman is inherited by her daughters (Ezenwoko et el, 2014, p. 151). This is where the conflict between brothers of the deceased and the wife arises, especially when the man dies without a child or the children are still young. Since a woman cannot inherit the property of a man, then the brothers come for it.

On the other hand, in the pre-colonial period, the method by which family property was shared among the members of a monogamous family differed from the way family property was shared in a polygamous family. On the death of the head of a family, his eldest son exclusively inherited his personal "*ofo*" (symbol of authority) and other objects of worship. The eldest son also exclusively inherited his late father's Obi (the house where he lived and died), distinct plot of land known as "*ala isi obi*" or "*ani isiobi*" – a plot of land specifically meant for the head of the family (Nwogugu, 1974), furniture and dresses. The other properties, such as farm land, farming implements, economic trees, livestock, etc., were shared among his male children (Chubb, 1961). The eldest son was accountable to his other brothers. If he desired to sell or lease any of the plots of land, he had to inform his brothers who were also stakeholders. However, family inheritance generated a lot of conflicts in Igbo society because some eldest sons, after inheriting their father's property, especially landed property converted some to themselves by planting economic trees, like palm trees, on them. Attempt by the other brothers to reclaim such property from their eldest brother usually leads to conflict.

CONFLICT RESOLUTION

Conflict resolution is the process by which two or more parties in conflict reach a peaceful resolution to a dispute. It is the methods and processes involved in facilitating the peaceful ending of <u>conflict</u>. It can also be thought to encompass the use of nonviolent resistance measures by conflicted parties in an attempt to promote effective resolution. Shedrack (2014) sees conflict resolution as a sense of finality, where the parties to a conflict are mutually satisfied with the outcome of a settlement and the conflict is resolved in a true sense (p. 94). On the question, if conflict can truly be resolved? Shedrack avers that "some conflicts, especially those over resources, are permanently resolvable." Conflict can be said to be resolved when the basic needs of the parties in conflict have been met and their fears defused. Conflict resolution can either aim at resolving or terminating conflicts in an open and predictable process in accordance with legal principles or focus on efforts to increase cooperation among the parties to a conflict and deepen their relationship by addressing the conditions that led to the dispute, fostering positive attitudes and allaying distrust through reconciliation initiatives, and building or strengthening the institutions and processes through which the parties interact.

The overall objective of conflict resolution in African society was to uphold and promote peaceful co-existence among and between community members. It is in the light of this that the following guiding principles had informed the African approaches to conflict resolution.

1. **Impartiality:** In traditional conflict resolution, no case was treated as an isolated entity. The elders tried to be as neutral and unbiased as possible, siding or supporting no party.
2. **Transparency:** All issues emanating from conflicting situations were placed at the public domain for all to see and hear.
3. **Fairness, Justice and Equality:** Traditional conflict resolution distributes equitable justice to all and sundry, irrespective of the status.
4. **Award:** Traditional African conflict resolution dreaded the issue of "winner takes it all." Conflict resolutions were aimed at stabilizing the bond of relationship in the society. This was done through celebration of reconciliation.

UMUNNA

Umunna is an Igbo word from the Eastern part of Nigeria. It is a compound word. "*Umu*" means children or sons and "*nna*" means father. When brought together it could mean "children of the father" or "sons of the father". *Umunna* is translated 'kindred' or 'kinsmen', to mean the extended family of one's ancestral village. It is a form of patrilineage maintained by the Igbos, which is a male line of descent from a founding ancestor with groups of compounds containing closely related families headed by the eldest male member. So, *Umunna* simply means, sons of the same father. The *umunna* kindred are often named after the founding ancestor. *Umunna*, the cornerstone of Igbo structure, defines the arrangement of every individual in a family structure and describes their social position in the community. *Umunna*, the weekly assembly of only male members of the clan/kindred, is another traditional method of resolving conflict. The *umunna* is made up of elders and male members of families bonded by some ancestral ties. These elders have overtime stood as peace builders that built strong and virile communities that have witnessed a prolonged peaceful co-existence (Ebisi, 2016). The terms, 'village group council' and 'village assembly,' are used interchangeably to refer to the Igbo central authority, while *umunna* village-group and *ndiamala* refer to the more locally derived authority headed by the *okparas*, elders and *Ozo* title holders at the village level.

As family groups which share a common ancestry, *umunna* kindred is the next political structure above the family. The kindred assembly is presided over by the eldest *okpara*. The kindred union is similar to the family meeting, except that it ordinarily deals with issues that affect the kindred. The village union handles issues and problems that concern the entire village. Individuals can, nevertheless, take their complaints to the village union, especially if they are not satisfied with the decisions taken at the kindred union, or if the dispute is between people from different kindreds within the village. Therefore, *umunna* is another form of arbitration. Arbitration has been one of the significant methods of resolving conflict in traditional Igbo society. It has produced great level of trust, confidence and mutual understanding in traditional Igbo society. The arbiters or arbitrators, who are mostly elected leaders of the clan in conjunction with the elders, have lived up to their expectation of being impartial and interpreted the customs and norms creditably suitable to issues of conflict handled in the arbitral proceedings. In Igbo land, there is a court, if the parties have tried negotiation and mediation and it did not work, they move to the court, which might be the town hall where *umunna* meet weekly, king's palace, village square, or in the shrine (as a last resort). Supporting this statement, Charles (2016, p.7) said "Africa used council of elders, king's court, people's assemblies" in resolution of conflict. The judges in town hall, village square or market place are the elders and traditional rulers, who in judging, use the norms and belief of the land.

The eldest man in the kindred is the holder of the kindred *ofo* and acts as the chairman of the *umunna* assembly. *Umunna* village assembly is in charge of resolving conflicts between individuals from different families in the same clan and village. The *Umunna* assembly resolves conflicts, such as; land boundary and inheritance conflicts. Simple cases of fighting and stealing are treated by the *umunna,* either on their "*awurawu*", that is, weekly gathering of all the male members of the community or, if it involves a female during the moonlight, as the community gathers at the village square. As it was, the family constituted the lowest court in the traditional African system, whereas the king and his council formed the highest court of appeal. They constitute what might be called 'third party intervention' in conflict management. In traditional thought, philosophy and religion, the third party is expected to be neutral and possess the capability to diffuse tension, listen to all sides, restore peace and put social mechanisms in place for conflict management. Their task is to re-establish the energy flow within individuals, families and communities so as to re-build social harmony.

According to Matudi (2016), "Traditional African conflict resolution is embedded in the cultural heritage or values of the society." They seek to promote serial harmony or togetherness illustrated by the proverb which says that, "when people gather in the village square moonlight, it is not because they cannot see the moon in their individual houses" (Achebe, 1959). Conflict resolution in the African society by the *umunna* was a drama where there were neither actors nor spectators. The process of conflict resolution was triangular, involving the parties in conflict, witnesses and the audience. Conflict resolution by the *umunna* involves the celebration of settlement of disputes. There was no loser or winner in the conflict resolution in Igbo traditional society. Concerted efforts were geared toward establishing and sustaining ontological balance between the society and the supernatural world.

UMUNNA WITHIN THE CONTEXT OF *IGWEBUIKE* PHILOSOPHY AND CONFLICT RESOLUTION

Kanu, the founder of *Igwebuike* philosophy, gave a succinct description of *Igwebuike* in this way: "*Igwebuike* is an Igbo word; one of the major dialects in Africa. It is a principle that is at the heart of African thought, and in fact, the modality of being in African ontology" (2017, p. 6). He went on to say that it can be employed as a word or used as a sentence: as a word, it is written as *Igwebuike*, and as a sentence, it is written as, *Igwe bu ike*, with the component words enjoying some independence in terms of space. The three words involved are: '*Igwe*' is a noun which means 'number' or 'population,' usually a huge number or population. '*Bu*' is a verb, which means 'is.' '*Ike*' is another verb, which means 'strength' or 'power' (Kanu, 2016). Thus, put together, it means 'number is strength' or 'number is power;' that is, when human beings come together in solidarity and complementarity, they are powerful or can constitute an insurmountable force. Its English equivalents are 'complementarity', 'solidarity' and 'harmony'. The preferred concept, however, is 'complementarity' (Kanu, 2017, 2018 & 2019).

However, applied to African traditional conflict resolution, Kanu writes that:

> *Igwebuike*, an Igbo-African philosophy is, therefore, employed as a system of conflict resolution which would help Africans to incorporate African traditional categories in the resolution of conflicts, promotion of peace, justice, freedom, human dignity, sustainable development and better quality of life. *Igwebuike* as an indigenous wholistic Igbo philosophy is generated to emphasize that indigenous peoples have worldviews and means of relating to the world. This worldview is rooted within indigenous epistemologies, cultures and traditions with the understanding that we are all related- each aspect relates with the whole: the dynamics of realty are based on the relationships and experiences of interrelationships and interconnections (2017, p.2).

Conflict resolution in *Igwebuike* philosophy is viewed like a person with headache which sends the person to bed. The headache is on the head but it has affected the whole body. So, unless the head stops aching, the whole body will continue to be in discomfort. Applying this to *Umunna*, the head is the one in conflict, while the rest of the body symbolizes the kindred. The kindred will never have rest when there is conflict amongst its members. It (*Igwebuike*) celebrates in a deep cultural and philosophical modality our relatedness, our interconnectedness, our common humanity, our common responsibility towards one another and for one another (Kanu, 2015a&b). *Igwebuike* is an innate human quality. For, deep in the recesses of the heart of everyone are found the qualities of and hunger for complementarity, solidarity, compassion, reciprocity, dignity and harmony (Kanu, 2017. P.7). This, in reality, is what *umunna* stands for. It gives everyone, both young and old, the sense of belonging. Kanu opines that;

> *Igwebuike* as an indigenous method of peace and conflict resolution has a community-based approach. It is an outcome of the wisdom of traditional African conflict management practices drawn from the values of host communities, and founded on the custom and tradition of the African people which has been developed over a long period of time- it is entirely based on culture and emphasizes the fundamental part which culture plays in the lives and actions of people. It is more of a healing process in which individuals contribute positive energy with the sole aim of re-establishing the energy flow within individuals, families and communities for the purpose of rebuilding social harmony (p. 8).

In relation to conflict, *Igwebuike* philosophy does not understand conflict merely as a fracas between two persons, or two groups, it rather understands conflict as a fracas touching on the harmony of reality. Thus, it is not just about justifying the one and condemning the other, it works towards a compromise for the reconciliation of both parties and the restoration of balance or the harmony of reality. It is relatively informal and, thus, less intimidating, as those involved are at ease, and are in a familiar environment.

This is the case with the *umunna* in Igbo land, which settles conflict during the weekly gathering, which is on a particular market day, at an open family hall or *"awurawu"* of the kindred, as it is called in some parts of Igbo community. On this market day, all palm-wine tapped in the kindred belongs to the kindred. A person designated by the kindred goes round to all those tapping wine to collect the wine. At the time for the meeting, all the male members of the kindred gather at the kindred hall and the meeting begins with the breaking of the kolanut by the eldest in the kindred. After the kolanut is broken and shared, issues of the day are discussed. During this time, anyone who has conflict presents the issue with four (4) pieces of kolanuts. After he has finished presenting his case, the eldest in the kindred, who also serves as the leader, invites the second party in the conflict to give his own side of the story. This is followed by cross-examination, witness and consultation. At the end, the conflict is resolved by the most elderly member of the kindred, using words of wisdom. Shedrack (2014), avers that, "The words of our elders are words of wisdom. The wise man (or woman) hears and gets wiser" (p. 99). They sometimes receive input from other members of the community present, but the verdict comes from the elders. The aim of the verdict is to reconcile the parties in conflict, promote community solidarity, and not to blame either party. The conflict can be said to have been resolved when the parties in conflict display any of the signs of reconciliation; shaking of hands, hugging, sitting together, etc.

When all the issues of the day have been presented and treated, the palmwine that has been collected earlier are brought out for celebration of the conflict resolution, not without the eldest pouring some on the ground to appease and appreciate the gods/ancestors for their intervention in the conflict. It is a process of socialization for every male member of the community, a learning process for the younger generations. This is why younger male members do more of listening and observing of the elders than participate in contributing. This is because, in the words of Shedrack, "Indeed younger people are typically not to be heard" (2014, p. 100). It is important to note that it is not all kinds of conflict the *umunna* resolves in Igbo land, some serious conflicts are reserved for elders and elders-in-council or for the chief priest. This is so because, since the *umunna* is the gathering of all male members of the community, some conflicts are too big for the minds and ears of younger members of the community.

However, *umunna* conflict resolution is informal, cost-effective and expeditious. The parties often sit together and resolve their dispute within a sitting or two. This way, the poor and indigent clients are carried along in a system that is just and less expensive. The elders acting as arbiter resolve conflict in the kindred, knowing all the ramifications of personal relationships within their small community, for most of these important factors are not brought out in the case, but are presumed to be known to all hearers. In this regard, they act as peacemakers and keep the community running smoothly. The *Umunna* has contributed a lot to the resolution of conflicts in Igbo land and their role in conflict resolution has been very interesting and effective. Judging by the guiding principles of conflict resolution in pre-colonial Africa, elders in the *Umunna* are impartial; they display neutrality and unbiased attitude in resolving conflicts. The process has always been transparent, since all issues are placed at the public domain for all to see and judge. There is fairness, justice and equality in judgment.

CONCLUSION

The process of conflict resolution by the *Umunna* involves getting the parties and their families together, and getting to the root of the conflict to ensure the underlying causes of conflict are resolved and the parties reconciled. The Igbo world has many other indigenous mediatory bodies for conflict management and resolution. The family is the first in the process of conflict resolution in cases concerning the family. If the crisis is between neigbours, the families involved are required to come for a dialogue. Where the family or families are unable to resolve their problem, the *umunna* institution comes in to help. *Umunna* is called upon where families cannot resolve their problem. The weekly gathering of *Umunna* was not only to settle or resolve conflict; when there is no conflict, the *Umunna* gather to strengthen the bond of family ties. They do a lot of conflict prevention and also take proactive measures to ensure that conflicts do not arise amongst members. The major aim of the *umunna* is to keep the brotherhood in unity. In Igbo land, drinking palm wine together is the sign of unity and friendship. It is also a sign of communion, bonding them together. Thus, the overall objective of conflict resolution in *Igwebuike* philosophy is to uphold and promote peaceful co-existence among and between members of the kindred. It has produced a great level of trust, confidence and mutual understanding in traditional Igbo society, and reconciliation has apparently been the end product of the *umunna* conflict resolution mechanism.

REFERENCES

Achebe, C. (1959), Things Fall Apart, Greenwich: Fawcett.

Charles, M.O. (2016). *Tiv and Igbo Conflict Management Machanism: A Comparative Study*, Portharcourt, Centre for Conflict and Gender Studies (CCGS), 5(7), 22-29.

Chubb L.T. (1961). *Ibo Land Tenure*, 2nd Edition. Ibadan, O.U.P.

Ebisi, N. (2016). The challenge of Peace and conflict Resolution a clue from Igbo cultural Group of Nigeria. *Journal of Arts Humanities and Social Sciences.*1 (14)

Ezenwoko, F.A. and Osagie I. J. (2014). *Conflict and Conflict Resolution in Pre-colonial Igbo Society of Nigeria.* Benin city, University of Benin.

Kanu I. A. (2015b). *A hermeneutic approach to African traditional religion, theology and philosophy.* Nigeria: Augustinian Publications.

Kanu, I. A. (2015a). *African philosophy: An ontologico-existential hermeneutic approach to classical and contemporary issues.* Nigeria: Augustinian Publications.

Kanu, A. I. (2016). Igwebuike as an Igbo-African hermeneutic of globalization. *IGWEBUIKE: An African Journal of Arts and Humanities. 2. 1.pp.* 1-7.

Kanu, A.I. (2017). *Igwebuike as an Igbo-African Modality of Peace and Conflict Resolution,* A paper presented at the 2017 Igbo Studies Association International Conference held at Great Wood Hotel, Owerri, Imo State, pp.1-10.

Kanu I. A. (2017). Igwebuikeconomics: Towards an inclusive economy for economic development. *Igwebuike: An African Journal of Arts and Humanities. Vol. 3. No. 6.* 113-140.

Kanu I. A. (2017). Sources of *Igwebuike* Philosophy. *International Journal of Religion and Human Relations.* 9. 1. pp. 1-23.

Kanu, A. I. (2016a). *Igwebuike* as a trend in African philosophy. *IGWEBUIKE: An African Journal of Arts and Humanities. 2. 1.* 97-101.

Kanu, A. I. (2017c). *Igwebuike* as an Igbo-African philosophy of inclusive leadership. *Igwebuike: An African Journal of Arts and Humanities.* Vol. 3 No 7. pp. 165-183.

Kanu, A. I. (2017d). *Igwebuike* philosophy and the issue of national development. *Igwebuike: An African Journal of Arts and Humanities.* Vol. 3 No 6. pp. 16-50.

Kanu, A. I. (2017f). *Igwebuike* as an Igbo-African Ethic of Reciprocity. *IGWEBUIKE: An African Journal of Arts and Humanities. 3. 2. pp.* 153-160.

Kanu, I. A. (2016a). *Igwebuike* as an Igbo-African Hermeneutics of Globalisation. *IGWEBUIKE: An African Journal of Arts and Humanities*, Vol. 2 No.1. pp. 61-66.

Kanu, I. A. (2016a). *Igwebuike* as the consummate foundation of African Bioethical principles. *An African journal of Arts and Humanities* Vol.2 No1 June, pp.23-40.

Kanu, I. A. (2016b) *Igwebuike* as an Expressive Modality of Being in African ontology. *Journal of Environmental and Construction Management. 6. 3.* pp.12-21.

Kanu, I. A. (2017). *Igwebuike* as an Igbo-African Philosophy for Christian-Muslim Relations in Northern Nigeria. In Mahmoud Misaeli (Ed.). *Spirituality and Global Ethics* (pp. 300-310). United Kingdom: Cambridge Scholars.

Kanu, I. A. (2019). *Igwebuike* research methodology: A new trend for scientific and wholistic investigation. *IGWEBUIKE: An African Journal of Arts and Humanities* (IAAJAH). *5. 4.* pp. *95-105.*

Kanu, I. A. (2018). *Igwe Bu Ike* as an Igbo-African hermeneutics of national development. *Igbo Studies Review. No. 6.* pp. 59-83.

Kanu, I. A. (2018). *Igwebuike* as an African integrative and progressive anthropology. *NAJOP: Nasara Journal of Philosophy.* Vol. 2. No. 1. pp. 151-161.

Kanu, I. A. (2018). New Africanism: *Igwebuike* as a philosophical Attribute of Africa in portraying the Image of Life. In Mahmoud Misaeli, Sanni Yaya and Rico Sneller (Eds.). *African Perspectives on Global on Global Development* (pp. 92-103). United Kingdom: Cambridge Scholars Publishing.

Kanu, I. A. (2019). *Igwebuikeconomics*: The Igbo apprenticeship for wealth creation. *IGWEBUIKE: An African Journal of Arts and Humanities* (IAAJAH). *5. 4.* pp. *56-70.*

Kanu, I. A. (2019). *Igwebuikecracy*: The Igbo-African participatory cocio-political system of governance. *TOLLE LEGE: An Augustinian Journal of the Philosophy and Theology. 1. 1.* pp. 34-45.

Nwogugu E.I. (1974). *Family Law in Nigeria*, Ibadan, Heinemann.

Nwolise O.B.C. (2004). Traditional Approaches to Conflict Resolution Among the Igbo People of Nigeria: Reinforcing the Need for Africa to Rediscover its Roots. *AMANI.*

Matudi, G.I (2016). Unpublished lecture Note on African Approaches to Conflict Resolution, Yola, MAUTECH.

Shedrack, G.B. (2014). "The Methods of Conflict Resolution and Transformation." in Shedrack G.B. (ed.), *Introduction to Peace and Conflict Studies in West Africa*. Ibadan, Spectrum Books Limited.

THE CONCEPT OF IGWEBUIKE IN IGBO KNOWLEDGE INTEGRATION

Obinna Victor Obiagwu, PhD
Directorate of General Studies
Federal University of Technology, Owerri
obinnaobiagwu71@gmail.com

EXECUTIVE SUMMARY

Igwebuike, as a concept in Igbo ideology, is that of strength in numbers, where togetherness in one accord remains the watch word and the spirit of engagement. It aims towards the promotion of a sustainable development and also improvement of economic, social, cultural and political purity within the Igbo-speaking people in comparison with their neighbours of other languages and nationalities. The Igwebuike philosophy, therefore, becomes the force behind the Igbo indigenous knowledge holders in making their own decisions as it affects their future life endeavours, which define them as a people among others of different cultures. What it implies then is that Igwebuike application is inherent in self-determination and consistent with socio-cultural and other developmental relativity. Igwebuike ensures equity and justice in Igbo integration of knowledge through its nature of all hands being on deck.

Keywords: Igwebuike, Philosophy, Kanu Ikechukwu Anthony, Igbo Knowledge

INTRODUCTION

According to Posey (1998), there will be nothing 'new' if we do not develop new methodologies for dialogue with local knowledge holders. He goes further to say that until indigenous people have political and economic parity with development forces that is only when a positive result will be achieved on indigenous knowledge development.

Looking at the case of Igbo knowledge integration, one can be tempted to ask how indigenous Igbo people can assert their traditional cultural values within their social environment in a way that it will be fair to all concerned. The simple answer to this question is the "**Igwebuike**" concept.

The concept of "**Igwebuike**" is a concept that was articulated by Professor Kanu Ikechukwu Anthony. It captures and communicates the Igbo-African world. *Igwebuike* is the form and symbolic of the Igbo-African mental being and the gateway to Igbo-African philosophy. Beyond the literal understanding of *Igwebuike* (*Igwe-* number; *bu*-is; *ike*-strength) as "there is strength in number", it captures the Igbo philosophy of relationality, complementarity and interconnectedness of reality (Kanu 2014; 2015; 2016; 2017; 2018; 2019). It concatenates Igbo forms, symbolism, signs, media, meaning, anthropologies, universal cosmic truths, functions, semantic powers, physics, phenomena, faculties, and Igbo environ-mentalities, and symbolizes the propositional powers of Igbo knowledge, perception, identity, phenomenalism, physics, metaphysics, logic, history of analytic character, speculative mindset and positive provisions for definitions of facts (Kanu 2020).

Parity, in this context, involves equal relations among the indigenous peoples of Igbo extraction, whose knowledge is being integrated with the other worlds, knowing full well that knowledge integration involves the synthesization of multiple knowledge models, or representation into a common one. Knowledge integration has also been studied as the process of incorporating new information into a body of existing knowledge with an interdisciplinary approach (Wikipedia). Integration, therefore, occurs when separate ideas or things are brought together, just like in the amalgamation of northern and southern protectorates of Nigeria in 1914 by Lord Frederick Lugard, the then Governor General of the combined colony of Nigeria.

The *Igwebuike* spirit of parity is, therefore, seen as the ability of the Igbo indigenous knowledge holders to make autonomous decisions about their future, based on a set of principles derived from their own collective ontology. The Igbo integration of knowledge must be based on people's understanding of the world, rather than from imposed assumptions. Parity of Igbo knowledge integration is inherent in self-determination and consistent with cultural relativity. Parity ensures equity and justice, just like in "**Igwebuike**", where all hands must be on deck without any pranks.

IGBO KNOWLEDGE INTEGRATION OF WESTERN EDUCATION

Western education, no doubt, has come to stay in Igbo cultural milieu. But the issue here is "educational diversification." This is important to meet individual differences as regards interests and abilities. The emphasis here is on specialization.

According to Eliot (1949), education is the process by which the community seeks to open its life to all the individuals within it and enable them to take their part in it. It attempts to pass on to them its culture, including the standards by which it would have them live. In furtherance to the emphasis on education, Okafor (1974) states that education is a process of acculturation by which the individual is helped to attain the maximum activation of his potentialities according to right reason and to achieve thereby his perfect self-fulfillment. Looking at the two above,

214

one can observe that the *Igwebuike* concept of Igbo knowledge integration has a major role it is already playing. The issue of Western education is at present a collective concern of the Igbos. One can easily observe the community efforts in the establishment of schools and training of individuals. In most Igbo communities, some indigenous people attended various levels of education, through communal efforts, believing that any educated mind among them is a major asset to the community. Through the *Igwebuike* concept, the Igbo communities from 1950s till date still build schools, in order to ensure that Western education does not elude them. They also endeavour to see that their people are educated, by going further to make contributions towards the education of some of their sons and daughters. They as well made earlier donation of lands to the White Missionaries for the establishment of educational institutions, even before the advent of community schools.

That is actually the concept of *Igwebuike* in the Igbo Western education knowledge integration. The "**Igwebuike**" spirit of oneness helped so much in this direction, even till date. Western education is still very important to the majority of the Igbos that the issue of scholarship award is still common among the people, just to make sure that those who cannot afford Western education on their own can benefit from such awards.

Going through studies and researches on "**Igwebuike**" concept of the traditional Igbo attitudes and values with a view to formulating educational procedures responsive to the good in the Igbo background have inescapably brought into sharp focus the importance the Igbos attach to educational realities. They have quite acknowledged the fact that Western education is an integral and prevailing factor among the people.

IGBO KNOWLEDGE INTEGRATION OF CHRISTIANITY

Christianity is agreeable to Igbo culture – a culture of deep spirituality, maximized religious values and quite theocentric in outlook. This fact was very evident in the early centuries when parts of Igbo land first came in contact with the Christian religion. Christianity, therefore, is an excellent example of what renascent Igbo should incorporate into her cultural fabric.

However, distinction must be made between Christianity as practiced by discrete individuals and groups and Christianity in its essential substance. In the words of Okafor (1974), over the centuries, certain individuals and groups did, in fact, run into behavioural mud water in the practice of Christianity; but still over the centuries, many individuals and group did succeed in exemplifying in their lives the perfection that was essentially embedded in Christianity. Okafor also goes further in his work to remind us of the fact that, that many do not measure up to the ideal does not remove the validity or the reality of the ideal. In spite of individual failures, Christianity still remains the most civilized of all religions. It remains the religion better than which none can be found.

Looking at its nature, one can observe that Christianity remains that unique religion, which by all means holds the greatest potentialities of meeting up with the dilemmas and challenges of the modern Igbo race. It is so simply because of the fact that Christianity puts into consideration a mysterious combination of the essentials of the traditional Igbo religions and those principles which constitute the badge of civility to contemporary man.

In comparison with the Christian religion, the Igbo traditional religion also accommodates certain Christian doctrines like forgiveness, patience, brotherhood, blessing of the peace-makers and the merciful, kindness, malice towards none, charity, etc. All these and others are agreeable to the Igbo man. They not only touch at the heart of the traditional Igbo religion but also reveal any imperfections that might be present in them.

The Igbo man, in his "**Igwebuike**" spirit, accepted the Christian religion holistically and has been making concerted efforts to enroute Christianity into the cultural norms of the Igbos. This is being achieved through communal efforts, just like in the case of Western education. The Igbo communities have invested much in the building and establishment of churches of different denominations, with a good number of Igbo sons and daughters going into various religious professions. Prayer itself has become a central survival strategy of the Igbo people.

CONCLUSION

It will be totally wrong and a great social misgiving for one to think that there is nothing good, admirable or worth preserving in the Igbo of the old. There are a lot of things that are quite good, highly admirable, and worthy to be preserved in the Igbo traditional knowledge norms. Same is also applicable to that of the other worlds. Every group of people is naturally endowed or structured with some characteristic assets and blessing. Taking into consideration the fact that humans are structured as a community of brotherhood, which makes the assets of any sector of humanity a common property for all to share. As such, there must be a kind of unity in diversity. Just as Whitehead (1982) states that a diversification among human communities is essential for the provision of the incentive and material for the odyssey of human spirit. Other nations of different habits are not enemies; they are god-sends. Whitehead goes further to explain that men require of their neighbours something sufficiently akin to be understood, something sufficiently different to provoke attention and something great enough to command admiration.

As a result of speedy communication of development in these contemporary times, the world has been brought closer, together than it has ever witnessed. This has also made the issue of knowledge integration quite imperative. One sector of the global arrangement, therefore, must influence another socially, politically and economically, as well as in their different cultural norms.

In a situation like these, the Igbos, propelled by their "**Igwebuike**" philosophy, need a proper integration of their knowledge with other nationalities of the world. They are expected to conform to what Okafor (1974) described as judicious selective integration of culture. The old norms of knowledge must be treated with respect, as a legacy for the newer ideas. But it must also be refined, given new meaning, expression and direction. Anything undesirable in the old knowledge must be dropped as history of the old, so as to pave way for the new normal.

To cope with the present challenges, the Igbos must approach their plan of action with every atom of definition. They should not allow the mystical past to conscript them, nor allow themselves to be consumed by the indecision of the present. They should be clear about the present situation, and avoid building castles in the air. In the best "**Igwebuike**" team spirit, the Igbo should collectively be realistically guided in their cultural spectrum.

REFERENCES

Eliot T. S., (1947). Notes Towards the Definition of Culture, New York: Harcourt, Brace & Company.

Kanu, A. I. (2016a). *Igwebuike* as a trend in African philosophy. *IGWEBUIKE: An African Journal of Arts and Humanities. 2. 1.* 97-101.

Kanu, A. I. (2017c). *Igwebuike* as an Igbo-African philosophy of inclusive leadership. *Igwebuike: An African Journal of Arts and Humanities.* Vol. 3 No 7. pp. 165-183.

Kanu, A. I. (2017d). *Igwebuike* philosophy and the issue of national development. *Igwebuike: An African Journal of Arts and Humanities.* Vol. 3 No 6. pp. 16-50.

Kanu, A. I. (2017f). *Igwebuike* as an Igbo-African Ethic of Reciprocity. *IGWEBUIKE: An African Journal of Arts and Humanities. 3. 2. pp.* 153-160.

Kanu, I. A. (2012). The problem of being in metaphysics. *African Research Review: An International Multi-Disciplinary Journal.* Vol.6. No.2. April. pp. 113-122.

Kanu, I. A. (2012). The problem of personal identity in metaphysics. *International Journal of Arts and Humanities.* Vol.1. No.2. pp.1-13.

Kanu, I. A. (2012a). The concept of life and person in African anthropology. In E. Ezenweke and I. A. Kanu (Eds.). *Issues in African traditional religion and philosophy* (pp. 61-71). Nigeria: Augustinian.

Kanu, I. A. (2012b). Towards an Igbo Christology. In E. Ezenweke and I. A. Kanu (Eds.). *Issues in African traditional religion and philosophy* (pp. 75-98). Nigeria: Augustinian.

Kanu, I. A. (2013). African identity and the emergence of globalization. *American International Journal of Contemporary Research*. Vol. 3. No. 6. pp. 34-42.

Kanu, I. A. (2013). African Identity and the Emergence of Globalization. *American International Journal of Contemporary Research*. Vol. 3. No. 6. pp. 34-42.

Kanu, I. A. (2013). Globalisation, globalism and African philosophy. C. Umezinwa (Ed.). *African philosophy: A pragmatic approach to African probems* (pp. 151-165). Germany: Lambert.

Kanu, I. A. (2013). On the sources of African philosophy. *Filosofia Theoretica: Journal of African Philosophy, Culture and Religion, Vol. 2. No. 1*. pp. 337-356.

Kanu, I. A. (2013). The dimensions of African cosmology. *Filosofia Theoretica: Journal of African Philosophy, Culture and Religion, Vol. 2. No. 2*. pp. 533-555.

Kanu, I. A. (2014). A historiography of African philosophy. *Global Journal for Research Analysis. Volume. 3. Issue. 8*. pp. 188-190.

Kanu, I. A. (2014). Being and the categories of being in Igbo philosophy. *African Journal of Humanities. Volume 1. Issue 1*. pp. 144-159.

Kanu, I. A. (2016a). *Igwebuike* as the consummate foundation of African Bioethical principles. *An African journal of Arts and Humanities* Vol.2 No1 June, pp.23-40.

Kanu, I. A. (2016b) *Igwebuike* as an Expressive Modality of Being in African ontology. *Journal of Environmental and Construction Management. 6. 3*. pp.12-21.

Kanu, I. A. (2017). *Igwebuike* as an Igbo-African Philosophy for Christian-Muslim Relations in Northern Nigeria. In Mahmoud Misaeli (Ed.). *Spirituality and Global Ethics* (pp. 300-310). United Kingdom: Cambridge Scholars.

Kanu, I. A. (2017). *Igwebuike* as an Igbo-African Philosophy for the Protection of the Environment. *Nightingale International Journal of Humanities and Social Sciences.* Vol. 3. No. 4. pp. 28-38.

Kanu, I. A. (2017). *Igwebuike* as the Hermeneutic of Individuality and Communality in African Ontology. *NAJOP: Nasara Journal of Philosophy.* Vol. 2. No. 1. pp. 162-179.

Kanu, I. A. (2017a). *Igwebuike* and Question of Superiority in the Scientific Community of Knowledge. *Igwebuike: An African Journal of Arts and Humanities.*Vol.3 No1. pp. 131-138.

Kanu, I. A. (2017b). *Igwebuike* as a Complementary Approach to the Issue of Girl-Child Education. *Nightingale International Journal of Contemporary Education and Research.* Vol. 3. No. 6. pp. 11-17.

Kanu, I. A. (2018). *Igwe Bu Ike* as an Igbo-African Hermeneutics of National Development. *Igbo Studies Review. No. 6.* pp. 59-83.

Kanu, I. A. (2018). Igwebuike as an African Integrative and Progressive Anthropology. *NAJOP: Nasara Journal of Philosophy.* Vol. 2. No. 1. pp. 151-161.

Okafor F. C., (1974). Africa at the Crossroads, Philosophical Approach to Education. New York: Vantage Press, Inc.

Purcell T. W. & Onjoro E., (2004) Models of Knowledge Integration; In Harvesting & Sharing Indigenous Knowledge in Africa (Eds) Okere T. I. & Nkwocha L. Owerri Assumpta Press.

Nwaka G. I., (2004) Using Indigenous Knowledge to strengthen Local Governance and Development in Nigeria, in Harvesting & Sharing Indiginoud Knowledge in Africa. (Eds) Okere & Nkwocha L. Owerri Assumpta Press.

Whitehead A. N., (1919a (1982). An Enquirty Concerning the Principle of National Knowledge. Cambridge: Cambridge University Press.

ABOUT THE AUTHOR

Ikechukwu Anthony KANU, O.S.A is a Friar of the Order of Saint Augustine, Province of Nigeria. He is Professor of African Philosophy and Religion, Tansian University, and a Tenured Professor of Orthodox Studies at The University of America, San Francisco, USA. The former Rector of Villanova Polytechnic, Imesi Ile, Osun State and currently an Adjunct Professor to the University of Jos, Plateau State, Veritas University Abuja and Saint Albert the Great Major Seminary, Abeokuta. He is the President of the Association for the Promotion of African Studies (APAS) and the Global President of the World Cultural Studies Research Association (WCRA).

Printed in the United States
by Baker & Taylor Publisher Services